HIGHER EDUCATION IN THE DEVELOPING WORLD

Recent Titles in
Greenwood Studies in Higher Education

Internationalization of Higher Education in the United States of America and Europe: A Historical, Comparative, and Conceptual Analysis
Hans de Wit

Academic Staff in Europe: Changing Contexts and Conditions
Jürgen Enders, editor

HIGHER EDUCATION IN THE DEVELOPING WORLD

Changing Contexts and Institutional Responses

EDITED BY
David W. Chapman
and Ann E. Austin

Greenwood Studies in Higher Education
PHILIP G. ALTBACH, *Series Editor*

GREENWOOD PRESS
Westport, Connecticut • London

Library of Congress Cataloging-in-Publication Data

Higher education in the developing world : changing contexts and institutional responses / edited by David W. Chapman and Ann E. Austin.
p. cm.—(Greenwood studies in higher education, ISSN 1531–8087)
Includes bibliographical references and index.
ISBN 0–313–32016–0 (alk. paper)
1. Education, Higher—Developing countries. I. Chapman, David W. II. Austin, Ann E. III. Series.
LC2610.H55 2002
378'.009172'4—dc21 2001054713

British Library Cataloguing in Publication Data is available.

Library of Congress Catalog Card Number: 2001054713
ISBN: 0–313–32016–0
ISSN: 1531–8087

First published in 2002

Greenwood Press, 88 Post Road West, Westport, CT 06881
An imprint of Greenwood Publishing Group, Inc.
www.greenwood.com

Printed in the United States of America

The paper used in this book complies with the
Permanent Paper Standard issued by the National
Information Standards Organization (Z39.48–1984).

10 9 8 7 6 5 4 3 2 1

Published in cooperation with the Center for International Higher
Education and the Program in Higher Education, Boston College,
Chestnut Hill, Massachusetts.

Contents

Figures and Tables

FIGURES

TABLES

Series Foreword

Greenwood Studies in Higher Education publishes current research and analysis on higher and postsecondary education. Higher education in the twenty-first century is a multifaceted phenomenon, combining a variety of institutions and systems, an interesting diversity of students, and a range of purposes and functions. The challenges of expansion, technology, accountability, and research, among others, require careful analysis. This series combines research-based monographs, analysis, and reference books related to all aspects of higher education. It is concerned with policy and practice in a global perspective. Greenwood Studies in Higher Education is dedicated to illuminating the reality of higher and postsecondary education in contemporary society.

Higher education is a central enterprise of the twenty-first century and a key part of the knowledge-based economy. Universities are the most important source of basic research, and are therefore key to the development of technology. They are also the repositories of the wisdom of society—their libraries and other facilities are in many ways the institutional memory of civilization. University faculty provide not only education and training, but are involved in the creation and interpretation of knowledge. Universities are central to the civil society. Higher education is a key to the social mobility and progress of large numbers of people.

Universities and other postsecondary institutions are increasingly complex. They are large and multifaceted. Academe is also diverse, with a wider range of institutions, a less homogenous student population, and a mixture of public and private support. This series is dedicated to illuminating these complexities. It is also committed to the improvement of one of the most important parts of society—postsecondary education.

Philip G. Altbach

Part I

Introduction and Overview

Chapter 1

The Changing Context of Higher Education in the Developing World

David W. Chapman and Ann E. Austin

Half of the students enrolled in higher education worldwide live in developing countries (World Bank, 2000). By some estimates, the 65 million students enrolled in colleges and universities in 1991 will grow to 97 million by 2015 (World Bank, 2000). It is little wonder that extending access and strengthening the quality of higher education are emerging as key national priorities of governments across much of the developing world. This intensified interest in higher education is driven by demographics, politics, economic challenges, the changing nature of the workplace, and national pride. Yet, at the same time, many governments are facing serious economic constraints and intensified competition for public funds from other sectors that are limiting their ability to respond solely by investing more money in campus construction, faculty salaries, and student stipends. Government and education leaders across much of the developing world are intensively engaged in a search for more creative (and presumably less expensive) ways to extend and improve higher education.

Leaders are finding, however, that reaching consensus and implementing needed changes in how governments and higher education institutions relate and how colleges and universities operate is more difficult than many had anticipated. Efforts to reshape and reform higher education have spawned perplexing issues as government officials and educators struggle to define new structures, new rules, new procedures, and new relationships with one another. Each change in the structure and operation of higher education has rippling consequences that affect other aspects of institutions' relationships with their students, faculty, citizens, and government.

One premise of this book is that many of the international efforts over the last three decades to strengthen higher education in the developing world were focused at the institutional level. A widely held belief was that meaningful higher education reform depended on improving the management capacity within the institutions themselves. This led to an array of partnering arrangements between institutions in different parts of the world, university linkage projects, faculty and administrator exchanges, administrative training programs, and internships intended to strengthen the management and instructional functions of the participating institutions (Chapman & Claffey, 1998). These efforts tended to concentrate on helping colleges and universities develop stronger budgeting systems, enrollment management systems, student and facilities tracking systems, course credit policies, and procedures for systematic curriculum design. While many of these efforts have been successful and will continue to be needed, the main challenge of the next decade centers on how institutions define and shape their external relationships with government, on one hand, and with the larger citizenry, on the other. The development of administrators' skills and the introduction of management tools will continue to be important but will not be sufficient to address the complex political, social, and economic pressures that now shape the future of higher education in the developing world.

This book identifies five particularly critical issues with which higher education institutions in the developing world must grapple as they respond to changing contexts, offers examples of institutional responses to these issues, and considers them within a systems perspective which recognizes that each response impacts how institutions respond to other critical issues. Critical issues include:

1. *Seeking a new balance in government-university relationships.* Shifts toward privatization and decentralization characterize the changing relationships between governments and higher education institutions. As new relationships are forged, goals sometimes collide and system components change at different rates. Conflicts that emerge among rules, operating procedures, and incentive systems can threaten to undermine the very changes being sought.
2. *Coping with autonomy.* Institutions often want more independence in governance without giving up their dependence on public funds. Governments often want colleges and universities to be more financially self-sufficient, but may not want to relinquish state authority over the operations of higher education institutions. The search for balance is one of the central challenges of higher education reform in the developing world. The benefits of autonomy are often clearer than the costs, on both sides of the equation.
3. *Managing expansion, while preserving equity, raising quality, and controlling costs.* There is generally a tension, and sometimes a direct trade-off, among the political necessity to expand enrollments, the moral imperative to increase equity, the educational desire to raise quality, and the overwhelming need to control costs. Governments are being forced to choose between the politically

prudent, the socially important, the academically desirable, and the financially feasible.

4. *Addressing new pressures and forms of accountability.* The downward pressure on quality associated with rapid enrollment increases, the financial autonomy being granted to many public institutions, the rise of private institutions, and the growing prevalence of online courses give new importance to the design and control of quality assurance procedures.
5. *Supporting academic staff in new roles.* The pattern of underpaying university faculty while allowing (and encouraging) them to supplement their income through private consulting has been a rather common way of subsidizing higher education across the developing world. One consequence of low academic salaries, however, is that institutional administrators have little control over faculty time. Initiatives to channel faculty time to improving instruction, conducting research, or providing service are often lost to faculty members' struggles to maximize their income.

THE RENEWED INTEREST IN HIGHER EDUCATION

During the 1960s and 1970s the development of higher education was viewed as a national priority across much of the developing world. In support of emerging nations' priorities, national governments and international assistance organizations (such as the World Bank, regional development banks, and bilateral assistance agencies) made substantial investments in higher education throughout the developing world. During the 1980s that commitment languished as priorities shifted and international assistance agencies refocused their attention and money on expanding access to and improving the quality of elementary and secondary (i.e., "basic") education (Chapman & Claffey, 1998). The inability to secure external assistance for higher education dampened national investment in this sector.

The shift away from higher education over the last two decades stemmed from three main factors. First, support of higher education in the developing world during the 1960s and 1970s failed to yield the expected payoffs to national development in some parts of the world. The impact of the investment was dissipated by brain drain, government neglect, politicization of higher education, and the financial crises confronting many countries. Second, in many countries higher education institutions remained detached from domestic problems (i.e., food security, illiteracy, and disease prevention). Third, basic education was seen to have a higher "rate of return." Twenty to 30 children could be educated at the primary level for the cost of one year of college education, and the basic literacy and numeracy skills they gained were often more consistent with the needs of the immediate labor market than was university training. Economists and educators concluded that public investment in college and university education tended to be of far greater long-term advantage to individual students than to the larger society. As a consequence, international assistance agencies were reluctant to fund college and university projects (Chapman & Claffey, 1998).

While there is renewed interest in the development and strengthening of higher education, the years on the sidelines took a toll. In many countries, government and institutional leaders lack clear systems and well-developed strategies for improving the operations and the impact of their colleges and universities. While there are pockets of vision and examples of successful initiatives, those are not yet the dominant experience.

The renewed attention to higher education on the part of national governments and international assistance organizations arises from the convergence of six trends (World Bank, 1994, 2000). First, the success of many countries in raising primary school participation and retention rates has created an enrollment bubble that is rapidly working its way up the system, resulting in extraordinary pressure for expanded access to higher education. Governments understand that failing to accommodate this new demand for access comes at considerable political risk. Most governments can ill-afford to alienate this growing group of students or their families by limiting their access to better employment and life opportunities (perceived or real) (Chapman & Claffey, 1998).

Second, in some parts of the world, the intense focus of investment at the primary level over the last 30 years has resulted in an imbalance in the skills available in the workforce. Governments increasingly recognize the need for greater balance in the output of their education system to ensure that enough citizens have the advanced technical and managerial capacity needed to foster and sustain development in an increasingly technology- and information-based economy. Moreover, the participation rate and quality of basic education in many countries has now reached a level that allows more attention to be given to higher levels of schooling.

Third, the forces of economic globalization have changed the knowledge and skill mix needed in the workplace (and hence the workforce) for a country to compete effectively in the modern economy. The wealth of nations is no longer measured solely in terms of natural resources or level of industrialization. The new emphasis on higher education reflects the changing international economy in which knowledge is the new capital and information is the currency of exchange (World Bank, 2000). The increasingly technological nature of international communications and trade requires a workforce with more advanced education.

Fourth, the changes in national political systems from centralized to more democratic approaches that are sweeping many regions of the world are creating a new environment within which a society's institutions must function (cf., International Renaissance Foundation, 1997). These shifts in national political environments are creating both the opportunity and the necessity for higher education institutions to rethink and rework their relationship with government.

Fifth, many of the changes in the structure and operation of higher education are being forced by heightened competition with other sectors for public funds. Even the strongest advocates of education acknowledge the threats posed by degradation of the environment (pollution, deforestation), the rise in HIV/AIDS and other health threats, persisting poverty, and continued urbanization (Asian Development Bank, 1997; Beyrer, 1998; Bloom & Godwin, 1997; Bruestle, 1993; Chapman, 1998, 2000; Corbin, 1998; Feldman & Miller, 1998; Imai, 1998; Jalal, 1993; Linge & Porter, 1997; Panayotou, 1993; Park, 1995; Rogers, 1993; Tan & Sanderson, 1996; United Nations, 1997). It is not that education is viewed as less important, but that other issues have taken on more urgent dimensions.

Sixth, technological advances are providing new delivery possibilities for higher education. With the widespread introduction of online course delivery, national governments no longer necessarily control what higher education programs are offered within their borders. New approaches to the design and delivery of higher education itself are forcing a rethinking of how institutions are organized, how instructional quality is monitored, and the role of government in the oversight of higher education (Burbules & Callister, 2000; Katz & Associates, 1999; Maslen, 2001; Palloff & Pratt, 2001; Phipps & Merisotis, 1999).

The convergence of these pressures has created a serious dilemma for both government and higher education institutions. Increasing public demand for access to higher education and the need for a more highly educated workforce clash with sharp financial constraints, changing political environments, entrenched incentive systems, and normal organizational resistance to change. How these dilemmas are resolved in the current era will do much to define the shape of higher education in the developing world well into the new century. It is essential, then, that the responses of governments and higher education institutions to these trends be culturally appropriate, economically sensible, operationally manageable, and strategically effective.

Much of the literature on higher education in international settings has focused on describing the organization and operation of national systems in selected countries. Several recent volumes have made important steps toward a more analytic examination of issues in higher education development (Ajayi, Goma, & Johnson, 1996; Altbach, 1998; Kempner, Mollis & Tierney, 1998; Postiglione & Mak, 1997; World Bank, 2000). This book builds on and extends this analytic approach by concentrating on specific institutional and system responses to external pressures and on strategies for strengthening the operation, contribution, and relevance of higher education institutions themselves.

The volume is grounded in a systems perspective, in which higher education institutions are understood as complex organizations composed of multiple, interconnected subsystems (Weick, 1976). Furthermore, higher education institutions function as subsystems within larger national systems. Changes affecting any particular subsystem have implications that ripple through and affect other subsystems, sometimes in unanticipated ways. For example, efforts to enhance access may unintentionally undercut commitment to equity by disadvantaging some people in the population. Adopting technology-based delivery options may broaden access, but simultaneously may raise questions about quality and create new pressures for institutional accountability. Efforts to strengthen institutional autonomy may lead to diminished government support, therein threatening faculty financial security which, in turn, may foster faculty resistance.

A tenet of good national planning is that planners need to anticipate and provide for the cross-impacts of the interventions they advocate. Only as government and education leaders understand the interwoven nature of the problems now facing colleges and universities and the interconnections among the intended solutions they seek to implement can they offer effective leadership in charting a course that strengthens the quality and improves the relevance of higher education in their countries.

The five issues addressed in the remainder of this book are, by their very nature, deeply interwoven. Solutions pertaining to one issue will have consequences relating to each of the other issues. Planning at both the central government and institutional levels will only be effective as government and education leaders understand these relationships and actively anticipate the interconnectedness and wider consequences of their actions. It is to this end that the authors of this book are committed.

The book draws on recent experience of the higher education systems in the developing world, but it is *not* intended to provide full descriptions of higher education in particular countries. Rather, the focus of the book is on identifying critical issues and examining institutional strategies in response to those issues. Space constraints required choices among countries and issues to be included in this volume. Chapters were selected to focus on high profile issues in higher education, involve authors with extensive experience and insight about the national contexts about which they were writing, and illustrate a range of institutional responses to changing external pressures. They were not selected to represent the full variety of educational systems in the developing world or to achieve geographical balance. In the end, important examples of institutional responses were found in small education systems (Laos, Mongolia) as well as in larger, higher profile systems (South Africa, Brazil, China).

In the remaining portion of this chapter, we elaborate on the five central themes of the book and offer an overview of the arguments offered by the chapter authors. Following this first chapter, Jamil Salmi provides an overview and probing analysis of the current state of higher education across the world, asserting that higher education systems and institutions are at a turning point. He argues that three interwoven forces are fueling this revolution—economic globalization, the increased importance of knowledge as a driver of growth, and the pervasiveness of relatively low-cost, high-speed information and communication systems.

Significant implications, he argues, follow from these forces. First, higher education systems must meet new demands to provide training and education for workers needing higher level skills and lifelong learning opportunities. The emphasis of education and training is shifting away from basic knowledge acquisition to developing the ability to access, use, and apply knowledge. Second, traditional higher education institutions face increasing competition from institutions around the world offering online learning options and from new institutions sponsored by corporations. Third, new education and training needs and new forms of competition will push traditional higher education institutions to reform their governance, organizational structures, internal processes, and modes of operation.

A key element in Salmi's analysis pertains to the way in which growing emphasis on high technology in business and industry is a major force accelerating the demand for more advanced education throughout the developing world. At the same time, the use of technology to deliver postsecondary education is changing the way higher education institutions operate. The introduction of online, distance education creates new avenues for student access to higher education as it decreases the importance of physical distance. It opens new pedagogical opportunities when, for example, a single class can involve students from several countries in discussion and debate. Perhaps most importantly, online instruction is already changing the financial underpinnings of higher education as colleges can offer courses to large numbers of students using part-time faculty, without the heavy infrastructure costs of classrooms and campuses.

At the same time, these forms of distance education also raise perplexing questions about national oversight of higher education and the reach of unwanted cultural influences. In some countries, they threaten the national government's use of higher education as a source of national identity and international prestige. At the institutional level, online, distance education is reshaping academic appointments and careers. No longer is the presence of full-time professors necessarily a key determinant of institutional quality. These mechanisms for course delivery also are changing the pattern of competition for students across institutions. Salmi points out that in both Thailand and Turkey, national open universities enroll about 40 percent of the total student population in each country.

While the growth of online instruction offers important new options for extending higher education in the developing world, these programs pose dilemmas that go well beyond technology, to the very heart of the higher education enterprise. Among the challenges now facing colleges and universities are how they will prepare their instructional staff to operate in this environment, how universities in resource-scarce parts of the world can afford the investments in high-technology needed to compete with universities in countries with greater resources, and how governments will ensure the quality of instruction that comes from outside their borders.

Salmi emphasizes that traditional higher education institutions are facing immense challenges that require them to take a proactive approach to transformation. His analysis of the rapidly changing environment within which higher education institutions are functioning provides a thoughtful preface to the particular issues addressed in the following sections.

SEEKING A NEW BALANCE IN GOVERNMENT-UNIVERSITY RELATIONSHIPS

Organizational change nearly always involves shifts in benefit streams that require a rebalancing of competing interests. Improving the effectiveness and efficiency of an education system does not necessarily work to the benefit of those groups most central to the operation of that system, and may directly work against those interests. Changes that serve the best interest of a higher education system do not necessarily serve the self-interest of individual constituents whose support is crucial to the success of those changes. Inevitably some groups benefit more than others. Even dysfunctional systems produce benefit streams that some find worth protecting. Consequently, from a systems perspective, an essential element in implementing organizational change is an analysis of cross-impacts.

Too often, seeming solutions create new problems, some worse than the original problem they were intended to address. In other cases, demonstrably successful interventions are opposed, even by groups that would appear to benefit from the changes. While these dynamics are not new to education planning, the failure to anticipate the cross-impacts of proposed policies and practices persists. At times this is due to the power of wishful thinking—decision makers clinging to unfounded optimism for lack of any better alternatives. At other times it is because decision makers fail to clearly understand the different incentive systems that operate across key constituent groups. Strengthening and expanding a higher education system, then, not only requires a clear vision of a better system, but also a strategy for helping groups find a new balance of interests that serve their individual needs.

D. Bruce Johnstone and Olga Bain, in Chapter 3, argue that the move by higher education institutions to become more financially self-sufficient has often entailed a loosening of traditional legal and social ties between higher education and government. They discuss the interplay of three forces—privatization, decentralization, and autonomy—on universities, with particular attention to the Russian Federation. Each of these dimensions, they argue, is being driven, in part, by the need for a more responsive, efficient, and financially self-sufficient system of higher education. They examine the extent to which the interaction of these factors operates to encourage better university management and greater responsiveness to the needs of students and society versus the extent that it leads to the fragmentation of universities, the breakdown of the university's unifying role, and the loss of academic quality.

Interests are in conflict. The desire to serve national economic interests brings higher education and government into closer alliance, even while the desire of universities for institutional autonomy tends to pull universities and government apart. In some countries, there is fear that government may use higher education's own move toward privatization, decentralization, and autonomy as a cover for financial disengagement, casting institutions into precarious financial circumstances in the guise of honoring requests for autonomy.

In Chapter 4, the clash of interests between government and higher education is illustrated in David N. Plank and Robert E. Verhine's analysis of university resistance to institutional autonomy in Brazil. At present, a smaller share of the relevant age group is enrolled in tertiary education in Brazil than in virtually any other country in the region. Educators and government officials recognize that Brazil needs to expand its university system. A major impediment to that expansion, however, is the high cost of the federal system, much of which is more the result of inefficiencies than legitimate expenditures needed to maintain high academic standards. For example, the determination of staffing levels, salaries, and criteria for promotion are centralized at the national ministry. Institutional level administrators have little control over the allocation of faculty time or reward structures.

To improve efficiency, the Ministry of Education (MEC) tried to devolve greater responsibility and authority for institutional administration to the individual universities within the federal system. Increasing institutional autonomy was intended to give institutional administrators more flexibility to address inefficiencies and to create a structure in which savings would stay at the campus level for reallocation to higher priority uses. This precipitated fierce opposition on the part of faculty, staff, and students who feared that greater autonomy would reduce the benefit stream they had come to expect from the national government.

While there is widespread agreement in Brazil that the present system cannot be sustained, greater autonomy threatens to change the distribution of power and resources. Faculty, staff, and students all stand to lose if efficiency measures are introduced. Faculty retain generous salaries and light teaching loads. Staff keep job security in a heavily overstaffed system. Students seek to retain free higher education, which disproportionately benefits students from middle- and upper-class families.

Plank and Verhine argue that there is no capacity within universities for collective purpose or shared sacrifice. Yet, while the interests of faculty, staff, and students diverge, there is a common interest in maintaining the benefit flow provided by the inefficiencies of the present system. This leads faculty, staff, and students to be allies in resisting the pressures toward greater institutional autonomy. This, in turn, leads to coalitions among faculty, staff, and students to protect their separate benefit streams at the expense of the larger public who must then pay for these benefits through higher taxes. While higher education systems in many parts of the world eagerly seek greater autonomy from government control, Plank and Verhine's case study illustrates how such changes can have unexpected negative consequences when greater autonomy alters incentive systems in ways that were not fully anticipated.

David W. Chapman, in Chapter 5, addresses another face of the same problem in his analysis of the relationship between national government and higher education in the Lao People's Democratic Republic. The financial imperative for public colleges and universities to generate more of their own funding is widely advocated as a positive reform in higher education. Proponents argue that, since the long-term benefits accrue so heavily to the graduates themselves, students should carry more of the cost than is presently the case in many countries. Faculty, too, are being expected to contribute to the development of new income streams, such as the sale of research and consulting services through university research centers. While the development of new funding streams is absolutely essential for many institutions, the pursuit of funds can distort the incentive system in ways that undercut the core functions of the university in unanticipated ways. Chapman illustrates this with a case study of the National University of Laos (NUOL).

The Lao government uses the National University to build national identity and pride by incorporating three highly symbolic features into its system of higher education: (1) all instruction is in the Lao language; (2) no tuition is charged; and (3) a complex formula is used to allocate university places across provinces in an effort to provide equity in admissions. When, due to high inflation, the government was unable to meet the recurrent budget needs of NUOL, faculty were allowed to offer special English language evening courses in a variety of subjects for which a hefty tuition was charged and for which no scholarships were available. This effectively limited enrollment in the special evening courses to students of affluent families living in the capital city. It essentially created an informal, private university system operating within the structure of the formal, public system, but at considerable variance to the rules governing that formal structure—courses were in English, tuition was charged, and regional equity in admissions was ignored.

The money from these special evening courses went to subsidize the university budget and provide a supplemental income stream for faculty. In doing so, the special evening program distorted faculty incentives and diverted their attention from the regular day program of the university to the special evening program where they could earn additional money. This, in turn, undercut the quality of the regular academic program of the university. In the end, efforts to strengthen the financing of the university, necessary to improve the quality of instruction, had the opposite effect.

COPING WITH CHALLENGES OF GREATER AUTONOMY

The call by campus leaders for more institutional autonomy is a common theme across much of the developing world. Many governments are beginning to agree, but not for the same reasons. Faced with the increasing number of secondary graduates wanting access to college, escalating higher education costs, and competing financial priorities, governments in many countries have shown new interest in reformulating their relationship with higher education. The form of those new relationships varies widely across countries, but the debate often centers on rebalancing financial responsibility and operational control. Institutions often want more operational autonomy while continuing to receive public funds. Governments often want colleges and universities to be more financially self-sufficient but may still want to keep their authority over institutional operations. The resolution of that debate is taking a variety of forms, but with some cross-cutting issues.

The benefits of greater autonomy come at a cost. As institutions are granted greater academic freedom and wider institutional discretion in the use of their budget, those costs are now emerging. While university leaders sometimes complained about decisions made far away from campus, they are now realizing that distance had a useful insulating effect. They could blame the government authorities for decisions that are now being shifted to individual campuses. Some of the complexities once handled by others are now theirs to solve. Campus leaders are now being assailed for their administrative decisions by faculty and students on their own campuses. With autonomy, something is gained but something is also lost.

In Chapter 6, Jairam Reddy offers a broad survey of how national governments and higher education institutions have sought to balance government control and institutional autonomy in the post-independence development of higher education in Africa. National independence meant loosening ties with university systems of the colonial powers. In a relatively narrow period of time, 30 to 40 years, higher education institutions across many countries of the African continent confronted a series of decisions about curriculum, appropriate standards, internal governance, and mechanisms of quality control. Over that time, the postcolonial models inherited from (mostly) the French and British systems have been reshaped into a diverse set of institutions. But the battles frequently were fierce and, in some countries, still continue.

Financial pressure on virtually all African economies (and the economic collapse of some) led to diminished support for higher education, government intrusion into university affairs, and new pressures on campus leaders. The national higher education systems across Africa responded in very different ways, yielding to central government influences in Sudan and Nigeria while maintaining more decentralized management in Uganda and Kenya.

Perhaps the most dramatic pressures on higher education have occurred in countries making a rapid transition from centrally controlled political and economic systems to more democratic, market-based systems. In Chapter 7, John C. Weidman and Regsurengiin Bat-Erdene trace the tension between government and higher education institutions over control of resources and decision making in Mongolia. They point out that during times of rapid transition not all components of the higher education system embrace reform at the same rate and not all participants agree on the shape of the new structure toward which they are moving. Their case study captures the struggle to build new consensus, especially when policies and regulations intended to implement the transition are not all made at once, but are phased in incrementally. This results in misalignments. Policies do not work as intended because supporting economic structures, legal frameworks, and social views are not yet in place. The chapter illustrates the misunderstandings, both intentional and unintentional, that emerge during times of rapid transition, as collective interests give way, at least in part, to more divergent self-interests of both government and higher education institutions.

In finance, for example, institutions are now allowed to charge private tuition, but levels are capped by government regulations. Institutions responded by implementing other income producing strategies, but then had to fend off government claims on those funds. In admissions, quotas established by government gave way to a system more responsive to student demand. However, that student demand was not well aligned to actual employment opportunities, as students had little or no information on prospective labor market needs or the career ladders associated with different jobs. Moreover, institutions' need to ensure tuition flow sometimes has overshadowed merit in student selection.

Gerard A. Postiglione, in Chapter 8, examines the effects of expansion and greater institutional autonomy on the core functions of higher education—teaching, research, and service—in China. China educates one-quarter of the world's students on one percent of the world's education budget (Zhang, 1999). He describes a government apparatus that has transferred much autonomy and responsibility for teaching and research to individual institutions. Faced with explosive growth in its higher education system (the number of regular colleges and universities increased from 598 in 1974 to 1,080 by 1994), administrators in higher education must focus on financing expansion. In the meantime, universities face a shortage of qualified academic staff, and those in place are underpaid. At the same time, current faculty members are coming under new pressure to teach in different ways, improve the quality of their instruction, and revise their curricula to reflect the changing nature of the national economy (more market-based). Postiglione examines the strategies employed by institutions dealing with greater autonomy as they must adapt to the pressures of enormous enrollment growth in the face of limited funds.

ACHIEVING EQUITY WHILE MANAGING EXPANSION

The tensions among university efforts to expand access by increasing the size or the number of higher education institutions, improve equity by admitting a more diverse group of students, improve quality by raising admissions or graduation standards, and contain costs to government are widely understood by policy makers. While the tensions are clear, the trade-offs are not.

Higher education across much of the developing world is caught in a set of paradoxes. On one hand, higher education systems have come under enormous political and social pressure to accept more students while, at the same time, many of those systems are experiencing declining levels of per student support from government. Government and education leaders call for higher quality education, even though rapid enrollment increases typically are accompanied by declines in quality indicators. Moreover, expanded access in the face of declining resources does not always bode well for greater diversity in who actually enrolls. The access-equity-quality-cost squeeze has generated sharp interest in ways that colleges and universities can generate increased revenues through the introduction of private tuition and the more entrepreneurial use of faculty. However, these efforts to promote greater financial independence have costs as well as benefits.

Less well understood than the financial implications of rapid enrollment increases is the relationship between rapidly expanding enrollments and equity in admissions. Improved equity in higher education admissions is the stated goal of virtually all countries experiencing rapid enrollment increases. The presumption is that lower tuition and fees allow more students to attend higher education and that more students in the system mean a broader set of students enjoying the benefits of higher education. Public policies often assume that heavy subsidization of higher education (low to no tuition and fees) will provide greater equity in access for a larger segment of the population coming from lower and lower-middle income families.

In Chapter 9, Darrell R. Lewis and Halil Dundar challenge these assumptions, arguing that the rapid growth in the number of places has not necessarily led to greater equality of opportunity. Rather, expanded access to higher education has often come at the expense of equity.

They argue that proportionate access to higher education by lower income groups is not materially improved by low- and no-tuition policies. There is often a regressive effect in which middle or higher income groups receive a disproportionate benefit from the no-tuition policy. Consequently, keeping higher education costs low does not necessarily benefit students from the lowest income backgrounds. Too often the poorest families inadvertently end up subsidizing richer families.

Lewis and Dundar argue that the strongest economic influences on access are not tuition and fees, but the other private costs of attendance. These other costs work against students from rural areas that lack an adequate supply of higher education places. These students then have to relocate to an urban area to gain higher education access, making their costs of attendance higher than the costs for students already residing in the urban areas. They suggest that the quality of the secondary schooling that students receive, the geographic location of higher education institutions, and differential access to program options within higher education can limit the greater equity that would appear to be gained by maintaining a low- or no-tuition and fee policy.

NEW PRESSURES AND FORMS OF ACCOUNTABILITY

The relationship between higher education institutions and their national governments often are operationalized through rather formal systems of government oversight of higher education. Among the more prominent oversight mechanisms are the institutional accreditation and quality assurance procedures that are employed by government. As Elaine El-Khawas argues in Chapter 10, quality assurance procedures can be a powerful means of institutional improvement or a tool of control and external manipulation.

The rapid enrollment increases that sometimes put downward pressure on quality, the greater financial autonomy being gained by some public institutions, the rise of private, for-profit institutions, and the emergence of virtual universities that offer online programs across borders all conspire to give new importance to quality assurance procedures in both developing and more industrialized countries. One of the sharpest concerns of the last decade is how to ensure quality in higher education in the face of multiple pressures that could easily threaten it.

As government-university relationships change, government still has a legitimate and necessary role to play in protecting the public interest and ensuring that the higher education offered meets minimum standards. El-Khawas discusses the choices countries confront in their efforts to ensure quality. For example, there are serious questions as to the general purpose of quality assurance—improving education, enhancing relevance, raising standards, ensuring quality control, or correcting deficiencies. Moreover, the particular quality assurance procedures adopted by governments can have a significant impact on instructional quality, faculty morale, and the ability of higher education institutions to prepare graduates with the skill mix most relevant to the needs of the country.

She points out the political dimensions that often underlie the particular quality assurance strategies that have evolved in particular countries. El-Khawas combines an insightful discussion of the purposes and issues involved with quality assurance in higher education with an informative discussion of how a variety of countries actually undertake and implement quality assurance procedures.

SUPPORTING ACADEMIC STAFF IN NEW ROLES

Underpaying university faculty while expecting them to supplement their income through private consulting has been a rather common way of financing higher education. It is a functional system of mutual benefits in which instructors gain the prestige of having an academic title and affiliation that serves them well in their entrepreneurial ventures while colleges and universities secure a distinguished faculty at a low price. One consequence of this practice, however, is that institutional administrators have little control over the non-instructional time of academic staff. While this issue arose in earlier chapters (e.g., Chapman's chapter on Laos), this section explores the wider implications and challenges that university administrators and academic staff face as they define and clarify new roles and relationships.

In few places in the world have changes in higher education occurred with the magnitude and speed of those experienced in China during the last several decades. Higher education enrollment in Chinese colleges and universities in 2000 was three times the enrollment in 1980, a dramatically faster expansion of the higher education system than had been anticipated or sought. This, in turn, has resulted in sharp increases in the demand for new faculty and for instructional space. At the same time, the more open and global economy emerging in China has resulted in new pressures on higher education institutions to revise curriculum and pedagogical practices to ensure that Chinese graduates are competitive in a world market. All of these changes are expensive and, consequently, have fueled intense pressure on institutions to expand and diversify their sources of funding.

It is against this backdrop that Yvonna S. Lincoln, Bryan R. Cole, Wang Xiaoping, and Yang "Sherry" Xiaobo, in Chapter 11, present a force-field analysis of the pressures shaping faculty work life in Chinese higher education. Their chapter explains that, in the context of the expansion of higher education in China, reform is underway pertaining to financing, administrative and governance processes and structures, and curriculum. The consequences of these reform efforts pose significant implications for the academic staff. With 80 percent of the full professors nationwide expected to retire by 2005, new faculty members must be attracted and retained. Some changes in the academic workplace—such as reduced retirement—may diminish interest in academic careers.

Reformulating incentive systems to attract new faculty members is needed, but improved incentives alone will not be enough. Reform of higher education also means changes in the nature and organization of faculty work. In China, faculty members are facing expectations to teach larger classes, expand their research agendas, revise curricula, and take on institutional leadership and governance roles. Since, historically, institutional structures and governance were centrally controlled in China, greater autonomy and faculty participation involve new roles and challenges for academic staff.

The issues for academic staff in China are not unlike those in other countries. Faculty members are being asked to do more work and take on new responsibilities. These expanded roles often must occur in contexts where institution-level administrators lack experience in managing and leading decentralized organizations and where tight financial resources constrain institutional spending for research and teaching facilities. Furthermore, many faculty members lack the skills needed to revise and improve the curriculum and their own instructional practices to meet new demands for quality and relevance. To that end, many institutions will need coordinated, sustained faculty development programs.

Ann E. Austin, in Chapter 12, examines the emerging movement to institute formal faculty development programs in higher education across the developing world, with particular attention to South Africa. She traces the relationship between faculty and their institutions during apartheid and how that changed with the end of apartheid. With the breakdown of apartheid, there was a need to racially integrate faculty and student bodies, revise curricula to align with the dramatic changes in social policy, address quality issues in higher education institutions, prepare faculty members to work with a broader range of student academic abilities, move from teacher-centered to student-centered instructional practices, and do all these things within tight fiscal constraints. Given this context, Austin discusses the role of faculty development and suggests practical strategies for establishing a faculty development program.

The faculty development activities she proposes have wide applicability beyond South Africa. As countries move to a market economy, faculty are coming under new pressure to offer instruction better aligned with the knowledge and skills graduates will need in the labor market, to give more emphasis to fostering students' critical thinking and problem-solving abilities in their instruction, and to assist students in their college-to-work transitions. Only as education leaders provide the necessary support for faculty development are these goals likely to be achieved.

In Chapter 13, Ann E. Austin and David W. Chapman offer a series of observations about fostering innovation in the developing world and revisit the central thesis of this book. Among other things, they point out that many of the most pressing issues facing higher education institutions are not directly educational issues and that successful reform requires more than formulating clear goals.

CONCLUDING REMARKS

Several key themes weave through and connect the chapters in this book. First, higher education institutions throughout the world are facing changing contexts and new demands that call for institutional response. Second, while the unique circumstances of each national and institutional situation must be recognized, the challenges created by these changing contexts and new demands are similar for higher education institutions across the developing world. Third, these issues are best understood and institutional responses most effectively developed within a systems perspective. While each section of this book highlights a particular critical issue, readers will discern that the chapters often reveal the interrelationships among the issues. In determining their responses to each issue, institutional leaders are wise to examine the multiple dimensions of each issue, and how actions to respond to one challenge may affect other aspects of institutional mission, functioning, quality, responsiveness, and effectiveness.

Higher education leaders across the world—in both developing and developed countries—are well served to consider how other institutions, in other countries, are responding to the challenges created by changing contexts. Useful examples of institutional strategies and approaches can be found in many countries, large and small, developing as well as developed. The book's final chapter looks across the particular institutional and national examples offered in previous chapters to offer cross-cutting observations and relevant lessons for those concerned with higher education innovation and change.

REFERENCES

Ajayi, J.F.A., Goma, L.K.H., & Johnson, G. H. (1996). *The African experience with higher education.* Athens: Ohio University Press.

Altbach, P. (1998). *Comparative higher education: Knowledge, the university and development.* Greenwich, CT: Ablex Publishers.

Asian Development Bank. (1997). *Emerging Asia: Changes and challenges.* Manila: Asian Development Bank.

Beyrer, C. (1998). *War in the blood: Sex, politics, and AIDS in Southeast Asia.* New York: White Lotus Books.
Bloom, D., & Godwin, P. (Eds.). (1997). *The economics of HIV and AIDS: The case of South and Southeast Asia.* New York: Oxford University Press.
Bruestle, A. E. (1993). East Asia's urban environment. *Environmental Science and Technology, 7,* 2280–2284.
Burbules, N. C., & Callister, T. A., Jr. (2000). Universities in transition: The promise and the challenge of new technologies. *Teachers' College Record, 102*(2), 271–293.
Chapman, D. W. (1998). *Technical working paper on trends, issues and policies in education management and efficiency in Asia.* Paper prepared for the Asian Development Bank project on Regional Trends, Issues and Policies in Education, Manila: Asian Development Bank.
Chapman D. W. (2000). Trends in educational administration in developing Asia. *Educational Administration Quarterly,* 36(2), 283–308.
Chapman, D. W., & Claffey, J. (1998, September 25). Higher education and international development: Some new opportunities worth taking. Point of View commentary. *Chronicle of Higher Education,* p. B6.
Corbin, J. (1998). *Recent HIV seroprevalence levels by country: July 1998.* Health Studies Branch, Washington, DC: U.S. Bureau of the Census.
Feldman, D. W., & Miller, J. W. (1998). *The AIDS crisis: A documentary history.* Westport, CT: Greenwood Press.
Imai, R. (1998). *Population, energy, and the environment: Can Asia keep them in balance in the coming century?* Tokyo: Institute for International Policy Studies.
International Renaissance Foundation. (1997, July 4–6). *Education in Ukraine in the time of transition.* Discussion paper prepared for the seminar, "Strategic development of education policy in Ukraine," Kiev (under IRF project, *Society and State: Education Policy Dialogue*).
Jalal, K. F. (1993). International agencies and the Asia-Pacific environment. *Environmental Science and Technology, 27,* 2276–2279.
Katz, R. N. and Associates. (1999). *Dancing with the devil: Information technology and the new competition in higher education.* San Francisco: Jossey-Bass.
Kempner, K., Mollis, M., & Tierney, W. (Eds.). (1998). *Comparative education.* ASHE Reader Series. Needham Heights, MA: Simon and Schuster.
Linge, G.J.R., & Porter, D. (Eds.). (1997). *No place for borders: The HIV/AIDS epidemic and development in Asia and the Pacific.* Academy of Social Sciences in Australia, St. Leonards, Australia: Allen and Unwin.
Maslen, G. (2001, March 9). Students at Australian colleges are attacking a plan to create a global online university. *Chronicle of Higher Education,* p. A39.
Palloff, R. M., & Pratt, K. (2001). *Lessons from cyberspace: The realities of online teaching.* San Francisco: Jossey-Bass.
Panayotou, T. (1993). The environment in Southeast Asia: Problems and policies. *Environmental Science and Technology, 27,* 2270–2274.
Park, J. (1995). *Financing environmentally sound development: Asian Development Bank's Office of the Environment.* Manila: Asian Development Bank.
Phipps, R., & Merisotis, J. (1999). *What's the difference? A review of contemporary*

research on the effectiveness of distance learning in higher education. Washington, DC: The Institute for Higher Education Policy.

Postiglione, G., & Mak, G. (Eds.). (1997). *Asian higher education: An international handbook and reference guide.* Westport, CT: Greenwood Press.

Rogers, P. (1993). The environment in Southeast Asia. *Environmental Science and Technology, 27*, 2269.

Tan, J-P., & Sanderson, W. C. (1996). *Population in Asia.* World Bank regional and sector studies series. Brookfield, VT: Avebury.

United Nations. (1997). *Population and environment dynamics, poverty and quality of life in countries of the ESCAP region* (Asian Population Studies Series, number 147). United Nations Economic and Social Commission for Asia and the Pacific. New York: United Nations.

Weick, K. E. (1976). Educational organizations as loosely coupled systems. *Administrative Science Quarterly, 21*, 1–19.

World Bank. (1994). *Higher Education: Lessons from experience.* Washington, DC: The World Bank.

World Bank. (2000). *Higher education in developing countries: Peril and promise.* Report of the Global Joint Task Force on Higher Education, Washington, DC.

Zhang Baoqing. (1999, January 10). *Zhonggong zhongyang dangxiao—Baogao xuan* [Party school of the Chinese Communist Party—selected reports], no. 1, pp. 2–17, as quoted in *Chinese Education and Society, 33*(1), 53–60. New York: M.E. Sharpe.

Chapter 2

Higher Education at a Turning Point

Jamil Salmi

> It is not the strongest species that survive, nor the most intelligent, but the ones most responsive to change.
>
> —Charles Darwin

Imagine a university without buildings or classrooms or even a library. Imagine a university 10,000 miles away from its students. Imagine a university without academic departments, without required courses or majors or grades. Imagine a college open 24 hours a day, seven days a week, 365 days a year. Imagine a college proposing a bachelor's degree in Individualized Studies or in Interdisciplinary Studies, with a catalogue of more than 4,000 different courses. Imagine a degree valid only for five years after graduation. Imagine a college willing to reimburse its students if they do not find a suitable job within six months after graduation. Imagine a higher education system where institutions are ranked not by the quality of their teachers, but by the intensity of electronic wiring and the degree of their Internet connectivity. Imagine a country whose main export earnings come from the sale of higher education services. Imagine a socialist nation which charges market-rate tuition fees to obtain full-cost recovery in public higher education. Are we entering the realm of science fiction? Or are these evocations real-life stories of revolution in the world of higher education at the dawn of the twenty-first century?

In the past few years, many countries have witnessed significant transformations and reforms in their higher education systems, including the emergence of new types of institutions, changes in patterns of financing and governance, the establishment of evaluation and accreditation mechanisms, curriculum reforms, and technological innovations. But the tertiary education landscape is not changing as fast everywhere. Some universities have proudly tried to maintain their traditions, good or bad (World Bank, 1998). At Oxford University, New College is a venerable sixteenth-century institution. At Bob Jones University in South Carolina interracial dating was banned until only recently. These unbending institutions are not alone; other universities throughout the world have been passive in the face of crisis. The oldest university on the American continent, the Autonomous University of Santo Domingo in the Dominican Republic (established in 1538), is about to collapse under the pressure of its 80,000 students crowding facilities originally designed to accommodate only 6,000. The largest classical university in Latin America, the National Autonomous University of Mexico, was paralyzed for ten months in 1999–2000 by a strike over the rector's decision to increase tuition fees by the equivalent of US$140 per year. In this rapidly evolving world, what is likely to happen to those higher education institutions which are not willing or able to change?

To approach this problem, this chapter is divided into two parts. It looks first at the new challenges characterizing the environment in which higher education institutions operate and compete at the beginning of the twenty-first century. Second, it examines some concrete implications of these challenges for higher education leaders, looking at promising trends and experiences in countries and institutions that have taken the lead in introducing reforms and innovations.

THE NEW CHALLENGES

There are three major, intertwined new challenges which bear heavily on the role and functions of higher education: (1) economic globalization, (2) the increasing importance of knowledge as a driver of growth, and (3) the information and communication revolution.

Economic Globalization

Globalization is the complex integration of capital, technology, and information across national boundaries in such a way as to create an increasingly integrated world market, with the direct consequence that more and more countries and firms have no choice but to compete in a global economy. Globalization may not be a new phenomenon. The conquest of America by the Spanish and Portuguese invaders at the end of the fifteenth century, the triangular cotton and slave trade in the seventeenth and eighteenth centuries, the construction of the trans-Atlantic telegraph cable in the 1860s, and the colonization of most of Asia and Africa until the middle of the twentieth century were key factors of economic integration and determinants of economic growth on a global scale. But there has undoubtedly been an acceleration of the phenomenon in the past two decades, as demonstrated by the increase in international trade and the growing interdependence of capital markets.

Emphasizing globalization as an important economic trend does not imply a value judgment, either positive or negative. Many people see this evolution as a major source of opportunities, while critics decry the dangers of interdependency and high volatility, such as the risk of transferring financial crises from one country to the other. But globalization is happening, whether one approves of it or not, whether one likes it or not, and every country in the world, every firm, every working person is affected by it and is very likely a part of it.

The Increasing Importance of Knowledge

The second dimension of change is the growing role of knowledge. Economic development is increasingly linked to a nation's ability to acquire and apply technical and socioeconomic knowledge, and the process of globalization is accelerating this trend. Comparative advantages come less and less from abundant natural resources or cheaper labor, and more and more from technical innovations and the competitive use of knowledge. The proportion of goods with a medium-high and high level of technology content in international trade has gone from 33 percent in 1976 to 54 percent in 1996 (World Bank, 1998). Today, economic growth is as much a process of knowledge accumulation as of capital accumulation. It is estimated that firms devote one-third of their investment to knowledge-based intangibles such as training, research and development, patents, licensing, design, and marketing. In this context, economies of scope, derived from the ability to design and offer different products and services with the same technology, are becoming a powerful factor of expansion. In high-technology industries like electronics and telecommunications, economies of scope can be more of a driving force than traditional economies of scale (Banker, Chang, & Majumdar, 1998). New types of companies, called producer services companies, have begun to prosper as providers of specialized knowledge, information, and data supporting existing manufacturing firms. Experts see them as the principal source of created comparative advantage and high value added in advanced industrialized economies (Gibbons, 1998). At the same time, there is a rapid acceleration in the rhythm of creation and dissemination of knowledge, which means that the life span of technologies and products gets progressively shorter, and obsolescence comes more quickly. In chemistry, for instance, there were 360,000 known substances in 1978. This number had doubled by 1988. By 1998, there were three times as many known substances (1,700,000). Almost 150,000 new "patent equivalents" were added to the Chemical Abstracts database in 1998, compared to less than 10,000 a year in the late 1960s. Perhaps the best illustration of the short life span of new information and products comes from the computer industry, where the monopoly of the Intel microprocessing chip has decreased spectacularly in duration with each new version. With its 386 microprocessor, Intel dominated the market for more than three years in the late 1980s. Ten years later its competitive edge lasted only three months with Pentium II. Even more dramatic, Pentium III was supplanted by AMD's Athlon microprocessor after being on the market for only a few weeks.

In addition, many fields see the distance between basic science and technological application narrowing or, in some cases, disappearing altogether. The implication is that pure and applied research are not separate any longer. Molecular biology and computer science are two salient examples of this evolution.

The results of a recent survey of technical innovation in U.S. manufacturing firms underscore the strategic importance of academic research in the development of new industrial products and processes. On average, 19 percent of new products and 15 percent of new processes were directly based on academic research. The proportion was even higher, 44 and 37 percent, respectively, in high-technology industries such as drugs, instruments, and information processing (Mansfield, 1991). There is also a significant geographical dimension to this relation between academic research and industrial applications, as underlined by a rich body of evidence on the regional development impact of universities and the spillover effects of academic research on industrial research and technology and local innovation (see, for example, Jaffe, 1989).

The Information and Communication Revolution

The third dimension of change is the information and communication revolution. The advent of printing in the fifteenth century brought about the first radical transformation in the way knowledge is kept and shared by people. Today, technological innovations are revolutionizing again the capacity to store, transmit, and use information. Rapid progress in electronics, telecommunications, and satellite technologies, permitting high capacity data transmission at very low cost, has resulted in the quasi abolition of physical distance. Sixty years ago a phone call from New York to London cost the equivalent of US$300 per minute, today that same call costs only five cents per minute. In 1985, the cost of sending 45 million bits of information per second over one kilometer of optical fibers was close to 100 dollars; in 1997, it was possible to send 45,000 million bits per second at a cost of just 0.05 cents (Bond, 1997). For all practical purposes, there are no more logistical barriers to information access and communication among people, institutions, and countries.

IMPLICATIONS FOR HIGHER EDUCATION

What are the implications of these challenges for higher education? They herald (1) radical changes in training needs, (2) new forms of competition, and (3) new configurations and modes of operation for higher education institutions.

Changing Training and Needs

A trend toward higher and different skills has been observed in OECD countries and in the most advanced developing economies. In knowledge-driven economies, ever greater numbers of workers and employees need higher level skills. This is illustrated by recent analyses of rates of return in a few Latin American countries (Argentina, Brazil, and Mexico) which show a rising rate of return for tertiary education, a reversal of earlier trends in the 1970s and the 1980s (Barros & Ramos, 1996; Lächler, 1997; Pessino, 1995). Moreover, in Organization of Economic Cooperation and Development (OECD) countries, highly skilled white collar employees account for 25 to 35 percent of the labor force.

The second dimension of change in education and training needs is the growing importance of continuing education needed to update knowledge and skills on a regular basis because of the short "shelf life" of knowledge. The traditional approach of studying for a discrete and finite period of time to acquire a first degree or to complete graduate education before moving on to professional life is being progressively replaced by practices of lifelong education. Training is becoming an integral part of one's working life, and takes place in a myriad of contexts: on the job, in specialized higher education institutions, or even at home. As Shakespeare wrote with prescience several centuries ago,

> Learning is but an adjunct to ourself,
> And where we are our learning likewise is.

The evolution of training needs means that, in the medium term, the primary clientele of universities will no longer be young high school graduates. Universities must now organize themselves to accommodate the learning and training needs of a very diverse clientele: working students, mature students, stay-at-home students, traveling students, part-time students, day students, night students, and weekend students. One can expect a significant change in the demographic shape of higher education institutions, whereby the traditional structure of a pyramid with a majority of first degree students, a smaller group of postgraduate students, and finally an even smaller share of participants in continuing education programs will be replaced by an inverted pyramid with a minority of first-time students, more students pursuing a second or third degree, and the majority of students enrolled in short-term continuing education activities. Already in the United States, almost half of the student population consists of mature and part-time students, a dramatic shift from the previous generation. In Russia, part-time students represent 37 percent of total enrollment. Finland, one of the leading promoters of continuing education in Europe, has 150,000 young people enrolled in regular higher education degree courses and 200,000 adults in continuing education programs.

Another important consequence of the acceleration of scientific and technological progress is the diminished emphasis in tertiary education programs on the learning of facts and basic data per se. We now see a growing importance of what could be called *methodological knowledge* and skills (i.e., the ability to learn in an autonomous manner). Today in many disciplines, factual knowledge taught in the first year of study may become obsolete before graduation. The learning process now needs to be increasingly based on the capacity to find, access, and apply knowledge to problem solving. In this new paradigm, where learning to learn, learning to transform information into new knowledge, and learning to transfer new knowledge into applications are more important than memorizing specific information, primacy is given to information seeking and analysis, the ability to reason, and problem solving. In addition, competencies such as learning to work in teams, peer teaching, creativity, resourcefulness, and the ability to adjust to change are among the new skills which employers value in the knowledge economy.

The third dimension of change in training needs is the growing attractiveness of degrees and credentials with international recognition. In a global economy, where firms produce for overseas markets and compete with foreign firms in their own domestic markets, there is a rising demand for internationally recognized qualifications, especially in management-related fields. Many entrepreneurial university leaders have been quick to identify and capitalize on this trend. In the United States, a rapidly growing number of online universities are reaching out to students in foreign countries. Jones International University, for instance, which already serves students in 38 countries, is the first online university in the world that has been formally accredited by the same agency that accredits traditional universities such as the University of Michigan or the University of Chicago. In Asia and Eastern Europe, there has been a proliferation of so-called overseas "validated courses" offered by franchise institutions operating on behalf of British and Australian universities. One-fifth of the 80,000 foreign students enrolled in Australian universities are studying at off-shore campuses, mainly in Malaysia and Singapore. Also, each year hundreds of thousands of students in Commonwealth countries take exams organized by UK examination boards such as the Institute of Commerce and Management or the London Chamber of Commerce and Institute (Bennell and

Pearce, 1998). In the Middle East, the American universities of Beirut and Cairo have always attracted significant numbers of young people eager to earn a U.S. degree. In China, one of the fastest-growing private education institutions is a school specializing in preparatory courses for American colleges, called the New Oriental School, which already boasts 50,000 students in Beijing alone (Doyle, 2000). In Germany, where higher education is predominantly public, a number of private business schools have been recently established, either as independent institutions or subsidiaries of existing public universities. Following the example of a rapidly growing number of MBA programs in the Netherlands and France, programs in these schools are taught in English, and international students are actively sought.

New Forms of Competition

The decreased importance of physical distance means that the best universities of any country can decide to open a branch anywhere in the world or to reach out across borders using the Internet or satellite communication links, effectively competing with any national university on its own territory. The president of the University of Maryland wrote an article of complaint in the *Washington Post* in April 1999, vehemently protesting the opening of a branch of the University of Phoenix in Maryland. The California-based University of Phoenix, one of the most dynamic distance universities in the United States, uses an incentive system to reward professors on the basis of the labor market outcomes of graduates and boasts an enrollment of 68,000 students. The British Open University has inundated Canadian students with Internet messages saying more or less "we'll give you degrees and we don't really care if they're recognized in Canada because they're recognized by Cambridge and Oxford. And we'll do it at one-tenth the cost" (The Maclean's Guide to Canadian Universities, 1999). It is estimated that, in the United States alone, there are already more than 3,000 institutions offering online training. Thirty-three states in the United States have a statewide virtual university; 85 percent of community colleges are expected to offer distance education courses by 2002 (Olsen, 2000). Distance education is sometimes delivered by a specialized institution set up by an alliance of universities, as is the case with Western Governors University in the United States and Open Learning Agency in British Columbia. The proportion of U.S. universities with distance education courses has grown from 34 percent in 1997–1998 to about 50 percent in 1999–2000, public universities being much more advanced than private ones in this regard (Mendels, 2000a). The Mexican Virtual University of Monterrey offers 15 master's degree programs using teleconferencing and the Internet that reach 50,000 students in 1,450 learning centers throughout Mexico and 116 spread all over Latin America. In Thailand and Turkey, the national open universities enroll respectively 41 and 38 percent of the total student population in each country.

Corporate universities are another form of competition that traditional universities will increasingly have to reckon with, especially in the area of continuing education. It is estimated that there are about 1,600 institutions in the world functioning today as corporate universities, up from 400 ten years ago. Two significant examples of successful corporate universities are those of Motorola and IBM. Recognized as one of the most successful corporate universities in benchmarking exercises, Motorola University, which operates with a yearly budget of $120 million representing almost 4 percent of its annual payroll, manages 99 learning and training sites in 21 countries (Densford, 1999). IBM's corporate university, one of the largest in the world, is a virtual institution employing 3,400 professionals in 55 countries and offering more than 10,000 courses through intranet and satellite links. The 1999 recipients of the Corporate University Awards sponsored by *Financial Times*, which recognize the most innovative corporate university initiatives of the year, were TVA University, IDX Institute of Technology, Dell Learning, IBM Corporate University, and ST University (Authers, 1999).

Corporate universities operate under one of three modalities, or any combination of these: (1) with their own network of physical campuses (e.g., Disney, Toyota, Motorola), (2) as a virtual university (e.g., IBM, Dow Chemical), or (3) through an alliance with existing higher education institutions (e.g., Bell Atlantic, United HealthCare, United Technologies). A few corporate universities, such as the Rand Graduate School of Policy Studies and the Arthur D. Little School of Management, have been officially accredited and enjoy the authority to grant formal degrees. Experts are predicting that, by the year 2010, there will be more corporate universities than traditional campus-based universities in the world, and an increasing proportion of them will be serving smaller companies rather than corporate giants.

The third form of unconventional competition comes from the new "academic brokers," virtual entrepreneurs who specialize in bringing together suppliers and consumers of educational services. Companies like Connect Education, Inc. and Electronic University Network build, lease, and manage campuses, produce multimedia educational software, and provide guidance to serve the training needs of corporate clients worldwide (Abeles, 1998). Rennselaer Polytechnic Institute coordinates and delivers degree programs from Boston University, Carnegie Mellon, Stanford University, and MIT for the employees of United HealthCare and United Technologies (Motti, 1999). Nexus, a UK-based company advertising itself as the "world's largest international student recruitment media company," organizes fairs in many East Asian and Latin American countries, bringing together higher education institutions and students interested in overseas studies. At the shadier extreme of the academic brokering industry, one finds Internet-based essay mills offering to help students with their college assignments. Described by their promoters as mere research tools, they are under attack from the academic community who decry their capacity to increase plagiarism and cheating.

Some "traditional" higher education institutions have been quick to catch on to the potential of education and training brokering arrangements. St. Petersburg Junior College recently entered into a partnership with Florida State University, the University of Central Florida and the UK Open University to offer four-year degree programs at some of its sites (Klein, 1999). The University of California at Santa Cruz, having set up its own corporate training department ten years ago in the middle of Silicon Valley, has established successful partnerships with a number of corporate universities, notably those operated by GE and Sun Microsystems. It has even managed to attract additional state funding on a matching grant basis (Clark, 1999).

The emergence of these new forms of competition is likely to change the nature of quality assurance bodies, mechanisms, and criteria. It is doubtful that the philosophy, principles, and standards routinely applied to evaluate or accredit campus-based programs can be used without significant adjustments to assess the quality and effectiveness of online courses and other modalities of distance education. Appropriate and reliable accreditation and evaluation processes are needed to reassure the public that the courses, programs, and degrees offered by the new types of distance education institutions meet acceptable academic and professional standards. Less emphasis is likely to be given to traditional input dimensions such as qualifications of individual faculty and student selection criteria, and more on the capabilities of graduates. Such a shift would reflect the results of effective teamwork among designers of pedagogical support materials, facilitators of resource-based course delivery, mentors of students, and evaluators of learning outcomes. Western Governors University's initiative to move to competency-based evaluations performed by an independent agency has created an interesting precedent which may ultimately have consequences extending even to traditional universities.

At the national level, higher education authorities are increasingly challenged by the availability of foreign programs through distance education, franchise institutions, and online courses. Very few developing nations have established accreditation and evaluation systems, let alone access to the necessary information on these foreign programs or the institutional monitoring capacity to be able to detect fraud and protect their students from low quality offerings. Many Latin American countries, for example, find themselves in the awkward situation of having more distance education doctoral programs proposed by Spanish universities than conventional doctoral programs offered in their national universities.

> Distance learning is a world of extremes, when you look at the best university education around the world, some of it is now distance learning, when you look for the worst, all of it is distance learning. Bad distance learning may now be given a new lease on life by the brave new world of online teaching. (Daniel, 1999, quoted in Olsen, 2000)

For those countries which cannot afford to develop their own information system, there is always the possibility of participating in international accreditation and evaluation networks or requiring from foreign tertiary education institutions the same quality assurance obligations as demanded in their country of origin.

Changes in Structures and Modes of Operation

Faced with new training needs and new competitive challenges, many universities need to undertake drastic transformations in governance, organizational structure, and modes of operation.

A key aspect will be the ability of universities to organize traditional disciplines differently, taking into consideration the emergence of new scientific and technological fields. Among the most significant ones, it is worth mentioning molecular biology and biotechnology, advanced materials science, microelectronics, information systems, robotics, intelligent systems and neuroscience, and environmental science and technology. Training and research for these fields requires the integration of a number of disciplines which have not necessarily been in close contact previously, resulting in the multiplication of inter- and multidisciplinary programs cutting across traditional institutional barriers. For example, the study of molecular devices and sensors, within the wider framework of molecular biology and biotechnology, brings together specialists in electronics, materials science, chemistry, and biology to achieve greater synergy. Imaging technology and medical science have become closely articulated. At the University of Glasgow, physicians and mechanical engineers conduct research together in the field of control engineering, trying to develop technologies to help paraplegic patients. In Denmark, environmental science programs are taught by a group of specialists who include not only scientists and engineers but also theologians and political scientists responsible for teaching relevant ethical and political economy dimensions. At Roskilde University near Copenhagen, traditional departmental borders were removed in the late 1980s. For instance, chemistry and life sciences are part of a single multidisciplinary department, as are mathematics and physics or technology and social sciences. In each department, the educational experience of undergraduate students follows a project-based learning approach. George Mason University in Virginia started what is called the New Century College with a bachelor's degree in Interdisciplinary Studies as its main academic program.

The University of Illinois at Urbana–Champaign and the University of Southern California have developed the "Team Engineering Analysis and Modeling" methodology based on the collaboration of researchers from a broad spectrum of the engineering and social sciences. The University of Warsaw's newly established Collegium for Interdepartmental Studies, which offers individually tailored undergraduate programs, is Poland's first attempt at interdisciplinary education (Bullag, 1999).

The new patterns of knowledge creation do not imply only a reconfiguration of departments into a different institutional map, but more importantly, the reorganization of research and training around the search for solutions to complex problems, rather than the analytical practices of traditional academic disciplines. This evolution is leading to the emergence of what some experts call "transdisciplinarity," with distinct theoretical structures and research methods (Gibbons, Limoges, Nowotny, Schwartzman, Scott, & Trow, 1994). McMaster University in Ontario, Canada, and the University of Maastricht in Holland were among the first universities to introduce problem-based learning in their medical and engineering programs in the 1970s. The University of British Columbia is promoting "research-based learning," an approach linking undergraduate students to research teams with extensive reliance on information technology for basic course information. Waterloo University in Western Ontario earned a high reputation for its engineering degrees—considered among the best in the country—through the successful development of cooperative programs that integrate in-school and on-the-job training. Such innovations have helped that institution achieve what Cambridge mathematician Alfred North Whitehead (1929) described, many decades ago, as the noble mission of the university:

> The tragedy of the world is that those who are imaginative have but slight experience, and those who are experienced have feeble imaginations. Fools act on imagination without experience. Pedants act on knowledge without imagination. The task of the university is to weld together imagination and experience. (p. 98)

Realigning universities on the basis of inter- and multidisciplinary learning and research themes implies not only changes in program and curriculum design, but also significant modifications in the planning and organization of the laboratory and workshop infrastructure. From the Georgia Institute of Technology comes a successful experience in developing an interdisciplinary mechatronics laboratory serving the needs of students in electrical, mechanical, industrial, computer, and other engineering departments in a cost-effective manner. Mechatronics is "the synergistic combination of precision engineering, electronic control, and systems thinking in the design of products and manufacturing processes" (Arkin, Lee, McGinnis, & Zhou, 1997, pp. 113–118). A unique partnership bringing together Penn State University, the University of Puerto Rico–Mayaguez, the University of Washington, and Sandia National Laboratories has permitted the establishment of "Learning Factory" facilities across the partner schools which allow teams of students from industrial, mechanical, electrical, chemical engineering, and business administration to work on interdisciplinary projects (Lamancusa, Jorgensen, & Zayas-Castro, 1997).

The use of modern technology has just begun to revolutionize the way teaching and learning occur. The concurrent use of multimedia and computers permits the development of new pedagogical approaches involving active and interactive learning. Frontal teaching can be replaced by or associated with asynchronous teaching in the form of online classes that can be either scheduled or self-paced. With a proper integration of technology in the curriculum, teachers can move away from their traditional role as one-way instructors toward becoming facilitators of learning. In Brazil, a few schools of medicine and engineering in federal universities have been experimenting with the use of computer-based programs to teach mathematics in first and second year, rather than having students attend regular classes. This change in pedagogical approach has resulted in a remarkable decrease in dropout rates—from 70 to 30 percent. In Australia, the University of Newcastle led the way in the use of a problem-learning approach in medical education. The University of Southern Denmark has cut dropout rates in its business administration program in half by replacing traditional teaching with project-based learning (Thulstrup, 1999). The Colorado Community College system is pioneering a two-year degree which is taught entirely online. In 1999, for the first time, a course of comparative education was taught simultaneously and interactively to groups of students in two separate New York State universities, SUNY Buffalo and SUNY Albany, combining videoconferences through satellite links and Internet sessions. This is also common practice at the University of Highlands and Islands in Scotland. St. Petersburg Junior College, Florida's oldest community college, has pioneered the use of two-way interactive video systems to regain the distance learning market invaded by institutions like the University of Phoenix.

However, modern technology is not a panacea. To create a more active and interactive learning environment, faculty must have a clear vision as to the purpose of the new technologies and the most effective way of integrating them in program design and delivery. They must then educate themselves in the use of the new pedagogical channels and supports. A recent report from the University of Illinois on the use of Internet classes in undergraduate education offers a few cautionary warnings (Mendels, 2000b). Quality online education is best achieved with relatively small class sizes, not to exceed 30 students. Moreover, it does not seem desirable to teach an entire undergraduate degree program only with online classes if students are expected to learn to think critically and interact socially in preparation for their professional life. Combining online and regular classroom courses gives students more opportunity for human interaction and development of the social aspects of learning through direct communication, argumentation, discussion, and consensus building. The Higher Education Council for England has recently allocated 30 million pounds over five years to fund the establishment of a Generic Learning and Teaching Center, based in York, to inform, guide, and support academic staff in the pedagogical use of new technologies. These program requirements apply also to the design and delivery of distance education programs which need to match learning objectives and appropriate technology support. In scientific fields like engineering, for example, the need for practical training is often overlooked. Computer simulations cannot replace all forms of applied training. In many science and technology-oriented programs, hands-on activities in laboratories and workshops remain an indispensable constituent of effective learning. Technology, however, does not only affect pedagogy.

The information and communication revolution will have far-reaching implications for how universities are organized and deliver services. Already in the United States new universities are designed and constructed without a library building because all students are expected to use computers to access online digital libraries and databases. CD-ROMs can replace journal collections in libraries. Cornell University, for example, has created the "Essential Electronic Agricultural Library," which consists of a collection of 173 CD-ROMs storing text from 140 journals for the past four years that can be shared with libraries at universities in developing countries. Wiring and Internet connectivity are becoming an important determinant of the attractiveness of a higher education institution. This is reflected by the recent publication, for the second consecutive year, of the results of a ranking survey which assesses U.S. universities on the basis of their computer and communication infrastructure and their level of Internet use for pedagogical and administrative purposes. Case Western Reserve University, MIT, and Wake Forest University were judged as the 1999 leaders in applying online services on campus (Bernstein, 1999). Case Western has established, in partnership with the Xerox corporation, an electronic network of 9,000 miles of cable and 15,000 information ports to dispense learning resources to students and faculty irrespective of their physical location.

Several economic factors weigh heavily in favor of the widespread adoption of electronic modes of organization and delivery of tertiary education services. The fiscal crisis faced by most countries, rich and poor alike, the rapid growth in the cost of higher education institutions in industrialized countries, especially in the United States, and the growing demand for tertiary education in developing nations and the former socialist countries of Eastern Europe and Central Asia all make it necessary to find more cost-effective alternatives to traditional models of higher education. The cost of producing a graduate from the UK Open University is about one-third that of a regular university. The cost of the Cornell electronic agricultural library mentioned earlier is about $10,000, as compared to the $375,000 it would cost any university to buy all the scientific journals included in the electronic database (McCollum, 1999). Yet, this differential can be somewhat misleading. University administrators must also keep in mind the high cost of information technology and infrastructure, which includes not only the initial capital outlays required to follow the advanced information and communication technology path, but also the recurrent budget outlays needed for expenditures on infrastructure maintenance, training, and technical support. It is estimated that these recurrent costs can represent as much as 75 percent of the life cycle costs of technology investments.

To be able to adapt to this changing environment, flexibility is very important. Increasingly, tertiary education institutions will need the capacity to react swiftly by establishing new programs, reconfiguring existing ones, and eliminating outdated programs without being hampered by bureaucratic regulations and obstacles. In many countries, however, university administrative procedures are very rigid when it comes to making changes in their structure, programs, or mode of operation. In Uruguay, it was only when confronted in the mid-1990s with competition from new private universities that the venerable University of the Republic—which for 150 years had exercised a monopoly over higher education in the country—started a strategic planning process and considered establishing postgraduate programs for the first time. Another example of institutional inflexibility occurred in Venezuela, where a dynamic private business administration institute called IESA had to wait several years to receive the official approval from the Council of Rectors for a new MBA program designed and delivered jointly with the Harvard Business School. The Brazilian Institute of Applied Technology (ITA), the most prestigious private engineering school in that country, had similar problems getting accredited. In Romania, CODECS, the first distance education institution of the country, created in the early 1990s, has had a hard time getting recognition of its degrees by the national higher education authorities. The only way it was able to achieve it was in an indirect manner, by forging an alliance with the UK Open University, whose degrees are recognized in Romania.

To increase flexibility in the design and organization of academic programs, many higher education institutions throughout the world have adopted the U.S. convention of credit-based courses. This evolution has affected entire national university systems (as in the case of Thailand), networks of institutions in a country (such as the Indian Institutes of Technology), and single institutions (such as the University of Niger) (Regel, 1992). The New Bulgarian University, one of Eastern Europe's most dynamic young private universities, is the first university in that country operating with a full academic credit system.

Higher education institutions are also changing their pattern of admission to respond in a more flexible way to student demand. In 1999, for the first time in the United States, a number of colleges decided to stagger the arrival of new students throughout the academic year, instead of restricting them to the fall semester. In China, similarly, a spring college entrance examination was held for the first time in January 2000, marking a sea change in the history of that country's entrance examination system. Students who fail the traditional July examination will no longer have to wait a full year to get a second chance.

Effective labor market feedback mechanisms, such as tracer surveys and regular consultations with employers and alumni, are indispensable for the purpose of adjusting curricula to meet the changing needs of industry. In Denmark, industry representatives, including presidents of large companies, commonly sit on departmental boards in universities to advise them on training and research priorities. Of course, there is no better linkage than when a new higher education institution is fully integrated into a regional development strategy as happened in Finland. The young University of Oulu has become one of the best universities in the Nordic countries, despite being located in a remote area very close to the Arctic circle. Its growth attests to the successful transformation of a small rural community into a high-technology zone. Winning companies (led by Nokia), science parks dedicated to applied research in electronics, medicine, and biotechnology, and the 13,000 student university function in symbiosis (*The Economist*, 1999). Palack University, in the Czech city of Olomouc, has received praise for its efforts to develop new law courses in response to the retraining needs generated by the reform of the legal system. The Michigan Virtual Automotive College is a focused learning partnership bringing together the state government of Michigan, the Detroit car industry, Michigan State University, and the University of Michigan.

An interesting example of willingness to change and adapt curricula and programs on a regular basis is provided by the University of South Florida in Tampa, one of the relatively younger public universities in the United States. The engineering department offers its graduates a five-year warranty not unlike the standard warranty against manufacturing defects which comes with any consumer good. If at any time during the five years following graduation an alumnus/a is required to apply skills in his/her work but had not received the requisite training during the time of studies at the university, he or she can re-enroll free of charge to acquire these skills.

Along the same lines, a university could very well achieve the dual objective of strengthening its financial sustainability and keeping its programs up-to-date by selling a "training for life" package. Under such a scheme new students would sign up and pay not only for their initial professional education, but also for all the retraining periods required throughout their professional career. Operating in the same geographical area as the University of South Florida, St. Petersburg Junior College boasts the ability to create a new program in just a few months to answer new educational needs in the local community (Klein, 1999).

At the same time, the need for more flexibility calls into question traditional modes and patterns of academic appointments and careers. In almost all countries, the administrative status of public university professors has usually been similar or very close to that of civil servants, with the benefit of strong employment guarantees and promotion based on seniority. In many private universities, especially in the United States, tenured appointments involve equivalent arrangements. Moreover, it has commonly been assumed that the presence of full-time professors was a key determinant of quality. In many Latin American countries for instance, where private higher education represents a significant proportion of overall enrollment—or even the majority as in Brazil, Colombia, the Dominican Republic, El Salvador, and Chile—one of the principal evaluation criteria applied by the accreditation authorities is the number of full-time professors. In Poland, when a new funding formula was introduced at the beginning of the 1990s to prop up quality in public universities, one of the two main parameters of the funding equation was the number of full-time professors with a doctorate.

But the need for higher education institutions to be able to respond rapidly to changing labor market signals and to adjust swiftly to technological change may require more flexible arrangements for the deployment of academic staff, including moving away from civil service regulations and abandoning tenure-track appointments. In Tunisia, an important dimension of the reform that initiated the successful establishment of a network of nonuniversity technology institutes at the beginning of the 1990s was a recruitment and remuneration scheme that permitted the full recognition of relevant professional experience and knowledge independent from the rigid rules about academic qualifications in force in the national universities. In Poland, university leaders have come to realize that overreliance on full-time professors does not allow the flexibility necessary to recruit, as part-time lecturers, practitioners required in key disciplines. At the Technology University of Warsaw, for example, the impossibility of offering adequate remuneration to qualified computer science specialists from the private sector is seen as a major obstacle (Interview with the rector of the Technology University of Warsaw, February 1999).

CONCLUSION

> We live in an era where everything is possible and nothing is certain.
> —Vaclav Havel, former playwright, president of the Czech Republic

Higher education is facing unprecedented challenges at the start of the twenty-first century, under the impact of globalization, knowledge-based economic growth, and the information and communication revolution. These momentous changes in the environment are stretching the traditional boundaries of higher education. The time dimension is altered by the requirement for lifelong learning while new technologies are doing away with space barriers altogether.

These challenges can be seen equally as terrible threats or tremendous opportunities for the world of higher education. Some observers have gone as far as predicting the end of the traditional university as we know it, seeing open and online universities as the only cost-effective answer to the massification challenge faced by many countries. Whether we are actually about to witness the disappearance of classical universities altogether, as distance education progressively replaces campus-based teaching and learning, remains to be seen.

> Many universities may die or may change beyond recognition as a result of the IT revolution. When asked what his light bulb would mean for the candle industry, Thomas Edison reportedly replied, "We will make electricity so cheap that only the rich will burn candles." We are entering an era in which most colleges and universities must decide whether to change a little (and thus remain in the academic candle industry) or a lot (and launch themselves into the academic electrical business). (Langenberg, 1996, quoted in Dator, 1998, p. 619)

What is certain is that the hegemony of traditional universities has been definitively challenged. Institutional differentiation is bound to accelerate, resulting in a greater variety of organizational configurations and patterns, and the emergence of myriad alliances, linkages, and partnerships within tertiary institutions, across institutions, and even reaching beyond the higher education sector. The recently announced alliance between MIT and Cambridge University, with financial support from the British government and private industry, is a symbolic illustration of these new trends. It is likely, under any scenario, that traditional universities will continue to play a major role, especially in advanced training and research. They will, however, undoubtedly undergo significant transformations prompted by the application of new education technologies and the pressure of market forces.

Countries and higher education institutions willing to take advantage of these new opportunities cannot afford to remain passive, but must be proactive in launching meaningful reforms and innovations. While there is no rigid blueprint for all countries and institutions, a common prerequisite may be the need to formulate a clear vision of how the higher education system can most effectively contribute to the development of a knowledge-based economy, how each institution elects to evolve within that system, and under what conditions the new technologies can be harnessed to improve the effectiveness and relevance of the learning experience. Preparation of the Dearing Report in the United Kingdom, the work of the National Commission for Higher Education Reform in South Africa, the Tertiary Education Green Paper in New Zealand, and the Plan for the University of the Third Millennium in France are recent examples of attempts to develop such a vision at the national level. They are a tribute to the wise words of the Roman philosopher, Seneca, who cautioned us two millennia ago that "there is no favorable wind for those who do not know where they are going." Washington State's Master Plan for Higher Education, released in January 2000, proposes a strategy to address the anticipated rapid growth of demand for tertiary education which relies heavily on the development of online education programs (Carnevale, 2000).

Strategic planning exercises undertaken by individual tertiary institutions serve a similar purpose. By identifying both favorable and harmful trends in their immediate environment and linking them to a rigorous assessment of their internal strengths and weaknesses, institutions can better define their mission, market niche, and medium-term development objectives and formulate concrete plans to achieve these objectives. For example, the exceptional growth of the University of Phoenix has been the result of a well-thought strategy involving a business model of university governance and management, a targeted clientele of working adults, a small number of professionally oriented programs, flexible arrangements to give credit for prior knowledge and experience, extensive use of education technology, and reliance on part-time, low-paid teachers well trained in technology-based pedagogy (Jackson, 2000). By contrast, for lack of strategic planning, many new distance education institutions have adopted inappropriate technologies, failing to assess their adequacy against the purpose of their programs, the competency of their professors, and the learning needs of their students.

A final word of caution is warranted to signal the danger of focusing exclusively on the implacable logic of technical change and globalization. Adapting to the changing environment is not only a matter of reshaping tertiary institutions and applying new technologies. It is equally vital to ensure that students are equipped with the core values necessary to live as responsible citizens in complex democratic societies. The small private University of Monterrey in northern Mexico has been able to compete effectively with the neighboring Technology Institute of Monterrey because of its deliberate inclusion of community-related courses and activities stimulating the development of appropriate values and social skills among students. A meaningful education for the twenty-first century should stimulate all aspects of human intellectual potential. It should not only focus on giving access to global knowledge, but also uphold the richness of local cultures and values, in support of which time-honored disciplines like philosophy, literature, arts, and social sciences will continue to remain essential. This overarching objective was artfully reemphasized by U.S. Supreme Court Justice Antonin Scalia in a speech at the 1998 graduating ceremony of William and Mary College in Virginia:

> Brains and learning, like muscle and physical skill, are articles of commerce. They are bought and sold. You can hire them by the year or by the hour. The only thing in the world not for sale is character. And if that does not govern and direct your brains and learning, they will do you and the world more harm than good.

REFERENCES

Abeles, T. (1998). The academy in a wired world. *Futures, 30*(7), 603–613.

Arkin, R., Lee, K-M., McGinnis, L., & Zhou, C. (1997, April). The development of a shared interdisciplinary intelligent mechatronics laboratory. *Journal of Engineering Education*, 113–118.

Authers, J. (1999, April 26). Keeping company with the campus. *Financial Times*, 11.

Banker, R., Chang, H., & Majumdar, S. (1998). Economies of scope in the U.S. telecommunications industry. *Information Economics and Policy, 10*, 253–272.

Barros, R., & Ramos, L. (1996). Temporal evolution of the relationship between wages and education of Brazilian men. In N. Birdsall and R. H. Sabot (Eds.), *Opportunity Foregone: Education in Brazil.* Washington, DC: Inter-American Development Bank/The Johns Hopkins University Press.

Bennell, P., & Pearce, T. (1998). *The internationalisation of higher education: Exporting education to developing and transitional economies* (pp. 193–214). Brighton: Institute of Development Studies.

Bernstein, R. (1999, May). America's 100 most wired colleges. *Yahoo! Internet Life*, 86–119.

Bond, J. (1997). The drivers of the information revolution—Cost, computing power and convergence. In *The Information Revolution and the Future of Telecommunications*. Washington, DC: The World Bank.

Bullag, B. (1999, December 3). Reforms in higher education disappoint Eastern Europeans. *Chronicle of Higher Education*, p. A55.

Carnevale, D. (2000, January 21). Master plan in Washington State calls for more online instruction. *Chronicle of Higher Education* (online).

Clark, S. (1999). Corporate-higher education partnerships: University of California customizes education for Silicon Valley titans. University of California Extension, Santa Cruz. http://www.traininguniversity.com/magazine/mar_apr99/corp2.html.

Dator, J. (1998). The futures of universities: Ivied halls, virtual malls, or theme parks? *Futures, 30*(1), 619.

Densford, L. (1999). Motorola university: The next 20 years. Online publication: http://www.traininguniversity.com/magazine/jan_feb99/feature1.html.

Doyle, D. (2000, January 19). China, Inc. *Education Week, 19*(19), 39.

Gibbons, M. (1998). *Higher education relevance in the 21st century*. Report prepared for the UNESCO World Conference on Higher Education. Washington, DC: The World Bank.

Gibbons, M., Limoges, C., Nowotny, H., Schwartzman, S., Scott, P., & Trow, M. (1994). *The new production of knowledge: Science and research in contemporary societies*. London: Sage Publications.

Jackson, G. (2000). University of Phoenix: A new model for tertiary education in developing countries? *TechKnowlogia, 2*(1), 34–37.

Jaffe, A. (1989). Real effects of academic research. *American Economic Review, 79*(5), 957–970.

Klein, B. (1999, June 5). SPJC aims for cutting edge of education. *The Tampa Tribune*.

Lächler, U. (1997). *Education and earnings inequality in Mexico*. Unpublished paper. Washington, DC: The World Bank.

Lamancusa, J., Jorgensen, J., & Zayas-Castro, J. (1997, April). The learning factory—A new approach to integrating design and manufacturing into the engineering curriculum. *Journal of Engineering Education*, 103–112.

The Maclean's Guide to Canadian Universities. (1999). Toronto: MacLean's Publishers.

Mansfield, E. (1991). Academic research and industrial innovation. *Research Policy, 20*, 1–12.

McCollum, K. (1999, December 12). Cornell University offers developing nations digital journals on agriculture. *Chronicle of Higher Education*, p. A44.

Mendels, P. (2000a, January 12). Government study shows a boom in distance education. *New York Times* (online).

Mendels, P. (2000b, January 19). Study on online education sees optimism, with caution. *New York Times* (online).

Motti, J. (1999, March 15). Corporate universities grow. *Internetweek*. Special Issue No. 756 (online).

Olsen, J. (2000, January–February). Is virtual education for real? *TechKnowLogia*, 16–18.

Pessino, C. (1995). *Returns to education in greater Buenos Aires 1986–1993: From hyperinflation to stabilization* (Working Paper 104). Buenos Aires: Centro de Estudios Macroeconómicos de Argentina.

Regel, O. (1992). *The academic credit system in higher education: Effectiveness and relevance in developing countries* (PHREE Background Paper Series No. 92/59). Washington, DC: The World Bank.

Survey: The Nordic Countries: Northern Light. (1999, January 23). *The Economist*, p. N11.

Thulstrup, E. (1999). University-industry cooperation with project based learning. In A. Kornhauser (Ed.), *University-industry cooperation: Learning strategies*. University of Ljubljana, Slovenia: Kornhauser, International Center for Chemical Studies.

Whitehead, A. N. (1929). *The aims of education and other essays.* New York: The Free Press.

World Bank. (1998). *World development report: Knowledge for development.* New York: Oxford University Press.

Part II

Seeking a New Balance in Government-University Relationships

Chapter 3

Universities in Transition: Privatization, Decentralization, and Institutional Autonomy as National Policy with Special Reference to the Russian Federation

D. Bruce Johnstone and Olga Bain

The term "in transition" has become a euphemism for changes that have swept over Russia and the other newly independent states of the former Soviet Union, as well as the other formerly socialist nations of Central and Eastern Europe. These changes, often wrenching and dislocating, have overturned entire economic and political systems, altered livelihoods and lifestyles, and forged entire new states. At the core of the transition has been a great reduction of state control over individual lives and productive activities and enterprises, including a lessening of state ownership, state regulation, and state (tax) funding. This diminution of state regulation and funding extends to the production and dissemination of knowledge by the universities, academies, and other institutions of higher education. For universities, "transition" has brought new freedom, both ideological and managerial, as well as new demands and new opportunities. In Russia and other countries, it has also brought universities instability and new levels of austerity.

Taking the place of central state control in much of the general goods and services sector of the economy is the guiding hand of the market, which (at least in theory) allocates capital and labor in the most efficient manner to meet changing consumer preferences and maximizes return on invested capital. The market has also supplemented and supplanted government or ministerial control of the universities in the transitional countries in the form of tuition-paying students (although still legally limited in percentages of total enrollments), the sale of faculty research and training capabilities, and greater financial self-sufficiency in the provision of dormitory and food services. Such measures are embraced by the concept of *privatization*. In addition, higher education, still primarily a public good, is also affected by the *decentralization* of government to the level of region or province or "subject" and, at least in the planning stage, to forms of publicly accountable but quasi-governmental "buffer" entities, akin to the U.S. public multicampus governing boards or state planning or coordinating councils. Finally, governments are granting more *autonomy* to institutions of higher education, allowing them to allocate resources more freely in pursuit of their institutionally determined missions. This chapter discusses the interplay of these three forces—*privatization, decentralization*, and *autonomy*—acting on universities in all countries, but especially within the transitional countries, and more especially within the Russian Federation.

UNIVERSITIES, CHANGE, AND THE STATE

Wrenching change, extending to universities, is by no means confined to those nations once thought of as the "Soviet Block," characterized by central economic planning and ideological regimentation. The combination of market capitalism and liberal democracy that has characterized the "West," epitomized by the member states of the Organization of Economic Cooperation and Development (OECD), while enormously productive and individually liberating, is also inherently destabilizing. Change, in fact, does not just *happen to* capitalistic economies or liberal democracies, it is the very essence of these systems, at least in their tendencies, absent regulations or public policies to the contrary. The increasingly global nature of markets and production systems, combined with the increasing speed of technological advances and their application, compounds the amount and pace of change with which modern universities in all countries must deal.

In reference to change, the university has always played two quite different, at times even contradictory, roles. On the side of change, the academy is devoted to inquiry, discovery, new knowledge, and learning. Its faculty is supposed to be skeptical, critical, imaginative, revisionist, and sometimes even radical. The university is a principal engine of economic competitiveness and individual self-betterment. All of these are clearly missions abetting change. At the same time (and reinforcing a natural conservatism), the university is a custodian, defender, and transmitter of culture and tradition. Whether it is, or is thought to be, controlled by the state, the faculty, or some form of management, it is controlled by those with power and status, and in turn transmits and thus perpetuates this very power and status. These are missions of continuity and stability and of likely resistance to change.

Some forces for change would strengthen the role of the state in the business of the university; others would weaken it. Among the former are increasing pressures to serve national economic interests, to serve society in ways defined by government, and to accommodate publicly determined values such as expanded participation or racial and ethnic tolerance. In most nations, higher education is thought to be more important to more people than ever before, and unequivocally a matter of national *interest*—whether or not it is necessarily a matter for government *ownership, regulation*, or *funding*. Government is also demanding that universities, whether public or private, be more accountable to students, families, and taxpayers, and prove to skeptical elected leaders that they are worthy of the public's trust and resources.

At the same time, there are centrifugal forces pulling universities away from the state, particularly from national or central governments, and drawing universities closer to clients—whether students, employers, or program sponsors—and to more regional or local interests. Such forces may stem from universities seeking greater autonomy, although autonomy itself, as we shall see below, is laden with complexity and nuance. Rectors or presidents, senior professors, faculty of lesser rank, and students may differ greatly on the attractions or fears that they perceive in either strengthened or weakened ties to the central state. For example, most rectors, and especially rectors of "classical," "flagship," or otherwise dominant universities generally seek maximum autonomy consistent with continuing their claim on public resources—and some may even "bargain away" part of these claims for additional freedom in allocating their resources and supplementing their governmental allocations with nongovernmental revenues. On the other hand, institutions of lesser prestige, with fewer opportunities to seek other-than-public revenue, and needing protection from the more hegemonic classical universities, may see greater protection in remaining under considerable governmental authority. In a similar fashion, rectors and other managers generally seek greater autonomy, while faculty and staff—particularly under conditions of financial austerity—may well see their jobs threatened by an unrestrained institutional management, and thus may see greater protection in a government that is likely to be more politically sensitive to the preservation of jobs than to the quality or adaptivity of the institution.

Finally, within—or perhaps looming over—these contests for control and authority is the struggle of universities almost everywhere with *austerity*, brought on by costs rising faster than revenues, especially those revenues from public treasuries. A partial solution, promoted by most Western economists and identified with the World Bank, is to shift more of the costs of higher education to nongovernmental, or other-than-taxpayer, sources, either by encouraging more private institutions of higher education, or by allowing or requiring public institutions to supplement public revenues with private funds. Such supplementation may entail partial or full tuition, full or nearly full-cost recovery on student living and dining arrangements, and revenue earned through entrepreneurial activities of the faculty. A related set of solutions is to seek greater efficiency, in part through practices that mirror those associated with the private sector, such as *downsizing, out-*

sourcing, performance budgeting, and *niche marketing.* (Johnstone, 1993; Johnstone, Arora, & Experton, 1998; World Bank, 1994; Ziderman & Albrecht, 1994).

This, then, is the global context of privatization, decentralization, (or regionalization or federalization), and institutional autonomy:

- *Privatization*, or an increasing orientation to markets and clients, an inclination to management practices associated with private enterprise, a lessening of financial dependence on the government or taxpayer, and a receptivity by the state to privately owned, tuition-dependent, institutions;
- *Decentralization*, or the devolution of control from the central or national government to regional (e.g., state, province, land, kray, oblast, or republic) governments. It may also include devolution to forms of public "buffer" entities such as constitutionally autonomous governing boards, university systems, or other publicly accountable planning or coordinating bodies, as in the United States (and increasingly examined with interest by other countries).
- *Autonomy*, or the freeing of the university from some measure of governmental authority or control, quite apart from public or private ownership or dependence on governmental or taxpayer revenue.

These terms describe trends in North America and Europe (including West, East, Central Europe and Russia), as well as other new states emerging from the former Soviet Union, and to many of the less industrialized countries of Latin America, Asia, and Africa. Governments are seeking a less regulatory relationship with universities and voluntarily divesting some of their authority, sometimes out of an ideology favoring privatization and market solutions, sometimes to divest themselves of financial burdens, and sometimes to find a more constructive balance between what van Vught (1994) calls the governmental "steering" balance between state *control* and state *supervision.* Each of these three important and exceedingly complex concepts in the governance and support of higher education is multidimensional and better understood not as "either-or," but as points along several continua.

PRIVATIZATION

Private universities and private nonuniversity forms of postsecondary education, either proprietary for-profit, or private not-for-profit, are playing larger roles in the provision of higher education in many countries. (The distinction between "private for-profit," or "proprietary," and "private not-for-profit" is critical in the United States, with the former generally signaling noncollegiate, vocational, short-cycle, and lower status, in addition to various legal and tax implications. The distinction, however, is less significant in much of the rest of the world, where "nonprofit," may be in fact, if not always in law, quite compatible with virtual personal or family ownership.) These private institutions, at least some of the not-for-profit kinds, may be among the most prestigious and selective colleges and universities, as in the United States, or they may be decidedly non-elite, or "demand absorbing," as in much of Latin America, India, Japan, South Korea, and the Philippines (Geiger, 1987; Levy, 1986). They may also be new and on the very edge of viability and acceptability, as in Russia, elsewhere in Eastern and Central Europe and the countries of the former Soviet Union, and China. This increase in private sector higher education activity may happen even where the government continues to regulate the mission, programs, and curriculum, and even the tuition that they may charge.

But "privatization," as we shall define the concept in this section, is also significant to traditional public universities and other public institutions of higher education. Declining tax revenues and increasing competition from other public sector needs (or the perceived need for tax relief) are causing many state-owned universities to turn more and more to other-than-governmental revenues. Most significant, but also problematic and controversial, is the shift in revenue dependence from government, or taxpayers, to parents and students through tuition and more nearly full-cost reimbursement for institutionally or governmentally provided food and lodging. No matter how small and supplemental this tuition may be compared to the total cost of instruction, any amount greater than a symbolic pittance amounts to a market transaction, with implications to consumer (both student and parent) demand, access and participation, and the "signaling" functions that prices play in a working market. Perhaps more important, and certainly more complex and controversial, are the social and political implications regarding the proper size and composition of the public sector generally, and the equity implications of a public higher educational sector, access to which is so highly correlated with social class and family status *even when fully subsidized*.

Reliance on nongovernmental revenue via tuition, as well as other forms of privatization, is found increasingly throughout the world. The privatization of public higher education in America is especially true of the high prestige public universities such as Michigan, Berkeley, or Wisconsin, to which in-state undergraduates may pay a third or more of full costs, out-of-state undergraduates may pay tuition that covers considerably more than full costs, and to which loyal alumni and friends give upwards of $100 million per year. The state taxpayer may actually cover less than a fifth of the total costs in such public universities. In China, all students began paying tuition in 1998 under official governmental blessing, which now proclaims, in language redolent of neoliberal economics, the social equity of having students who receive the benefits share in the costs of their higher education. Most of Europe, at the start of the twenty-first century, continues to resist tuition, although the Netherlands has charged tuition for some years; Britain began charging tuition in 1998 (surprisingly, under a Labor government); and Austria announced plans to do so in the year 2001 (Johnstone & Shroff-Mehta, 2000). In Russia, which has an historical, ideological, and constitutional history of free higher education, financial pressures on the universities and the need to supplement the grossly insufficient governmental allocations have forced universities to maximize the *conditional exceptions* to free higher education as specified by Article 43 of the 1993 Constitution of the Russian Federation. This article now allows universities to charge tuition to both public and private organizations that sponsor students, as well as directly to individuals who were not regularly admitted under competitive examinations and state quotas (Bain, 1998).

In this context, it is becoming increasingly difficult to say what it is that makes a university "private" as opposed to "public." The *privateness* or *publicness* of institutions of higher education, rather, must be viewed along the dimensions of (1) mission or purpose, (2) ownership, (3) source of revenue, (4) expenditure controls, (5) regulations or controls over other-than-expenditures, and (6) norms of management. Most importantly, each dimension has gradations of *publicness* and *privateness* such that an institution might be quite private on one or two dimensions, and quite public on others.

Mission or Purpose

The most private mission or purpose of an institution of higher education would be that of bringing profit to ownership in the manner of any other private business. This is the essential mission of the proprietary, for-profit, postsecondary institutions of the United States and many Asian countries. The usual form of higher education served by for-profit institutions is the provision of short-cycle vocational or professional training, which is willingly paid for by the client (the student or the family), and thus can be self-supporting and even profitable, particularly when delivered by institutions unencumbered with such "unbusinesslike" and potentially costly functions as shared governance and tenure. The reason that most advanced education and basic research are *not* served by proprietary institutions is that there is neither sufficient assurance of profit, nor sufficient trust on the part of government that it will get the full measure of what it is paying for, given the difficulty of measuring the outputs of fundamental research and advanced education.

In contrast, and on the clearly "public" end of the university mission continuum, would be a public mission established by government, paid for by public revenue, and assured by governmental monitoring and control. This mission might be fundamental research and the advanced education associated with the classical university, the much more applied research and practical education associated with the American Land Grant tradition, the more recent mission of egalitarian participation served by community and other open-access colleges, or the historic Soviet mission of meeting state manpower training plans.

Institutions that are state-owned and mainly or entirely governmentally-funded (and thus unequivocally public) might be thought more likely to act in the public interest (for example, the interest of the student) than would private, for-profit institutions acting in the interest primarily of their owners. However, public institutions, particularly if they enjoy a monopoly, and encouraged by traditions of faculty authority in governance and autonomy in the classroom (and especially if the faculty are protected by politically powerful civil service unions), may be inclined to act more in the interests of the faculty than of the student. In contrast, private institutions, either proprietary or nonprofit, operating in a context of competition and assuming legal safeguards against outright fraud, may be very responsive to student needs, not out of any individual or institutional nobility or any particular devotion to a public mission, but simply out of a need to continue attracting students and the revenue brought either by tuition or public payments. At the same time, any country experiencing private institutions of higher education for the first time (whether nonprofit or proprietary) will most likely lack the consumer knowledge and competition of a mature higher educational marketplace. Such countries—and Russia and the other "transitional" countries are among them—may have all the more need to regulate and hold accountable their emerging private sectors of higher education.

To complicate matters further, profit-making institutions, whether schools or businesses, make their profits by maximizing the difference between their revenues and their costs, with the positive difference, after providing for institutional reserves, going as profit to the owners. Private nonprofit universities, however, also try to maximize the positive difference between their revenues and their costs, with the only distinction being that the surpluses must go back into the institution, for institutional purposes, rather than to owners. The institutional behavior of maximizing revenues, holding down costs, and seeking surpluses to the degree possible, can be quite indistinguishable among universities that are legally *for-profit, nonprofit*, or even *public*. (Actually, public universities may be the least inclined to maximize surpluses between revenue and expense simply because to do so is to suggest that they were overfunded by the government in the first place.)

In between these extremes of the clearly private for-profit, and the clearly public governmentally determined, missions can be a range of missions established and maintained either by private *nonprofit* or by *quasi-public* institutions. The mission of a typical private nonprofit institution of higher education is established and maintained neither by owners, per se, nor by government, but by the institutional faculty under the direction of a lay governing board and an administration, or management, that is heavily influenced by tradition. The mission will be essentially public—and avowedly (by law) not for personal profit—but it will not be determined by the government. Similarly, a public university can be governed not by a ministry, but by some form of governing board that is ultimately controllable by the government (or occasionally, in the United States, directly by the electorate), but that is shielded, or *buffered*, from immediate governmental (executive or legislative) reach by lengthy, staggered terms of its members and frequently by constitutional protections. The effect is to weaken the control of a congress or parliament, or of a chief elected executive, and to strengthen the determination of mission by the faculty and administration, constrained, like the private not-for-profit institutions, by academic tradition and the isometric force of academic competition.

Ownership

The least ambiguous distinction between public and private higher education lies in ownership. But even this criterion has shades of meaning. The ownership of a university may be *clearly public*, as in a state agency or a state-owned enterprise, or *clearly private*, as in individual or corporate ownership. Or, the university—its name and all of its assets—may be held privately *but in trust for its designated public purpose*, as in the royal charters of the British or Dutch universities, or like the American nonprofit colleges and universities, granted corporate charters by their state government, but constitutionally protected from public confiscation by the 1819 United States Supreme Court decision in the Dartmouth College case.

Ownership is related to, but distinct from, mission. Public *ownership* should assure some form of public *mission*, but there are many different public missions, and different, equally public, institutions may (and desirably should) serve quite different public missions. On the other hand, private ownership can be quite compatible with a public mission, either when public revenue has been used to purchase the desired public mission, or when the public interest established by the government, and the private interests "established" by the market coincide—as in the provision of quality manpower training. This is the principle underlying state encouragement and even financial support of private (both nonprofit and for-profit) higher education. The head of the Russian Association of Non-State Universities declared in 1998 that many "non-state" universities have in essence very public state-inspired goals, such as training nationally needed personnel, creating new work places, doing research, and expanding access to higher education (Zernov, 1998).

There remains, however, a distinction between a private institution serving a public purpose because it suits the interests of the owners or the inclinations of the faculty, and a public institution that is perpetually under such a public obligation. Private nonprofit universities may be prohibited by law from serving the mission of private profit; but there is no assurance, beyond that brought about by explicitly earmarked public funding, that they will serve any *particular* public mission, or that they will serve it as directed by the government of the moment. Still, it is assumed by more and more countries—industrialized, less industrialized, and transitional—that the institutional or professional missions served by private nonprofit universities are so fundamentally in the public interest that government should encourage and protect the autonomy under which such institutions operate.

The expansion in Russia of the non state-owned higher education sector was quite dramatic in the 1990s, with 334 institutions licensed by the Ministry of General and Professional Education by the end of 1998, 35 percent of these in the cities of Moscow and St. Petersburg (Goskomstat, 1999, pp. 194–205). The typical private (or "non-state") institution, however, is small, with training in only a few fields (predominantly economics, management, languages, and law), leases space from a state university, and employs the faculty of the state university at a higher salary but with minimal financial obligations for pensions and no other benefits.

Source of Revenue

Revenue is generally thought "public" when it originates from the general citizenry, whether it is from direct taxation (as in taxes upon income, sales, or property) or from indirect taxation (as in taxes upon manufacturing value added or corporate profits, in both cases, presumably paid for by the consumer in higher prices) or from the confiscation of purchasing power by inflationary governmental borrowing or by the simple printing of money. Revenue is thought to be "private" when it originates from voluntary, private decisions, as in the payment of tuition, the making of a gift, or the purchase of research or other university services.

Most universities, whether publicly or privately owned, operate on a combination of public and private revenues: direct taxpayer-originated appropriations in combination with private tuition payments, the sale of services, private gifts and grants, and returns on privately held endowments. What may seem to be private revenues may actually be at least partly public: private tuition payments that come in part from public grants or from loans that are guaranteed and often further subsidized by the government at taxpayer expense; or private gifts encouraged by tax deductibility that removes revenue that would otherwise be owed to the government. And what of the lease of university property that is, or was, the public's? Or private gifts brought in, at least in part, through the efforts of staff whose salaries and/or pensions are supported by the government or taxpayer? Or university capital construction covered by bonds, the interest on which is low because of government guarantees or tax deductibility? Or a government-supported research grant won by the university in competition with other possible providers, public and private? In short, the source of revenue, while absolutely critical for all sorts of public policy considerations, is extremely complex and generally not a good indication of the "publicness" or "privateness" of a university.

The private flow of funds into Russian state universities has increased substantially. Anticipating privatization of university finance in the 1990s, the state in the mid-1980s began turning to indirect rather than direct allocation of state revenue (i.e., through research projects and limited training contracted by state enterprises). Later, with the emergence of a market economy and private sector, more extensive contract training brought more nongovernmental revenue to public universities. By the 1994 governmental decree, public universities were authorized to charge tuition on a limited number of individuals who had not been admitted by competitive examination within the publicly subsidized quotas. The amended Law on Education of 1996 raised the cap on tuition-paying students in the most demanded fields from 10 to 25 percent. By the end of 1998 Russian state universities and institutes enrolled more students on a fee-paying basis (70.2% of all tuition-charged enrollees) than non-state ones (29.8%). Overall, in the late 1990s every fifth student in the nation was charged tuition while admission to public institutions in Russia remained divided into those who are charged tuition and those admitted entirely at the expense of the state (Bain, 1998). Pressured to supplement state funds with revenue from nongovernmental sources, Russian state institutions of higher education on average generated 25 percent of their operating revenue from additional sources, and by 1998 this amount ranged from 30 to 60 percent.

Expenditure Controls

For some purposes, the *privateness* of a university is better signaled by the degree of institutional autonomy, or absence of state control over the expenditure of revenues (however "public" in origin) than by the public or private origin of the revenues themselves. A publicly owned university, for example, can be given an unrestricted grant of public revenues, which it can then co-mingle with various private revenues and spend as it perceives to be in the best interest of the institution. Such expenditures may include the setting of salaries, the purchase of real property, and even the incurring of debt, and may include the authority to carry over surpluses from current fiscal year operations—in short, to function quite like a private institution. Or, the same public university, with revenues from the same sources, can be treated like a governmental agency, with all expenditures controlled by the finance ministry. Insofar as universities seek to be treated more "privately," it is generally the absence of expenditure control, or governmental "preaudit," that they seek, rather than private ownership or a more private mission per se. Because all universities are labor intensive, with faculty and staff compensation accounting for three-quarters or more of current expenditures, fiscal flexibility, or expenditure autonomy, implies the ability to set compensation levels, hire or terminate staff, and move expenditure authority freely between compensation and other expenditures.

For a government to "let go" of expenditure controls requires trust on the part of the government that the university decisions, with fewer expenditure controls, or preaudits, will be neither *wrong* (in the sense of wrong priorities, or expenditures that will not, in fact, obtain the desired outcome) nor *corrupt* (in the sense of expenditures going to enrich or otherwise to aggrandize individuals rather than to serve institutional purposes). Trust does not come naturally, either to governments or to members of the universities and academies. The kind of trust necessary for sustained movement toward greater university autonomy requires changes in both culture and in processes, or systems. A *culture* conducive to trust requires: (1) a faith in the wisdom and/or integrity of individuals, especially of those in leadership positions (whether governmental or institutional); (2) a willingness on the part of those in the government (or, where still applicable, in the Party) to tolerate departures from the conventional ways that universities have been run in the past by the government—and even to tolerate occasional errors; and (3) a concomitant willingness on the part of institutional leaders to innovate, or "raise up one's head," or "stick out one's neck." Trust also requires the existence of, and a faith in, the *systems*, or *processes* that undergird trust such as audits, competitive bidding, independent judicial inquiries, and a free press.

Countries emerging from generations of rigid governmental authority and secrecy face the daunting task of building that culture of trust (and now, in addition, facing escalating corruption), as well as erecting, at considerable time and expense, those systems and processes such as transparent budgeting, good contracting procedures, sound internal auditing, and performance measures that allow rigorous postaudit, or "after-the-fact" monitoring of expenditures. In the meantime, absent such change in both culture and processes, and in spite of the considerable theoretical case to be made for greater institutional autonomy, there will continue to be resistance to it both from the central government, *from above*, and from the faculty, staff, and students, *from below*.

Regulations or Controls over Other-Than-Expenditures

Quite apart from expenditure controls, government can exercise—or choose not to exercise—control over a wide range of other aspects of university operations, such as

- the selection or final appointment of the chief executive officer (rector or president),

- the form of internal governance (especially the powers of the university faculty),
- the degrees or programs to be offered, or the curricular content thereof,
- terms and conditions of employment, including provisions for job security and the protection of pension rights, or
- the circumstances of student admission, including the grounds for selection or denial, or even the actual assignment of student to institution.

Many of these controls and regulations are for the protection of the consumer (generally, the student or family) or of the general public, and are similar to those consumer protection regulations applicable to other professional practices such as medicine, law, insurance, and banking. The private benefits of a higher education are presumed to be substantial, but they are also difficult to measure, are often not immediately appreciated or realized, and may be susceptible to reputations and "halo effects." Students and their families may thus be thought to be vulnerable to misleading promises or other forms of exploitation from universities, whether legally for-profit, nonprofit, or public. Hence, all countries have mechanisms for the accreditation or attestation of institutions, especially when they are starting up.

Norms of Management and Governance

Finally, "public" and "private" can refer to certain presumed norms of management, quite apart from the other dimensions of *privateness* or *publicness*. Among norms associated with *private*, for example, would be

- managerial decisiveness, toughness, affinity for numbers and other "hard" data, and even, where thought to be necessary (for profitability), ruthlessness;
- an eagerness for change and for all the current "re" jargon: *re*structuring, *re*newing, *re*engineering;
- close attention to the client or consumer (student, family, alumni, or potential donor); and
- close attention to image, advertising, and public relations.

These private norms stand in contrast to those associated with traditional university management, whether the university is public or private nonprofit:

- participatory governance, with openness, lengthy consultation, and consensus seeking;
- a flat organizational structure, an aversion to authority, and a disdain for "management," especially that which is permanent and/or is not associated with authority earned by scholarly competence;

- a sense that the academy is generally misunderstood, and probably not understandable anyway, especially to politicians and businesspersons;
- a related sense that the university has a special nobility or ethicality about it, which accounts for its clashes with norms that are merely *commercial* or *political*;
- a passionate concern for academic freedom, coupled with a tendency to view most threats to job security as threats to this much nobler principle.

In this sense, a move in the direction of privatization is a movement toward the first set of norms and away from the second set—again, quite apart from the public or private nature of mission, ownership, or source of revenue.

DECENTRALIZATION

Governments everywhere exercise some degree of decentralization, or delegation of authority or service delivery to regional subdivisions. Political decentralization may suggest *federalism*, in which the decentralization of state authority is constitutionally protected—that is, not easily removable or even amendable—and in which the region has some rights to shape its "own" governance as well as to select its own representatives to the central, or national, government. At one extreme, represented by Switzerland, the United States, or Canada, federalism limits the authority of the central government to that which is specifically constitutionally prescribed, with all residual authority (amounting in the extreme to virtual sovereignty) effectively maintained by the regional units. In other federal forms, such as Germany or Brazil, true sovereignty continues to be held only by the central state, which delegates authority in certain (perhaps very extensive) domains to the constituent regional units (see, e.g., Elazar 1987, p. 40 and ff.).

At the other extreme, decentralization may reflect neither history nor ethnicity, nor natural geographic features, but more of an arbitrary regional demarcation for the administrative convenience of the national government or a geographic unit for the mechanics of democratic representation. Such decentralization, evoking few political passions and implying no sovereignty, is especially compatible with different, even overlapping, geographic entities for different governmental functions such as judicial, financial, educational, or certain kinds of territorially specific environmental regulations.

The intensity of regional "pulls" and of the contests for hegemony over critical public institutions and functions like higher education will be heightened by the presence of distinctively regional ethnic, religious, or linguistic populations, as well as by the history of the region and even by sheer physical distance from the central capital city. Regional differences in wealth and predominant economic activity can also sharpen inclinations to stress local institutions and local policies. (Witness the compounding effect of these forces in Russia, China, India, Indonesia, and even Canada.)

Also sharpening the sense of regional identity and/or sense of sovereignty can be a history of political autonomy or existence antedating the larger national state. The region may have had a role in formation of the larger state, as the thirteen colonies (now states) had in the formation of the United States of America. Or, the region may have been forcibly subsumed by the larger state, as were certain of the republics of the former Soviet Union. Perhaps most complicating, at least when a central government is attempting to devolve authority to regional units of government, as in the Russian Federation, is a mixture of regional entities of very different characteristics: regions with distinctive ethnic and linguistic identities and even histories of sovereignty (albeit some quite distant and frequently enshrouded in myth), alongside other entities that are mainly subdivisions of the larger state for governmental administrative convenience, or even for the more effective control over these regions.

Finally, quite aside from these natural and historical forces for a weakening of the center vis-à-vis the regions, most of the mature industrialized democracies in the 1980s and 1990s have seen resurgent, and at times ascendant, political conservatism, standing for less government, less regulation, smaller public sectors, and less taxation. The United States, Britain, Germany, France, and Canada (to mention only a few) have moved politically rightward through much of the 1980s and 1990s—not always steadily, but nowhere more clearly manifested than by the ever-more centrist positions in the United States and Britain of the historic parties of the political left. This disfavor toward "big government" or central government favors the devolution of governmental authority and activity to the regions. Regional (state, provincial, subject, or even more local) government is thought, rightly or wrongly, to be more "in touch" with the needs of the people and less likely to exhibit the negative stereotypes associated in almost all cultures with *government* (e.g., excessiveness, remoteness, arrogance, or indifference). The fact that many democracies also elect representatives by *single member districts* increases the inclination of the members of the national parliament or legislature to act more in deference to local interests rather than to the interests of the nation as a whole.

Two other factors also contribute to this tendency toward regionalization or decentralization. The first is an increasing realization that most institutional or agency decisions, whether of a public university, a school, a health agency, or a department of public works, are better made in proximity to the people being served and to the management and professional staff delivering the service. Regionalization or decentralization can thus be associated with "good government" or "governmental reform": that is, fewer "layers" of seemingly unproductive and possibly stifling bureaucracy between government and citizen, as well as between government and agency (or university).

A quite different impetus toward regionalization, or political decentralization, is the difficulty of taxation, and the temptation of a central government to devolve not so much authority, but rather financial responsibility, to regions or other local units. Nothing plagues Russia and the other once centrally controlled economies more than the inability any longer to skim revenue from each public enterprise. Taxation is especially difficult when it is being visibly imposed for the first time, and when incomes and transactions in the emerging private sectors are so easy to hide from governmental scrutiny. For example, in 1997, the Russian government collected only an estimated 52 percent of the taxes that were due. In Moscow, with a population of some 10 million, only 120,00 persons filed their taxes on time. Thus, there is a powerful incentive on the part of the central government to shift public financial responsibilities to local or regional governmental units. The grip of the central ministry is then further loosened, and other dimensions of privatization (e.g., private ownership, private revenue, and private norms of behavior) are strengthened.

Decentralization of Authority: Over What, To What?

Decentralization of central governmental authority over higher education does not have to be to a devolution of all authority, nor does it have to be a devolution necessarily to the regional (or provincial, or subject, or Lander) unit of government. Different objects of authority—that is, the different things that matter in the institutional provision of higher education—can be retained by a central ministry, decentralized to other levels of government (or to other publicly accountable entities), or devolved to the university itself as an enhancement of institutional autonomy. For example, *what matters* to institutions of higher education includes:

- the right to exist or to operate (apart from the right to offer certain degrees or courses of study);
- the degrees and programs to be offered;
- the curricula, or content to be learned, associated with these degrees or programs;
- the hiring (and the retention or termination) of faculty, and the determination of their compensation and other conditions of employment;
- the admission of students, including standards for admission, retention, and graduation;
- the right to acquire (hold title to) and dispose of real property, including the incurring of indebtedness for such purposes; and
- the right to enter into contracts for the purchase and delivery of goods and services.

The levels of government, or other decentralized public entities or units of authority, to which these matters may, in theory, be delegated by the central government include:

- other ministries—especially the ministry of finance, but sometimes also (particularly in "transitional" countries) including a ministry or academy of science for the support of basic research, or production ministries with their "own" institutions of higher education;
- regional (state, provincial, Lander, or subject) ministries; or
- quasi-governmental *buffer* entities, generally removed from the direct political reach of government, but nonetheless publicly accountable and ultimately selected (and at least theoretically removable) either by government or by the electorate directly.

Buffer entities, in turn, may have authority over the governance of the university itself, including the all-important selection of the rector, president, or chancellor (the clearest example being the U.S. public multicampus system). The government may devolve to a buffer entity authority only over the allocation of an overall higher education budget among the several universities and other institutions of higher education. (This is the function of the *university grants commissions* modeled on the former British body of that name.) Finally, a publicly accountable buffer entity may be given authority over the chartering or accrediting of institutions, or of their programs or degrees. Accreditation, or the official recognition of some standard of minimal institutional (or program) quality, has in the United States been delegated to voluntary, institutionally controlled entities that serve much as "buffers" for the public regulatory and quality control purposes of the state and federal governments.

The larger point of the above explication is that *decentralization*, or the devolution downward of governmental authority, has little meaning without specification of the particular object of the decentralization and to what level of government, or quasi-governmental but publicly accountable buffer entity, the particular authority is to be devolved.

Decentralization in the Russian Federation

All of these factors enter into the willingness and ability of the Russian government to decentralize authority over universities and other institutions of higher education. The units of government to which Russia *might* decentralize begin with the 89 subjects of the Russian Federation. These subjects, according to the Constitution of December 1993, include 21 autonomous republics, six krays (provinces), 49 oblasts (regions), two cities of federal status (Moscow and St. Petersburg), one autonomous oblast and ten autonomous okrugs (districts). They differ considerably in size, natural extractive wealth and effective productive capacity (and thus in consequent tax-generating capability), as well as in characteristics such as ethnic and linguistic identity and sense of historical territorial integrity. But the subject level, while critical in the delivery of basic education, has as yet little role in higher education.

The central government has clung strongly to control over licensing-attestation-accreditation functions, including over emerging private institutions of higher education. There appear as yet to be no real ministries or other agencies at the subject level challenging the central government for ownership, authority, or control over Russia's 578 state institutions of higher education, although there may well exist a capacity in the future to move some of the advanced secondary vocational colleges, or *technicums*, into postsecondary status under *subject-level* agencies or ministries.

In as yet undefined ways, the subject governments are expected to assist in the "linkage" of university offerings to the needs of the regional economies. Thus, a September 1997 ministerial policy proposal assumed that the link between institutions of higher education, prospective regional employers, and executive officers of regional governments could be fostered by regional councils. It was further proposed that such a link could be institutionalized in a form of *university trusteeship*, extending some kind of university governance role to employer and subject representatives, possibly for the purpose of compensating for grossly inadequate funding from the central government with hoped-for new revenue from businesses and regional governments (Asmolov, Dmitriev, Klyachko, & Tikhonov, 1997, p. 13). Yet the precise authority of these proposed councils was not clearly specified, nor had policies yet been devised for the protection of academic freedom or the prevention of state university resources being diverted for personal profit. Many institutional and public leaders opposed the proposal as a tacit privatization of state universities. In any event, it does not appear, as of the end of the 1990s, that decentralization in Russian higher education means any significant devolution of authority to the subject level. Rather, according to an OECD (1998) review, as the central ministry sheds or devolves authority, it would seem more likely to be to the institution itself, or possibly to some as yet unspecified *systems* of institutions, while the role of Russia's 89 subjects (the oblasts, krays, and autonomous regions) in higher education remains unsettled but still minimal.

INSTITUTIONAL AUTONOMY

Autonomy is related to both decentralization and privatization. As applied to public institutions of higher education, autonomy suggests institutional self-governance, or freedom from state control. The more autonomous the institution, the more it will be allowed by the state to establish its own policies and programs and spend its money (public and otherwise) as it sees fit. But as with decentralization, it matters greatly which domains of decision making are to be delegated to the institution under the guise of autonomy. The easiest to delegate—indeed, domains that are difficult for the state *not* to delegate—are the curriculum (that which is to be taught and learned for a given program or degree), the methods of instruction, and the objects of scholarly inquiry. On the other hand, the domain that the state is unlikely to delegate is the determination of mission (that is, whether the institution is to be a comprehensive research-oriented university, or a polytechnic oriented more toward teaching and applied scholarship, or some other kind of institution). The state is also unlikely to give up the right of ultimate oversight, or quality control, at least over higher education that is supported by public revenue, and perhaps, for the purpose of public consumer protection, over privately supported higher education as well, although some governments may be willing to delegate that authority to a publicly accountable buffer entity.

The traditionally contested domains—but where the trend in much of the world is toward greater delegation to the university, or toward greater *institutional autonomy*—are:

- the appointment of the highest executive officer (president, rector, vice chancellor)—specifically, the role of the faculty and institutional governing board over this decision;
- the degrees and programs to be offered in accord with the established mission;
- the standards for admission to the institution or to certain programs (and indirectly the number of students that the institution may or must admit);
- the appointment of the faculty and the terms and conditions of their employment, including provision for academic freedom and job security; and
- the expenditure of revenues, including the right to allocate and reallocate funds among programs and between personnel and other expenditures.

There also may be a considerable issue as to whether "the institution" to which greater autonomy is being granted is (1) the president or rector, (2) the governing board (if there be one), (3) the academic management of several constituent faculties or schools, or (4) the faculty—as represented by some form of senate. The faculty, however, may have very disparate interests. In fact, some of the faculty may resist a larger measure of autonomy to the institution if "the institution" is perceived to mean only the president, or management, and if they perceive themselves or their jobs to be better protected by the ministry or the government than by their "own" president, rector, or dean. Similarly, rectors or presidents may actually resist greater measures of autonomy if they believe these to be mere devices for abetting further governmental financial disinvestment, or if they believe their institutions to be more vulnerable than other institutions in the competitive, market-driven world of academic entrepreneurship, or if they perceive that the greater autonomy would go not to themselves, as management, but to the faculty (or perhaps even worse to a governmentally mandated new governing council made up of faculty, staff, and students).

The role of quasi-public *buffer entities* may be critical in any national policy of enhancing institutional autonomy. A movement in the direction of greater university autonomy clearly means a weakening of the authority of the ministry and generally of the legislature or parliament. In theory, a *buffer entity* combines public accountability with institutional self-governance. Thus, a devolution of state authority from government or ministry to an entity such as a public governing board or a university grants commission is like a devolution of state authority to the institution to the degree to which the buffer entity, acting on behalf of "the public," embodies the traditions and the interests of the university (like a private university governing board), as opposed to the government itself. But such an entity, ideally, must also view its role as "benignly ministerial," serving a public interest by countering, when necessary, the misguided self-interests of either the university management or the faculty. (The danger, of course, is that a buffer board, lacking such a critical and highly nuanced balance of institutional and public interests, and possibly lacking both the culture and the processes of accountability and integrity, may become simply another source of either intrusion or corruption or both.)

Thus, when a central ministry declares its intention to "enhance university autonomy," it matters considerably what it intends to shed and what it will continue to hold. Also, it matters greatly whether the central government or national ministry is truly *granting institutional autonomy*, or is more accurately described as *decentralizing authority* to a subunit of government or to some kind of quasi-governmental entity—either of the latter two possibly turning out to be more intrusive over the affairs of the university than the central government.

University Autonomy in Russia

Absent viable subject ministries or established buffer entities to which the Russian Ministry can effectively devolve authority, the object of real devolution, at least in the mid- and late-1990s, would seem to be the university itself. In large part, a significant increase in institutional autonomy in Russia is inevitable given the breakdown of ideological controls over the curriculum and the absolute imperative for there to be substantial supplementation of central governmental revenue, mainly from the entrepreneurial activities of the institution and its faculty. In addition, there remains the very large number of institutions that are owned and operationally (if not academically) controlled by ministries other than the Ministry of General and Professional Education. These institutions pose particularly thorny problems for the government as many of them are small, narrow, and inefficient, and some are increasingly deficient both academically and in their physical plants and other assets. Yet merger and closure remain politically volatile, the more so given other competing ministerial "owners." Thus, although there remain strong and significant central ministerial controls over the processes of attestation and accreditation, over the nature and the granting of degrees, and over the numbers of students to be admitted under both "regular" and "fee-paying" status, other central controls, while still on the books, may be diminishing in effectiveness. Even the central determination of the base salaries and workload expectations of the faculty and staff, for example, is becoming almost moot as these salaries have become so inadequate that other ways have to be found by the institutions to compensate faculty.

Institutional autonomy in Russia, while clearly much greater now than under the former Soviet Union or even the early days of the Russian Federation, remains uneven (Bain, 1999). Figure 3.1 shows some of the key changes in the recent (1990s) devolution of autonomy to the Russian universities (Bain, 2001).

CONCLUSION

Privatization, decentralization, and autonomy are powerful and related, but complex and multidimensional, ideas that are changing the relationship between governments and universities. Each of these dimensions is being driven in part by the need for more efficient and responsive universities. Within these concepts may lie promises of:

- a more responsive university—to the students, economic enterprises, and governmental agencies that need its students and its research;
- a better managed university—meaning a university that better empowers the individual faculty member and that maximizes the impact of teaching, learning, and scholarship;
- a more accessible university, promoting equality and social unity.

It remains possible, however, that out of these same concepts, in North America and Europe, as well as in Russia and other transitional nations, will come increasing austerity, less participation, less academic quality, a fragmentation of the national universities, and a loss of the university's traditional unifying role that will not serve well the needs of any of these societies. The difference between these two scenarios may lie in the degree to which the government uses privatization, decentralization, and institutional autonomy to create more effective, efficient, and responsive universities—or, in contrast, as a cover for financial disengagement or a general collapse of state authority.

Figure 3.1
The Movement toward Greater Autonomy in Russian Universities

Former Soviet Centralized Model	**Current (1998) Russian Model**
Leadership, Governance, and Status of Faculty	
Rector appointed by national ministry.	Rector elected by conference representing faculty, staff, and students.
Governance "top down" and imposed by ministry for all universities; authority held by rector and party leadership.	Elected senate to be principal governing body; rector *ex officio* chair. Other governance machinery established by institutional charter.
Faculty employed for life.	Faculty employed by contract.
Allocation of University Resources	
Salaries established by state.	Minimal base salary and workload set by state and guaranteed by Labor Code; can be supplemented by university with own funds.
Line item budget determined by state, tied to standard ratios of expenditure per unit. Very limited reallocation authority; no fiscal year carry-forward.	Principle espoused of lump sum budgeting with substantial institutional reallocation authority; however, still no reallocation of major "protected" categories of salaries, taxes, or student stipends.
All funds from national government.	Nongovernmental revenues (currently averaging some 25%) encouraged from (1) tuition, (2) sale of faculty training and research services, (3) sale or lease of institutional assets, and (4) fees (from, e.g., special courses, early entrance exams, or issuing credentials).
Curriculum	
Curricular content and length of each program specified by state.	Curriculum for approved programs established by faculty. State attestation and accreditation assure comparability and standards.
Standards and Numbers of Students	
Admissions and total enrollments controlled by state for each program for each institution.	Admission numbers for state institutional support and student allowances established by state for each institution. Admission of nonsupported, fee-paying students up to institution, within state quota.
State entrance examinations administered by institutions.	State entrance examinations administered by institutions.
Awarding of Degrees	
Degrees awarded by the state within narrowly established categories.	Degrees still awarded by the state rather than the institution. Degrees are shorter, and conform more nearly to European and North American standards.

REFERENCES

Asmolov, A., Dmitriev, M., Klyachko, T., Kuzminov, Y., & Tikhonov, A. N. (1997, September 9). Everything is decided by human capital (Reform Proposal). *Uchitel'skaya Gazeta* [*Teachers' Newspaper*], pp. 11–14.

Bain, O. (1998, March). *Cost of higher education to students and parents in Russia: Tuition policy issues.* Paper presented at the Annual Meeting of the Comparative and International Education Society, Buffalo, NY.

Bain, O. (1999). Reforming Russian higher education: Towards more autonomous institutions. *International Journal of Educational Reform, 8*(2), 120–129.

Bain, O. (2001). *University autonomy: Case studies of four Russian universities.* Unpublished doctoral dissertation, State University of New York at Buffalo, NY.

Elazar, D. J. (1987). *Exploring federalism.* Tuscaloosa: University of Alabama Press.

Geiger, R. L. (1987). *Private sectors in higher education: Structure, function, and change in eight countries.* Ann Arbor: University of Michigan Press.

Goskomstat [The Russian Federation State Committee on Statistics]. (1999). *Regiony Rossii* [Regions of Russia], Vol. 2. Moscow: Goskomstat.

Johnstone, D. B. (1993). The costs of higher education: Worldwide issues and trends for the 1990s. In P. G. Altbach & D. B. Johnstone (Eds.), *The funding of higher education: International perspectives* (pp. 3–24). New York: Garland.

Johnstone, D. B., Arora, A., & Experton, W. (1998). *The financing and management of higher education: A status report on worldwide reforms.* Washington, DC: The World Bank.

Johnstone, D. B., & Shroff-Mehta, P. (forthcoming). Higher education finance and accessibility: An international comparative examination of tuition and financial assistance policies. In H. Eggins (Ed.), *Higher education reform.* London: Society for Research into Higher Education. Also available from the Center for Comparative and Global Studies in Education, State University of New York at Buffalo, or online at http://www.gse.buffalo.edu/org/IntHigherEdFinance/index.html.

Levy, D. (1986). *Higher education and the state in Latin America: Private challenges to public dominance.* Chicago: University of Chicago Press.

Organization for Economic Cooperation and Development (OECD). (1998). *Reviews of national policies for education: Russian Federation.* Paris: OECD.

van Vught, F. A. (1994). Autonomy and accountability in government/university relationships. In J. Salmi & A. M. Verspoor (Eds.), *Revitalizing higher education* (pp. 322–362). Oxford: Pergamon Press.

World Bank. (1994). *Higher education: The lessons of experience.* Washington, DC: The World Bank.

Zernov, V. A. (1998). Non-state higher education: Problems and prospects. *Magister* (Newsletter of the Russian Research Institute for Higher Education), *3.*

Ziderman, A., & Albrecht, D. (1994). *Financing universities in developing countries.* Washington, DC: The Falmer Press.

Chapter 4

Flight from Freedom: Resistance to Institutional Autonomy in Brazil's Federal Universities

David N. Plank and Robert E. Verhine

Standing before the cameras on July 27, 1999, Brazil's Minister of Education, Paulo Renato Souza, unveiled proposed legislation to grant financial and administrative autonomy to the country's 39 federally sponsored universities. The proposed law was designed to implement a principle that had been guaranteed in theory but not in practice by the Brazilian Constitution of 1988. It provided for the public funding of the federal university system through block grants, thereby making it possible for each institution to establish its own policies for allocating expenditures and handling personnel matters. The minister confidently announced that he would be sending the proposal to Congress within the week and that it would be in effect by the end of the year.

Diverse segments of the federal university community reacted to the university autonomy proposal with outrage. The National Association of Professors of Higher Education (ANDES) called the proposal "fascist" and "unconstitutional" and announced that if sent to Congress, the association, which has the legal status of a labor union, would call a national strike. The National Union of Students (UNE) reacted similarly, denouncing the bill as a veiled step toward charging student tuition fees at federal universities and warning that it would ultimately result in the privatization of the public system. The National Association of Presidents of Federal Institutions of Higher Education (ANDIFES) was also incensed, claiming among other things that the proposed financial allotment (to be based on 1997 budgetary levels and on indicators of institutional productivity) was totally inadequate in terms of university needs. Articles appearing in the national press, in many cases written by highly respected scholars, also rejected the initiative, linking it to the government's much criticized neoliberal approach to economic and social policy. Faced with this outcry, the minister of education, himself the former president of a public university, backtracked. Agreeing to discuss the autonomy issue publicly before submitting the bill to Congress, he went on the talk show circuit, set up a series of Internet debate sessions, and distributed pamphlets defending the proposal. These efforts to raise support proved fruitless. A year later, the much-touted bill had still not been sent to the legislature for consideration.

The university autonomy controversy in Brazil raises a key question: is change possible in a system that almost everyone agrees needs to be changed? In addressing this question, we seek to locate the origins of Brazil's relative backwardness in higher education, to explain the apparent incapacity of the country's federal universities to respond effectively to the problems they confront, and to evaluate the current government's approach for bringing about reform.

BRAZILIAN CORPORATISM

In general terms, we attribute the intractable problems of the federal universities to a deeply institutionalized tradition of corporatism in Brazilian politics, which finds its practical reflection in the rules of university governance. According to Kaufman (1977),

> The corporatist concept is best understood in contrast to the pattern of competition between spontaneously formed, fully autonomous voluntary associations that allegedly characterizes "liberal-pluralist" societies. The corporatist alternative envisions the monopolization of interest representation by noncompeting, officially sanctioned functional organizations, which are supervised by agents of the state bureaucracy. (p. 111)

Brazilian intellectuals have long recognized that corporatism is a deeply rooted characteristic of Brazilian society. In the 1920s, scholars attempted to explain Brazilian civilization through what became known as the Theory of Culturalism. The proponents of this viewpoint traced the corporatist tendencies predominant in Brazil's public sector to the feudalism and mercantilism that characterized the country's colonial experience. They saw corporatism as rooted in "patrimonialism," a term originally used by Max Weber. In a patrimonial system, political power is prized because public resources are "owned" by and deployed in the interest of those who control the state.

Efforts in Brazil to structure state-society relations along corporatist lines reached their apogee in the 1930s, under the regime of Getúlio Vargas. Over the course of the 1930s, key constituencies including labor unions and the major professions were incorporated into the state through the establishment of entities responsible for articulating and mediating relations between the corporations and the government, and through the progressive extension of privileges and rewards to new organizations and their members (Malloy, 1979). Under the corporatist model, the state was the sole arbiter of conflicts among organized interests, with each corporation directing its demands exclusively to and through state authorities.

In Brazil as elsewhere, the power of the state to control the principal corporations varies over time. During the Vargas era the state was generally successful in keeping pace with the political and financial expectations of its core constituents, and the corporatist model functioned relatively smoothly. The military regime that governed Brazil from 1964 until 1985 continued to mobilize rewards and sanctions for key groups in order to suppress active dissent or resistance. In recent years, in contrast, the number of constituencies demanding incorporation has dramatically increased, and the capacity of state actors to dictate the terms of incorporation, manage conflict, or mobilize sufficient rewards and sanctions has declined. As a result, negotiations between the state and its core constituencies are considerably more acrimonious than they once were. Nevertheless, the corporatist tradition under which these constituencies direct their demands to the state, and demand redress from the state, continues to define the goals and strategies of key actors in the Brazilian political system.

In our analysis of the political impasse in Brazil's federal universities we rely on a conceptual framework derived from game theory. We argue that the corporatist tradition manifests itself in a set of two-player games, in which each of the principal corporations (faculty, staff, and students) finds itself locked in a perpetual struggle with the Ministry of Education to gain additional resources for its members or to protect them against losses. The structure of these games ensures conflict, as the increasingly decrepit and dysfunctional state of the federal universities provides ample warrant for each constituency to advance its claims on additional resources. At the same time, none of the games produces change, as neither of the two parties has the power to impose losses on the other. Conflict either produces stalemate or results in costs that are borne by outsiders (i.e., taxpayers), or by reduction in the share of university budgets spent on anything (i.e., libraries, laboratories, and buildings) other than salaries. Finding a way out of this political impasse is urgently important to the survival of public higher education in Brazil. We argue that finding an exit will require a change in the structure of the game, and not just in the strategies of the players.

We begin by providing a brief review of the history of higher education in Brazil. We then discuss the crises currently facing Brazil's federal universities, basing our analyses on the manifestations and consequences of two interrelated phenomena: corporatism and state dependence. Our general focus is on recent attempts by the federal government to reform the federal university system by promoting institutional autonomy. We consider how the autonomy proposal and related initiatives affect key institutional players and explain the strong, organized resistance that these efforts have encountered. We conclude by assessing the likely outcome of the government's strategy. We argue that lasting institutional reform in Brazilian universities will require a set of interventions to alter the structure of the corporatist games that now obstruct changes in the higher education system.

THE HISTORICAL EVOLUTION OF THE BRAZILIAN UNIVERSITY SYSTEM

Public education in Brazil was not only born late but "born old," according to Anísio Teixeira. This is especially the case in higher education, where the origins and traditions of the Brazilian university remain powerful obstacles to innovation and adaptation to changing circumstances.

Universities were created elsewhere in Latin America as early as the sixteenth century, but Brazil's first university was not established on an accredited basis until 1920. In contrast to Spain, Portugal sought to make its South American colony totally dependent on the motherland, and this policy together with Brazil's slavery-based plantation economy meant that investment in higher education was seen as not only unnecessary but also counterproductive. During the nineteenth century, both before and after Brazil gained independence in 1822, a small number of single-purpose, professional colleges was established to train professionals in the fields of medicine, law, economics, and engineering. Efforts to create a national university were consistently rejected by Brazilian lawmakers, however, as both traditional oligarchs and progressive elements regarded the university as irrelevant or even hostile to their interests.

The federal government established the University of Rio de Janeiro in 1920, issuing an edict that joined three existing colleges under a single administration. The founding of Brazil's first university featured a number of elements that were institutionalized in the subsequent development of higher education, as a succession of regimes sought to oblige all higher education institutions to conform to the model of organization and governance pioneered in Rio. Among the most important of these was the tradition of top-down, federal control, under which universities were created and maintained as dependencies of the Ministry of Education (MEC). Others included the organization of universities as an assemblage of semiautonomous faculties linked by a weak central administrative apparatus and an almost exclusive focus on the preparation of professionals, minimizing the importance assigned to both general education and scientific research.

As late as 1945, Brazil had just five universities and a total higher education enrollment of only about 25,000 students. The system expanded markedly over the next two decades, however, and by 1964 (the year of the military takeover) the system included 37 universities, 564 single-purpose colleges, and nearly 150,000 students. During this period, the federal government continued to play a dominant role, federalizing and integrating state, municipal, and private institutions into a single system. In response to pressures from the growing middle class, the Ministry of Education also reduced fees at public universities until, by the early 1950s, students enrolled in federal institutions paid no tuition.

During this period university students emerged as a major political force, not only within the university community but in the broader society as well. The National Students' Union (UNE) was organized in the late 1930s under the auspices of the Vargas regime, in keeping with the regime's corporatist political strategy. The students increasingly turned against the government, however, and during the 1950s they constituted a militant, politically experienced, and ultimately powerful force. From the outset UNE focused its attention on university reform, seeking above all to democratize access (e.g., provide more openings, reduce or eliminate tuition, reduce the rigor of entrance exams) and to increase student participation in university decision making. For example, student organizations called for the adoption of the "one-third rule," under which the responsibility for university governance would be equally divided among students, professors, and functionaries, organized along corporatist lines.

By the early 1960s, criticism of the Brazilian university was coming not only from students but from other constituencies as well. As a nationalistic-developmentalist ideology became increasingly popular, the university was vehemently attacked for its lack of relevance to national goals and aspirations. Those on the right demanded that the university better serve the needs of the modern labor market, while those on the left called for the university to serve as a center for social criticism and eventual (if not immediate) social transformation. At the time of the military takeover in 1964, therefore, the pressure for university reform was intense. Committed to promoting national development and internal security through a political dictatorship and an economy linked to international markets, the military regime sought to integrate higher education into the modernization process and to diffuse and control campus-based political activity. Beginning in 1966 the government issued a variety of decrees that brought about major changes in the higher education system. The reform process culminated with the passage of a wide-ranging reform law in November 1968.

The new law (Lei 5540/68) required dramatic changes in all universities and colleges, public and private. Departments rather than faculties were designated as the fundamental administrative unit, and every university was required to promote not just teaching but also research and extension. Other reforms included the introduction of a semester system, course credits, enrollment by discipline, incentives for full-time faculty employment, a career ladder, graduate programs at both master's and doctoral levels, a cycle of basic studies followed by professional preparation, and the unification of entrance exams within institutions.

In many respects, the military's reforms responded to demands for university modernization that had been set forth in previous decades by a variety of groups, both within and outside the university. The reforms also had a decidedly corporatist and authoritarian character, however, in keeping with the interests of a right-wing military government bent on maintaining social order. At federal establishments, control over certain personnel matters was transferred from the university to the central government. The president of Brazil was granted the right to name rectors and college deans, and a representative from MEC was given a seat on the curator council of each institution. The powers of the Federal Council of Education, originally created in the 1930s to accredit institutions and define curricular standards, were expanded to permit the council to intervene in the affairs of specific institutions. In addition, all political activity on the part of students and faculty was outlawed, and federal intelligence-gathering agencies infiltrated the campuses. Academic freedom was strictly limited, the dismissal of professors and the expulsion of students became commonplace, and a general climate of fear and distrust prevailed at many institutions.

One of the justifications for the 1964 coup d'etat was the military's confidence that they could accelerate the growth of the Brazilian economy. In the short run they were extremely successful; the "Brazilian miracle" generated very rapid rates of growth, more than doubling the size of the economy in less than ten years. Economic growth was accompanied by a new willingness to invest heavily in higher education. Between 1964 and 1974, the number of students enrolled in postsecondary institutions increased more than fivefold. Much of this increase came about in private institutions, which were encouraged by federal policies, including loose criteria for accrediting new institutions and programs and special tax exemptions, credits, and subsidies. In addition, MEC introduced a student loan program targeted to students enrolled in private universities. The number of federal university students grew significantly during this period, but the number of those at private institutions increased much faster. As a result, the private/public enrollment ratio shifted decisively during this decade, with the share of all students enrolled in private institutions rising from 40 percent in 1964 to 60 percent in 1974. Most of the growth in private sector enrollments was concentrated in low-quality, single-purpose colleges whose students had failed to gain admittance to higher quality, more prestigious, and lower cost (i.e., user free) public institutions (Levy, 1986).

Since the first "oil shock" and the end of the "miracle" in 1973, university enrollments have increased much more slowly. Enrollments in federal institutions increased by only about 35 percent over the next 20 years. The slow pace of expansion can be traced to the high cost of maintaining research universities, which is the only type of university recognized under the 1968 legislation. A detailed analysis by Jacques Schwartzmann (1998) reveals that between 1973 and 1989 the total cost of the federal university system increased more than 500 percent, and the level of expenditure per student more than tripled. These trends were driven not only by major increases in the number of professors (117%) and functionaries (142%) employed in federal institutions, but also by increasing reliance on full-time staff and improvement in faculty qualifications. The number of professors employed full-time in federal universities climbed from 20 percent to 80 percent of the total faculty during the 1973–1989 period, while the share of those holding advanced academic degrees rose from under 14 percent to over 50 percent. Capital investments and other nonsalary expenditures were simultaneously curtailed, as Brazil experienced successive economic crises. In consequence, expenditures on personnel increased from 81 percent to 96 percent of total higher education expenditures.

The process of political democratization (*abertura*) that began in the 1970s brought about a significant shift in power within the higher education system, reaffirming corporatist political traditions and fostering conflict between the resurgent corporations and the central government. A nationwide professors' union (ANDES) was created in 1981, along with a similar (albeit weaker) union for university administrative and technical personnel (ASSUFBRA). UNE also reappeared, after two decades of repression by the military government. The three unions' efforts to advance the interests of their members have met with some success, but their actions have simultaneously raised powerful impediments to university reform. For example, the many nationwide strikes called by ANDES during the 1980s helped win a standardized career plan and salary schedule for professors in all federal institutions, as well as the de facto right of faculty, staff, and students to elect college deans and university presidents. At the same time, however, the strikes severely disrupted the norms and routines of academic life, caused huge losses of classroom and teaching time, and further politicized the institutional atmosphere. Moreover, the reliance on university-wide elections to choose institutional leaders often resulted in popularity contests that commonly involved the participation of national political parties.

Public discussion about the Brazilian federal university intensified in the late 1980s. Higher education was among the most contentious issues debated during the 1987–1988 constitutional convention, attracting the largest number of proposed amendments of any policy area. Defenders of the established public university model squared off against advocates of student fees and expanded support for private institutions, and the former were clearly the victors. The 1988 Constitution guaranteed that universities would be research-oriented, that public universities would not charge fees for tuition, and that federal university professors would enjoy job security and retirement rights that were even more generous than those granted to federal civil servants in general. Like other institutions of public instruction, the federal universities were guaranteed "democratic governance" and "didactic, scientific, administrative and financial autonomy." The new constitution thus reaffirmed and strengthened the traditional model of the public university that had been evolving since the first Brazilian university was created in 1920.

The current problems of Brazil's federal universities are the product of this historical legacy. Most importantly for our analysis, the corporatist political culture established in the 1930s organizes and divides university constituencies to this day. The 1968 university reform law that reaffirmed and strengthened the corporatist tradition still governs higher education in Brazil. In addition, federal universities remain dependencies of the state, almost entirely lacking administrative and financial autonomy. As a result, virtually all political conflicts are framed in terms of direct negotiations between the principal corporations and MEC. The expectation that the state should provide resources and resolve conflicts, persisting side by side with local resistance to dictates from Brasília, defines contemporary political struggles in the national higher education arena.

THE CURRENT CRISIS IN BRAZILIAN HIGHER EDUCATION

The Ministry of Education classifies tertiary institutions as either universities, university centers, multiple faculty institutions or single faculty ("isolated") facilities. These institutions can be administered by federal, state, municipal, or private authorities. In this chapter we focus on the most important component of the higher education system, the 39 federal universities (at least one per state). In 1998, the federal universities enrolled more than 400,000 students and employed over 40,000 professors (Brasil, 2000b). Although they enroll only about 19 percent of all tertiary level students, they employ nearly half of all professors holding doctorates. They consequently make a disproportionate contribution in terms of research output, graduate program offerings, and total higher education expenditure. In addition, they tend to attract the best (and often the most socially privileged) students in the country, both because of their relatively high quality and because they charge no tuition fees.

As can be seen in Table 4.1, enrollment in Brazilian universities grew significantly between 1980 and 1996 (85%), but the federal universities contributed only marginally to this expansion. Much of the growth in public university coverage has come from expanding state systems, which are often multicampus organizations of inferior academic quality geared to teaching rather than to research.

The recent expansion of higher education offerings has not corrected the

Table 4.1
University Enrollment Growth in Brazil, 1980–1996

Type of University	Enrollment Growth, 1980–1996	1980 Enrollment	1996 Enrollment	% of Total Enrollment, 1980	% of Total Enrollment, 1996
Federal	23%	305,099	373,880	47	31
State	151%	81,723	204,819	12	17
Municipal	179%	17,019	47,432	3	4
Private	139%	248,359	583,269	38	48
Total	85%	652,200	1,209,400	100	100

Source: INEP, as reported in Crawford and Holm-Nielson (1998).

fact that Brazil trails most other Latin American countries in the provision of higher education opportunities. As Table 4.2 shows, a far smaller share of the relevant age cohort is enrolled in tertiary institutions in Brazil than in virtually all other countries in the region and, sadly, the gap between Brazil and its neighbors has tended to widen in recent years. The problem of inadequate higher education coverage will likely grow worse in the near future because of the rising demand for university places created by rapid expansion in secondary school enrollment. In 1998, enrollment in secondary education was 85 percent higher than in 1991, and it is expected to continue to grow at a rate of 12 percent per year. Estimates by Hauptman (1998) indicate that within the next decade, 500,000 additional higher education places will be required just to maintain the participation rate at its current level.

One major factor inhibiting the growth of higher education enrollments is the fiscal drag created by the high cost of the federal system. In 1997, expenditures on the federal university system exceeded US$7 billion, or an estimated per student cost of US$14,500. This figure is somewhat bloated because it includes retirement benefits and the cost of university hospitals, but it remains high by international standards even when these two factors are removed. As can be seen in Table 4.3, the level of expenditure in Brazil on public higher education is greater than that of many far wealthier countries, including Germany, France, and Italy. Over 25 percent of all public spending on education in Brazil currently goes to higher education, although higher education comprises less than 2 percent of total public school enrollments. All told, expenditures on public higher education represent about 1.3 percent of Brazil's GDP and about 4 percent of the country's public sector spending.

It is a matter of common record that these elevated expenditure levels

Table 4.2
Growth in Coverage of Tertiary Education in Latin America

Country	% of Age Cohort, 1980	In Tertiary Education, 1993	% Increase in 1980 Coverage Rate in 1993
Brazil	11	12	9
Argentina	22	41	86
Chile	12	27	125
Colombia	9	10	9
Costa Rica	21	30	43
Mexico	14	14	0
Peru	17	40	135
Uruguay	17	30	77
Venezuela	21	29	38

Source: UNESCO data (1995) as reported in World Bank (1997) and in Crawford and Holm-Nielson (1998).

are more the result of inefficiencies than of the high cost of maintaining standards of academic excellence. Approximately 90 percent of the money spent by the federal universities goes to pay salaries (including those of retirees). Professors and technical and administrative staff are paid through the federal government's civil service system. These individuals enjoy a variety of benefits, including almost total job security and the right to retire at a relatively young age while receiving an annual pension that includes 100 percent of salary in the final year of employment plus any increases given subsequently to those who remain active. For the federal university system as a whole, there are only about nine students for each professor and five students for each member of the technical and administrative staff. As shown in Table 4.4, the student/professor ratio in Brazilian public education is one of the lowest in the world for the tertiary level, but one of the highest in the world at the primary and secondary levels. Added to these examples of inefficiency are the facts that about 40 percent of entering students never complete their studies and that a majority of those who succeed in graduating take longer to do so than the system officially anticipates.

The Ministry of Education in Brasília essentially determines staffing policy, budgetary allocations, and the number of students who are allowed to study. Universities cannot establish plans of positions, salaries, and criteria for promotion for either teaching faculty or technical and administrative personnel. MEC determines staff number and grades, and pay is uniform

Table 4.3
Expenditures per Pupil in Public Higher Education, Brazil and Selected Countries

Country	Per Pupil Expenditure (U.S. Dollars)
Switzerland	$12,900
Canada	$12,350
United States	$11,880
Japan	$11,850
United Kingdom	$10,370
Holland	$ 8,720
Brazil	$ 8,505
Sweden	$ 7,120
Germany	$ 6,550
Australia	$ 6,550
France	$ 6,020
Italy	$ 5,850
Spain	$ 3,770

Note: Brazilian costs do not include costs associated with retirees and hospitals.

Source: Education at a Glance—OECD indicators (1995), as reported in Durham (1998).

across the entire federal public system. Since approximately 90 percent of the federal funding goes to pay salaries, it is this factor, rigorously controlled by civil service legislation, which actually determines funding levels. A major element restricting personnel management, even on the level of MEC, is the 1987 Law of Isonomy, which establishes uniform salaries throughout the country for 354 federal job categories (including federal university jobs) and defines promotion policies that put a premium on length of service. The law is largely the outcome of a prolonged strike and is considered to be a major "conquest" by the unions that represent the professors and the administrative-technical staff. As an extension of this law, ANDES is currently lobbying fervently for a uniform career plan for professors, to be applied to all public institutions of higher learning, whether federal, state, or municipal.

Because federal universities are all officially research institutions, their professors are only required to teach eight hours per week. On the other hand, there is no effective mechanism for guaranteeing that the professors' remaining time is devoted to productive academic pursuits. Fewer than one-third of the professors in the federal university system hold a doctorate and the average number of publications per faculty member is very low by

Table 4.4
Average Number of Students per Professor in Public Systems of Education, Brazil and Selected Countries

Country	Primary Level	Secondary Level	Higher Education
Brazil	30.2	35.4	9.4
Canada	17.0	19.4	17.3
Mexico	28.8	18.1	9.6
United States	17.2	16.5	14.4
France	19.4	13.1	19.0
Italy	10.6	9.9	29.1
Spain	16.4	14.5	21.3
Turkey	27.9	23.7	21.5
Mean OECD	18.2	14.4	14.4

Source: Castro (1999).

international standards. A recent World Bank document notes an "absence of academic rigor and systematic evaluation of research performance, obsolete libraries and insufficient scientific equipment" (Crawford & Holm-Nielson, 1998, p. 20).

One powerful argument for university autonomy is the need to create incentives on the institutional level to reduce inefficiencies. As things stand now, savings from efficiency measures do not accrue to the individual institution so there are no incentives for promoting economies. Rectors who succeed in cutting expenditures often wind up receiving smaller budgets the following year. Likewise, money transferred to the university by the federal government and not spent by the end of the year is automatically reabsorbed by the central bureaucracy. Thus, instead of promoting efficiency, rectors are inclined to do exactly the opposite, as cost cutting causes them to suffer political pain while receiving no fiscal benefits in return. Similarly, since there is no penalty (either on the institution or on the student) if the student drops out or extends his or her period of study, there is no pressure to regularize student flows.

A solution to the problem of institutional inefficiency, therefore, is greater administrative and financial autonomy, meaning, in practice, both more organizational flexibility and greater institutional responsibility in matters relating to university management. As we have seen, however, many key actors see the promise of autonomy as a threat. This is especially true for those in weaker institutions, and for those who feel less secure about their own positions. Thus, the challenge is to devise a program for increased autonomy that is sufficiently attractive to be acceptable to the main stakeholders. Current structures may be totally inappropriate for achieving responsiveness and efficiency in the federal universities, but they are widely perceived as optimal when it comes to securing favorable employment conditions for faculty and staff.

It is apparent that manifest problems of access and quality in Brazilian higher education cannot be simplistically attributed to a lack of financial resources. A key question suggested by the data presented in Table 4.2 is not why Brazil invests so little in higher education, but rather why the Brazilian government spends so much and accomplishes so little in return. As we will argue below, providing additional resources would do little or nothing to improve matters. There is simply no more money to be had from the federal budget, and there is a profound need to find new sources of revenue and/or to reallocate available resources to uses other than the payment of salaries. This would require sacrifices from the main constituents of the university, however, and the corporatist traditions that govern university politics make these extremely difficult if not impossible to achieve. To better understand the obstacles to a meaningful reform of Brazil's federal university system, it is useful to more closely examine the problem of political impasse in terms of two interrelated factors: corporatism and state dependence.

CORPORATISM, DEPENDENCE ON THE STATE, AND POLITICAL IMPASSE

At least as striking as the depth of the crisis in which Brazil's federal universities are mired is the apparent impossibility of discovering a politically acceptable resolution. There is widespread agreement that the present situation cannot be sustained, both within the university and among external constituencies. Proposals for reform that promise substantial changes in the prevailing distribution of power and resources are invariably greeted by vehement protests, however, and sometimes by strikes and even riots. In the following section of the chapter we develop an account of the crisis in the federal universities that seeks to explain the perdurability of administrative and financial arrangements that are inimical to the improvement and indeed to the survival of public tertiary institutions.

Corporatism

As noted above, any serious attempt to address the fiscal crisis in Brazil's federal universities and open the way to reform and improvement in institutional performance will require sacrifices from one or more of the principal constituencies within the university. If the corporations were required to negotiate with one another, they might find some basis for shared sacrifice. In fact, however, each negotiates directly with MEC. Under these circumstances none of the corporations is prepared to sacrifice the interests of its members in favor of the abstract interest of "the university," nor can any of them be expected to make sacrifices in favor of the others. The consequence is political impasse that blocks virtually all significant proposals for change.

The fundamental obstacle to be overcome can be represented in terms of a classic problem from game theory, in which the first player to sacrifice for the common good receives the elegantly named "sucker's payoff." Students (and their parents) are unlikely to welcome the imposition of fees without the provision of some compensating advantage, or in the absence of assurances that others are being obliged to bear similar costs. Faculty will resist reductions in their salaries and privileges in all but the most dire circumstances, unless their conditions of service are improved in other ways, just as university functionaries will resist the loss of job security and increases in workload. Unfortunately, the present fiscal crisis in federal universities poses an almost insuperable obstacle to the provision of compensation to those who are expected to make sacrifices, which means that sacrifice is likely to be unrequited in all but the very long term. The short answer to the question of who is prepared to sacrifice their particular interests to advance the common good is therefore "No one." In the discussion that follows, we introduce the key players in the federal university arena and review their respective corporate interests.

The Faculty

Professors constitute the federal university system's strongest and most active interest group. They are organized in a very militant national labor union (ANDES), which has promoted strikes and work stoppages on a regular basis since its creation in 1981. Although such strikes are generally nationwide, not all universities necessarily participate, and within those that do, involvement on the part of the academic community tends to be very uneven. In truth, the academic community in Brazil's federal universities is far from homogeneous. A number of years ago, Castro (1989) claimed that it was composed of three distinct groups: the old guard (composed of aging intellectuals who dominated university life before the 1968 reforms), the young Turks (made up of recent Ph.D.'s with a strong commitment to scientific research), and the radical egalitarians (a group with few if any academic credentials who seek to compensate for their lack of scholarship by actively militating against meritocratic standards). In a more recent study, Schwartzmann and Balbachevsky (1996) revive Castro's typology (without the provocative nomenclature) and add a fourth classification. This group comprises professors who tend to hold master's degrees (but not doctorates), and who are therefore caught between professing values of professional achievement, and pursuing identity through group activity and collectivist ideals. Schwartzmann and Balbachevsky argue that it is this last group that now serves as the core of ANDES and its affiliated chapters. In contrast, the young Turks (who are no longer so young) tend to devote themselves to scientific careers and prefer to exert influence through scholarly writing, personal contacts, and participation in academic societies. They are rarely enthusiastic about the ANDES-led strikes, but they usually do not openly oppose them, preferring to use the free time to focus on their nonteaching academic pursuits.

Despite faculty diversity, however, the interests of the federal university professors tend to converge when it comes to three overlapping issues: job security, salaries and benefits, and *direitos adquiridos*, or vested rights. This convergence is reflected in faculty resistance to evaluation of individual or institutional performance and to demands for the protection of *isonomia salarial*, or salary equivalence. Together these pose substantial obstacles to improvement in the efficiency and effectiveness of Brazilian universities.

The salaries of retired faculty are on average higher than those of active faculty, and the salaries of the rapidly growing contingent of substitute professors are shamefully low. Under these circumstances it is obvious that across-the-board increases in faculty salaries will do nothing to improve the condition of Brazil's federal universities; indeed, because retired faculty capture a disproportionate share of any increase, it can be argued that raising faculty salaries without prior alterations in the terms of university employment actually harms the universities by shifting resources from more to less productive uses.

In addition, public university professors are protected by Brazil's generous civil service legislation. As a result, it is virtually impossible for professors to be fired, and the federal universities have no effective, institutionalized mechanism for evaluating professors, so competence and productivity have tended to go unrewarded. In a benign and prosperous environment, "the logic of confidence" may provide an attractive and sustainable basis for managing educational organizations (Meyer & Rowan, 1977). This is clearly not the case, however, in the turbulent and corporatist environment of Brazil's federal universities.

Direitos adquiridos are private entitlements, access to which is at best marginally linked to institutional interests. Examples are study leave that can be taken just prior to retirement and early retirement that can be followed by re-employment. It is clearly in the private interest of faculty to take full advantage of these opportunities, and simply foolish for any individual faculty member to forego the benefits and opportunities that are available to him or her. At the same time, it is equally clear that from the point of view of the university, the perpetuation of these and similar *direitos adquiridos* represents a large and continuing waste of scarce resources, as individual faculty members divert a growing share of institutional resources to private uses.

The principal of *isonomia salarial* establishes that all members of a given class or category of employment should receive the same salaries. Although the concept is a familiar feature of civil service employment, its extension to university faculty creates three kinds of problems in the federal university system. First, within each university it means that faculty with the same formal qualifications (degrees, years of service) receive the same remuneration, without regard to criteria of performance or productivity. There are consequently few incentives for faculty members to increase the time or effort that they invest in their academic work, and powerful incentives for them to shift as much of their effort as they can to other paid employment. Second, across universities it means that faculty with the same formal qualifications receive the same salaries, without reference to the states or regions in which they live. As the cost of living varies widely in Brazil, university employees in poor states receive substantially higher real incomes than those in more prosperous regions, despite the fact that the more productive universities tend to be located in the richer states. Third, constant salaries across academic areas mean that areas where private sector salaries are high, like medicine, law, and engineering, must rely heavily on part-time faculty.

The Students

Students have long constituted an organized and militant element on the national political scene. According to Simon Schwartzmann (1998), student demands are currently much narrower than in earlier times, focusing on things like cheap restaurants and no testing rather than on societal revolution. The movement away from the ideologically motivated political activism of the past is due to several factors, including lasting effects from the period of military repression and the fact that, with the expansion of enrollments, a larger percentage of today's students are older and already working. One key interest of the students, however, has remained unchanged: the maintenance of "free" higher education and thus continued resistance to the payment of fees. Free education represents a massive subsidy to the children of middle- and upper-class families, more than half of whom have attended private secondary schools in which they were obliged to pay fees. The transfer is particularly egregious because the best-off students generally attend the highest-prestige and highest-cost faculties, including engineering and medicine, while those poor students who manage to obtain admission to public universities tend to congregate in fields like teacher education and nursing. It is also worth noting that a disproportionate share of the public school graduates who pass the *vestibular* for admission to federal universities are recruited from the elite federal technical schools, and not from the public schools administered by states and *municípios* that enroll the vast majority of students.

As mentioned above, the students are not as militant as they used to be and now only rarely instigate strikes to achieve their ends. As a group, however, they tend to openly support the strikes initiated by the professors' union, even though they are the ones who ultimately lose the most from the interruption, in terms of both lost classroom time and the poor quality of teaching rendered during the rushed strike make-up period. Giannotti (1986) has referred to the students' support for professor strikes as an "implicit pact," in which the students exchange their "solidarity" for generous treatment at grade time and other favors.

The Functionaries

As with faculty, the interests of functionaries are focused on salaries and benefits, and on job security. These are important issues, especially because many Brazilian universities are vastly overstaffed by international standards. The political salience of this over-staffing is evidenced by the fact that *empreguismo* (patronage employment) is one of the time-honored strategies for building political support in Brazil, and federal politicians have in the past relied on the federal universities as a source of civil service jobs for their friends and supporters. This phenomenon was especially pronounced in the 1980s, during the carnival of *clientelismo* (the distribution of financial and other favors to political supporters) that accompanied the restoration of electoral politics in Brazil. The number of functionaries increased dramatically in virtually all federal universities during this period. More recently, most functionaries have entered employment through official civil service procedures (*concursos*), but the costly and inefficient reality of overstaffing will continue to persist unless positive and politically painful steps are taken. Given that a smaller number of functionaries means that those remaining must work harder, even efforts to reduce the size of the functionary contingent through attrition have tended to be strongly resisted.

Leading this resistance has been a national union (ASSUFBRA) which has become increasingly militant in recent years. Whereas in the past it was usually the national professors' union that initiated the nationwide strikes, today it is often the functionaries' union that takes the lead. One reason for this willingness to strike is that the federal government has frozen the level of pay for functionaries, but not for professors, since 1995, despite an accumulated inflation during the period of over 50 percent. Also, since existing legislation makes it very difficult to dismiss a university worker and since, for both political and legal reasons, salaries are almost never cut or held back during a public strike, an obvious question is "why not strike?" In the case of the professors, it is inevitably agreed as part of the end-of-the-strike negotiations that all lost class time is to be made up through a reduction in the vacation period. No such agreement has ever been made by the functionaries, however, in large part because the continuous, routine nature of their work is not conducive to an enforceable make-up requirement.

Added to the problems of overstaffing and frequent strikes is the fact that the functionaries are not organized into career hierarchies. As a result, advancements in position or salary level are almost impossible, thereby making it difficult to reward performance. Also, since lateral, but not upward, movement is permitted, many public university workers wind up occupying positions other than those for which they were originally employed and trained. This tendency together with the absence of articulated strategies for human resource development helps account for the low level of staff competence that plagues most of Brazil's federal universities.

The University's Central Administration

Federal university rectors (or presidents) are nominated for a fixed mandate by the president of the republic from a list of three candidates produced by the university's governing councils. Since the early 1980s, however, it has been customary for the governing councils to merely ratify the results of university-wide elections in which teachers, functionaries, and students participate with equal corporate weight. This process was officially altered by a law passed in 1995 (Lei 9192) which guarantees professors a 70 percent weight in elections for university leaders. Many universities have found ways to vitiate the 70 percent requirement, though, continuing to rely on the one-third rule (or some variation of it) instead. The result is that choosing the rector on the university level is a highly politicized process that often divides the institution along corporatist and/or ideological lines. Of course, since the elections are strictly advisory, the politicking continues long after they are over. Lobbying focuses first on the university councils responsible for formulating the list of three, and later on the president of Brazil, who makes the final choice in consultation with the minister of education.

Having the president select the rector from a list of three is intended to advance two purposes. First, it should help to ensure that candidates are people with legitimacy and leadership within their institutions. Second, it makes it possible for the government to choose someone who represents the interests of the broader society as well as his/her own institution. There are problems related to this nomination procedure, however. For example, the requirement that rectors be appointed from the faculty of their own universities is a powerful obstacle to reform. On the one hand, the rule strictly limits the pool of qualified candidates and prevents the professionalization of the university administration. On the other hand, the rule holds rectors hostage to the internal political dynamics of their own institutions, thus effectively minimizing the probability that they will be able to bring about significant changes. The fact that they must contest elections in order to gain appointment constrains their freedom of action, because a candidate who promises to attack the interests of one or more of the corporations is unlikely to win much popular support.

The federal university rectors are supported administratively by a set of pro-rectors (or vice presidents) who directly oversee specific administrative and academic areas. The rector has exclusive responsibility for filling these positions and often makes his or her choice based on election support and other political criteria. Many pro-rectors are faculty members with no prior administrative experience, and this along with the fact that they occupy their positions for a limited period of time tends to create a competency vacuum at the university's highest administrative levels. It is not surprising, therefore, that in reacting to MEC's university autonomy proposal, many rectors and pro-rectors argued that their institutions were not prepared to take on new responsibilities and that they would support such a reform only if it was implemented gradually. The obstacles to university reform are not just political; low levels of administrative competence also stand in the way.

Dependence on the State

In our view, the key consequence of the corporatist culture of Brazil's public universities is the dyadic games that it produces between the principal corporations and the federal government. The university is a federal dependency, and faculty and staff are employees of MEC. Each of the principal corporations negotiates directly with the state, seeking to advance the particular interests of its members, rather than with its counterparts at the local level. This makes the negotiation of shared sacrifice within the university to achieve common goals or protect shared institutional interests virtually impossible, as it is in the interest of each corporation to maximize its own private advantage in its negotiations with the state.

On the one hand, this situation produces perpetual conflicts, as we have discussed above. On the other hand, it leads to the abdication of local responsibility, as there is no capacity within the universities for the definition of collective purpose or the allocation of shared sacrifice. In addition, there is little or no articulation between the federal universities and local constituencies (e.g., employers), except perhaps the rhetorically romanticized poor, as the attention of all the major corporations is focused on Brasília rather than the local environment.

The political and professional cultures of the federal universities reflect their dependence on the state. On the one hand, the principal corporations within the university expend a great deal of time and energy demanding increased support and improved conditions of work from the federal Ministry of Education. In 1998 and again in 2000, for example, university professors promoted strikes that lasted about three months each, demanding increased salaries and other benefits from the federal government. On the other hand, they frequently decry the "interference" of the ministry in the affairs of the university when the ministry acts to address local issues. Again in 1998, the Federal University of Rio de Janeiro was closed for nearly four months because of protests over the minister's appointment of a rector who had not "won" election to the position among faculty, staff, and students within the university.

The dependence of the federal universities on the state has other consequences as well. One is the phenomenon of *isonomia salarial.* Another is that norms of regional equity and equity across states (reinforced by political pressures in the Congress and elsewhere) require that higher education investment be distributed so as to benefit all states rather than focused on the best or most productive institutions. Since the approval of the Brazilian Constitution in 1988, for example, four new states have come into being, each of which has been provided with a federal university. Whether this was the best available use for scarce resources in a system facing a virtually permanent fiscal crisis is at least debatable.

The most significant consequence of dependence on the state, however, is that it encourages constant recourse to Brasília by each of the principal corporations within the university, as they demand additional resources or assistance in resolving local political conflicts. Rather than assuming local responsibility for local problems, actors within the federal universities are encouraged to blame their problems on the federal government, and to insist that MEC solve their problems for them. This has two main consequences. First, it sets up the sterile two-player games described in the introduction. Second, it fosters local solidarities among the principal corporations that further limit the possibility for change in the universities. Each of the corporations engages in its struggle with MEC with the acquiescence or even tacit support of each of the others. Thus, for example, professors support the resistance of students to the imposition of fees, not because they were once students themselves, nor because their political orientation is generally critical of prevailing authority, nor even because they have children themselves who will one day be students. The overwhelming factor is that there exists a natural solidarity among the constituencies; gains for one are in a real sense gains for all, and they are in any case effectively costless for the other constituencies. Costs are imposed on outsiders (i.e., taxpayers), which sustains good relations within the university and affirms the importance of the work that each of the constituencies does.

These are games that no one can win. The problems described above will simply grow worse without changes in the corporatist relations between the principal constituencies and the ministry. As noted, it is in the interest of each constituency to perpetuate and protect its own privileges, and it is consequently in the interest of none to attack or undermine the privileges of the others (lest there be retribution against their own privileges). The consequence is political immobility, in which recurrent conflicts over familiar issues block change and blame is assigned to the ministry rather than to actors within the university. Long-term improvement in Brazil's federal universities thus requires a reform strategy that changes the structure of the games that now preoccupy the energies of the key constituencies within the higher education system.

THE PROSPECTS FOR REFORM: WHO TAKES THE HIT?

In assessing the prospects for reform in the federal universities, the key to success is finding a way out of the dyadic games between MEC and the principal corporations that block virtually all efforts to bring about significant policy change. Recent initiatives from MEC have sought to escape from these sterile and unproductive games by raising the stakes, adding players, altering the rules, and changing the arena of conflict. The government has managed to win approval of some important policy reforms in recent years, but resistance has been great and change has been sporadic and uneven at best. There is little solid ground for optimism. The twin traditions of corporatism and state dependence mean that virtually all efforts to implement change are met with a deeply institutionalized negative response. It will require all of the federal government's political agility to create a set of circumstances in which meaningful reform becomes possible, and even more to bring about its success.

As we have seen, the essential component of the present government's strategy for reforming the federal universities is the establishment of university autonomy. It is clear that the critical problems of Brazil's higher education system cannot be resolved under present governance arrangements, and some reassignment of responsibilities is therefore prerequisite to meaningful reform. It is equally clear, however, that shifting the responsibility for hard choices offers no assurance that the hard choices will be made or that the choices that are made will lead to real improvements in institutional performance. It is likely that some rectors will rise to the challenge of autonomy and develop innovative and successful strategies for the restoration and improvement of their institutions, but there is little reason to suppose that the capacity for innovative leadership is widespread within Brazilian universities, or that the opposition of established constituencies to changes that threaten the interests of their members will be easily vanquished. The most likely outcome of the move to university autonomy is therefore a further differentiation among institutions, in which universities with unusually effective leadership and cooperative employment relations will be able to take advantage of increased autonomy to resolve local problems and attract additional resources, while those that lack these attributes will persist in their present cycle of decline.

In closing it is worth noting that the reforms that the present government has initiated in basic education are unprecedented in their scope and effects.

These may set precedents for significant changes elsewhere in the education system, but the basic education system is different from the higher education system in two crucial respects. First, corporatism is not nearly as deeply entrenched in the basic education system, for a variety of reasons including the relatively low status of teachers and the continued importance of *clientelismo* in the appointment of administrators and functionaries to leadership positions. Second, the elite constituencies that obstruct reform in higher education are not deeply involved in the basic education system, because their children attend private schools. These differences mean that reform will be significantly more difficult in higher education than it was in basic education. The present government has won some small victories, but the institutional autonomy that is prerequisite to meaningful reform is not yet on the horizon. The condition of the federal universities is therefore likely to grow worse before it gets better.

REFERENCES

Brasil, Ministério da Educação, Instituto Nacional de Estudos e Pesquisas Educacionais. (2000a). *EFA 2000—Education for all: Evaluation of the year 2000*. Brasília: INEP.

Brasil, Ministério de Educação, Instituto Nacional de Estudos e Pesquisas Pedagógicos. (2000b). *Evolução do ensino superior—Graduação 1980–1998*. Brasília: INEP.

Castro, C. de M. (1989). What is happening in Brazilian education? In E. Bacha & H. S. Klein (Eds.), *Social change in Brasil, 1945–1985: The incomplete revolution* (pp. 263–309). Albuquerque: University of New Mexico Press.

Castro, M.H.G. (1999). O sistema educational brasiliero: Tendências e perspectivas. In J. P. dos Reis Velloso & R. C. De Albuquerque (Eds.), *Um modelo para a educação no século XXI* (pp. 35–117). Rio de Janeiro: José Olympio.

Crawford, M., & Holm-Nielson, L. (1998). *Brazilian higher education: Characteristics and challenges* (LCSHD Paper Series—Department of Human Development). Washington, DC: The World Bank.

Durham, E. (1998). *Uma política para o ensino superior brasileiro: Diagnóstico e proposta*. São Paulo: Núcleo de Pesquisas sobre Ensino Superior, Universidade de São Paulo.

Giannotti, J. A. (1986). *A universidade de ritmo de bárbarie*. São Paulo: Brasiliense.

Hauptman, A. (1998). *Accomodating the growing demand for higher education in Brazil: A role for the federal universities?* (LCSHD Paper Series, Department of Human Development). Washington, DC: The World Bank.

Kaufman, R. R. (1977). Corporatism, clientelism, and partisan conflict: A study of seven Latin American countries. In J. M. Malloy (Ed.), *Authoritarianism and corporatism in Latin America*. Pittsburgh: University of Pittsburgh Press.

Levy, D. (1986). *Higher education and the state in Latin America: Private challenges to public dominance*. Chicago: University of Chicago Press.

Malloy, J. M. (1979). *The politics of social security in Brazil*. Pittsburgh: University of Pittsburgh Press.

Meyer, J., & Rowan, B. (1977). Institutionalized organizations: Formal structure as myth and ceremony. *American Journal of Sociology, 83*, 340–363.

Schwartzmann, J. (1998). *Questões de financiamento nas universidades Brasileiras.* São Paulo: Núcleo de Pesquisas sobre Ensino Superior, Universidade de São Paulo.

Schwartzmann, S. (1998). *Higher education in Brazil: The stakeholders* (LCSHD Paper Series—Department of Human Development). Washington, DC: The World Bank.

Schwartzmann, S., & Balbachevsky, E. (1996). The academic profession in Brazil. In Philip Altbach (Ed.), *The international academic profession—Portraits of fourteen countries* (pp. 231–280). New York: The Carnegie Foundation for the Advancement of Teaching; Jossey-Bass.

World Bank. (1997). *World Development Indicators* 1997. Washington, DC: The World Bank.

Chapter 5

When Goals Collide: Higher Education in Laos

David W. Chapman

This chapter draws on the recent experience of the National University of Laos (NUOL) in negotiating a tricky path among three frequently competing national development agendas: (1) the government's use of higher education as a symbol of national identity and international prestige, (2) the university's effort to strengthen and expand the funding for higher education, and, (3) the effort of international donors and some university leaders to strengthen the quality and relevance of the education provided at the university. In the context of Laos, these factors interacted in unanticipated ways that ultimately threatened the attainment of all three goals. While this case study is based in the Lao People's Democratic Republic (Lao PDR), the lessons of Laos travel well. The message is one that has far broader applicability as higher education leaders across the developing world are struggling with this same convergence of pressures.

The story has a subtext. One of the most universal challenges across the developing world is how to preserve and strengthen core functions of the university (teaching, research, and service) in the face of limited resources and the frequently conflicting demands of multiple constituencies. This chapter argues that, due to the way academic staffs have been funded across many universities in the developing world, efforts to raise instructional quality, improve curriculum, encourage research, and promote a culture of service have met with limited success. The core functions of higher education have suffered. Improving the core functions of the university now requires a fundamental re-examination of the relationships of the university to the national government, and of university employees to their institution.

OVERVIEW—HIGHER EDUCATION IN LAO PDR

Laos has the lowest per capita enrollment in higher education of any country in the region. Only about eight of every ten school-age children enter primary school and only two of every 100 Lao children eventually complete secondary school and receive admission to the university. Nonetheless, higher education is the fastest growing segment of the education system in Laos. Between 1991–1992 and 1997–1998, new enrollment in bachelor's degree and university diploma programs increased by 315 percent (from 1,367 to 4,305 students); overall enrollment grew by 205 percent (from 6,004 to 12,296 students).

A major study of the education system in 1989 identified the lack of senior level administrative, managerial, and technical personnel as a significant impediment to national development and recommended that strengthening higher education in Laos be given a priority in the government's subsequent Five Year Plan (Asian Development Bank, 1989). The study also suggested that one strategy for accomplishing this goal would be to consolidate the existing postsecondary institutions to effect economies of scale and provide a new institutional framework to selectively start new postsecondary degree programs.

Based on recommendations from this study, the Ministry of Education (MOE), with assistance from the Asian Development Bank (ADB), undertook a project to consolidate three university-level institutions into a new structure, the National University of Laos. The intention was to eventually consolidate other postsecondary institutions into that structure and selectively open new colleges in high-priority subject areas (ADB, 1989; Weidman, 1997, 1999).

As a result, the National University of Laos (NUOL) was formed in 1995 through the consolidation of three existing postsecondary institutions: the College of Medicine, the Polytechnic, and the Teacher Training College. Additional colleges were then merged into this structure so that by mid-1998, ten colleges had been merged into NUOL. At present, the university consists of nine faculties, as described in Figure 5.1. NUOL now represents about 45 percent of the postsecondary enrollment in the country, while enrollment in special evening programs is about 15 percent. The remaining 40 percent of the enrollment is distributed across teacher training colleges and colleges sponsored by other ministries.

Students seeking entrance to the university take a common entrance examination that is administered in all provinces. Fifty percent of the places in the university are reserved for students from the provinces, though it is not always possible to fill that quota. Places not filled under the quota system are supposed to be filled on the basis of examination results.

The consolidation and expansion of the university has been a priority of the Lao government, largely for three reasons. First, the government rec-

Figure 5.1
Colleges within the National University of Laos

Colleges within the University	***Courses of Study Available***
College of Foundation Studies	A common core of courses taken by all students across the university; new in 1996–1997
Faculty of Sciences	Mathematics, Physics, Chemistry, Biology
Faculty of Humanities and Social Sciences	History, Geography, Lao Language, Literature, Foreign Languages (English, French, German, Russian)
Faculty of Engineering and Architecture	Civil, Electrical, and Mechanical Engineering, Architecture
Faculty of Medical Sciences	Medicine, Pharmacy, Dentistry
Faculty of Agriculture and Forestry	Agronomy, Animal Husbandry, Forestry
Faculty of Economics and Management	Economics, Management, Planning
Faculty of Law	Law
Faculty of Education	Education

Source: Department of Higher, Vocational, and Technical Education, Ministry of Education, Vientiane, Laos.

ognized the constraints on national development posed by the lack of highly trained personnel as well as the urgent need for more advanced administrative and technical skills in the work force. Second, the government was attracted by the symbolic need to have a university similar to those in neighboring countries, both as an international symbol of national development and as a way to demonstrate national progress to the country's own citizens. Finally, the government supported these efforts because they realized that higher education could also attract outside funding. It worked! Over the 1990s, the government received over US$25 million to support the formation of the National University of Laos (NUOL).

HIGHER EDUCATION AS A SYMBOL OF NATIONAL IDENTITY AND INTERNATIONAL PRESTIGE

Universities in the developing world walk a tightrope, serving as a showpiece of internal unity and a symbol of national progress while also trying to address the immediate needs of the labor force. Such is the case of higher education in Laos. The National University of Laos plays an enormously important symbolic function in national life. The government uses the university to build national identity and pride by incorporating three highly symbolic features into its system of higher education. First, instruction is in the Lao language. No instruction in other languages is allowed (except in foreign language classes). This honors the local language and culture and ensures that graduates who go on to important positions in government and business have a common language of communication. The use of Lao in higher education serves as a statement to the world that the Lao language is on par with other languages of international higher education. The use of Lao has serious ramifications for the quality of instruction, but these are discussed later.

Second, no tuition is charged. Government's provision of "free" higher education is intended as a message that a student's family background or ability to pay will not limit them from great achievements. While in practice there are substantial hidden costs to students, the symbolic message is salient.

Third, the MOE implemented a complex formula intended to provide equity in admission across all provinces. Approximately half of the student places in each college across the NUOL are allocated though the quota system, in which a fixed number of places are reserved for each province. Secondary school graduates wanting to attend NUOL must still take the university entrance examination, which is administered in every province each year. However, final selection of students for admission is made by the Provincial Education Director based on entrance examination scores, recommendations, and other considerations. Again, the message is one of national unification—that Lao citizens have an opportunity for higher education regardless of ethnic or regional affiliation.

The quota system, to the extent it is fairly administered, does ensure regional representation in student admissions. Quota students are required to return to their province upon completion of their university studies and remain in government service for five years, if their services are needed by government. This has not always worked smoothly, for several reasons: (1) students from rural provinces often do not want to return to their home provinces, preferring to remain in urban areas where employment options are more attractive; (2) graduates complain that the provincial administrations frequently do not assign returning students to work in the fields in which they were trained; (3) the requirement that graduates return is not consistently or effectively enforced—those who do not want to return to their province often do not.

The quota system ensuring provincial representation was also intended to help students from ethnic minority groups gain access to higher education. Since NUOL does not report enrollment by ethnic minority, the effectiveness of the quota system in meeting one of its central purposes is largely unknown. Nonetheless, the message to the country is one of open access.

UNIVERSITY EFFORTS TO INCREASE FUNDING FOR HIGHER EDUCATION

In the consolidation of campuses to form NUOL, the World Bank, the Asian Development Bank, and other international assistance agencies paid for capital construction, refurbishing of existing facilities, curriculum development, and staff training. Government was to pay for recurrent costs of operating the university (faculty salaries, supplies, etc.). However, two factors seriously jeopardized the financial underpinnings of the new university. First, the government didn't budget enough to cover the recurrent costs of operating NUOL (salaries, supplies, building cleaning, and maintenance). Second, the new university started operation just as the regional and national economic downturn made imports more expensive. In the first ten months of 1998 alone, inflation was 100 percent. This hit the university especially hard, since many of the materials, supplies, and staff training were purchased abroad, which required hard currency.

In the face of rapid price inflation, the instructional staff of the university, as members of the civil service, were caught in a particularly difficult bind. The salaries of university faculty were never particularly high. The average annual salary of university instructors (739,200 Kip in 1996–1997) is about 25 percent more than the salary of a primary school teacher (589,696 Kip in 1996–1997) and only about 3 percent more than the salary of an upper secondary teacher (719,830 Kip in 1996–1997), though they are expected to have significantly higher academic qualifications (ADB, 1998; Mingat, 1998). While allowances increase the financial benefit of being a university instructor, teacher compensation is relatively flat across levels of the education system. Moreover, in the face of sharp inflation, government was unable to raise salaries of civil servants. Faculty salaries, in real terms, declined by more than 50 percent in 1998 alone. Financially, the attractiveness of a university faculty position was marginal, and getting worse.

Consequently, NUOL faced serious financial problems both in meeting the operating cost of the university and in retaining faculty. To compensate for government inability to meet recurrent budget, NUOL allows faculty to conduct private consulting and operate small businesses using university facilities, in return for a small fee for overhead expenses. For example, instructors in engineering can consult with local engineering or construction firms, or they can operate their own engineering firms from university premises. Running a private business is quite doable, since work demands on instructional faculty are not excessive. NUOL instructors are expected to teach ten to twelve contact hours per week, including laboratory time, with some reduction in teaching load for instructors who also have administrative responsibilities. Once teaching responsibilities are met, instructors are free to leave campus, consult, and hold other employment.

The primary mechanism used by faculty members for responding to the financial squeeze was to initiate a series of private instructional programs, taught at NUOL in the evenings, for which they charge relatively high tuition (about 150,000 Kip per year) and provide no scholarships. These programs are in subject areas of particularly high demand, such as English language, and English language instruction in engineering and architecture. Demand has been substantial. For example, in 1997–1998, approximately 4,000 students took the examination for entrance to the special program in English language, for which only 600 places were available. This suggests that potential students are willing to pay private funds for advanced education in areas they believe are in high demand in the labor market.

Twenty percent of the private tuition is paid to NUOL for the use of their facilities and the balance is used to compensate the instructors. NUOL estimated that, in 1998, its share of the revenues for the evening English language engineering program alone amounted to 80 million Kip (about US$19,000). This means that engineering instructors teaching in these special programs generate about 320 million Kip (about US$76,000) in salary subsidy. This salary supplement is an important factor in faculty retention. The money also goes a long way toward meeting the government expectation that NUOL will generate at least 15 percent of its nonsalary recurrent funds each year.

It is unlikely that NUOL could retain its instructional staff or meet its own operating budget requirements without providing opportunities to earn additional income. These private business arrangements offer instructors a way to keep their professional skills fresh and maintain a current knowledge of labor market demand in their area of expertise.

At the same time, these salary subsidy arrangements, at least in Laos, have two negative effects. First, not all instructors participate in the evening programs or teach in specializations that offer consulting opportunities. The salary inequities can erode morale across the instructional staff. Second, the time and energy which instructors devote to special programs, private consulting, and business ventures draw their time and attention away from the regular program of the university. Indeed, administrators at NUOL express concern that faculty are shifting their time and attention away from their regular day courses and putting their energies into the preparation and delivery of their special evening courses, for which they get extra compensation (ADB, 1999).

This pattern (of giving the regular day program less attention) also threatens equity considerations that were a prominent condition of international funding for NUOL. Students in the regular day program of the university, mainly quota students from throughout the country, receive lower quality instruction while affluent students, predominantly from the capital city, receive a higher quality education. This arrangement reinforces existing patterns of advantage in the country, as children of the rich get a higher quality education than do others. It essentially undercuts the efforts of international organizations to ensure that NUOL address equity issues through a quota system in its admissions.

INTERNATIONAL DONORS' AND UNIVERSITY LEADERS' EFFORTS TO STRENGTHEN THE RELEVANCE AND QUALITY OF UNIVERSITY INSTRUCTION

While NUOL may have served a symbolic purpose within the country, the interest of the World Bank, ADB, and other international sponsors in providing financial support for university consolidation was anything but symbolic. These organizations were investing in human capital development. They expected a return on their investment in the form of graduates with advanced technical and management skills who would assume leadership positions in government, business, and industry. To that end, the international funding for the university project included substantial funds for upgrading the teaching staff at NUOL, upgrading laboratories and library resources, and for opening new programs in areas directly linked to national economic development (e.g., a college of economics). Better trained instructors working with better instructional materials would, they assumed, result in higher quality instruction.

These efforts to upgrade the quality and relevance of instruction encountered three largely unforeseen difficulties. First, given the exclusive use of Lao as the language of instruction, the limited availability of current textbooks and resource materials quickly surfaced as a serious problem. Since many students, faculty, and administrators did not have strong command of an international language, it limited their use of contemporary textbooks in English, French, or other international languages. Faculty members frequently did not have the language skills necessary to use international texts as references, even for their own lecture preparation. Textbooks available in Lao tended to be old and out-of-date. New textbooks are expensive to translate and, once translated, are often used beyond the life of their content. Students in some subject areas are learning material that is already obsolete.

Second, the use of Lao language instruction sharply curtailed the feasibility of sending Lao instructors abroad for training (particularly short-term training). While funding was provided for international training, the effectiveness of that training was limited by participants' language abilities. Similarly, efforts to improve instructional quality by using visiting instructors from other countries was seriously limited by language problems.

Third, the shortfalls in recurrent budget meant that laboratories and libraries were not well maintained. For example, students nearly ready to graduate in civil engineering had never conducted a concrete stress test and were not sure how to actually do one (though they had read about it). There just was not enough money available from the recurrent budget to cover the expendable supplies needed to conduct such experiments.

In the end, these factors converged to seriously threaten the quality of instruction at NUOL. The use of Lao language limited the use of international instructors, limited the ability of local instructors to upgrade their training, and forced the use of out-of-date textbooks and instructional materials. Efforts to promote a national identity (through the use of Lao) contributed to undercut the relevance and quality of instruction.

A SUMMARY OF THE LAO SITUATION—SYMBOLIC NEEDS, TECHNICAL SOLUTIONS

The investment by international organizations in higher education in the developing world is widely justified on technical grounds—economic growth is constrained by lack of a highly trained workforce; the provision of the requisite education is the central strategy for removing the constraint. While national governments share this view, they are frequently just as concerned with building national unity and social cohesion within a country (Heyneman, 2000). The technical and symbolic roles of higher education are not necessarily incompatible—social cohesion has significant economic benefits (Heyneman, 2000). Economic progress depends on people of different backgrounds working together toward a shared vision. However, the interplay of the two views (economic fix, symbol of unity) provide the ingredients for conflict.

So it was in Laos. International donors' investments in NUOL were driven by their belief that higher education would provide a technical fix to a human resources problem linked to national economic development. Labor market relevance, cost recovery, and sustainability were the key criteria of a successful effort. The Lao government faced more immediate problems—building national unity and a common identity within a country experiencing significant tensions among its ethnic groups, between urban and rural areas, and between rich and poor. University leaders had to find a stance from which they could respond to both sets of pressures. Their actions played upon and ultimately exacerbated the loosely coupled nature of higher education in Laos.

A loosely coupled system is one in which components operate somewhat independently of each other. Such systems are often characterized by a mismatch between the organizational plans and subsequent activities, jurisdictional ambiguities, and slow or absent coordination among units (Chapman, 1991; Firestone, 1985; Nagel & Snyder, 1989; Weick, 1976). While operating in a way that undercuts effective organizational planning, loosely coupled systems have some strengths. They often reduce conflict between system elements because in these situations such elements are not required to agree, interact with, or adapt to each other, creating fewer occasions for conflict (Deal & Celotti, 1980; Meyer & Rowan, 1977).

Higher education in Laos was caught between essentially conflicting demands. NUOL responded to the contradiction by decoupling formal structures from actual work activities in order to maintain *ceremonial conformity*. In the end, NUOL created a *planned contradiction*. As a matter of public policy, NUOL offered free tuition, equitable access to students from across the country, and instruction in Lao. In practice, quality instruction at NUOL was offered in English, at a high tuition, for children of affluent families in the capital city. The unintended impact is to give greater career advantage and employment mobility to students who already have greater wealth.

The use of the special evening courses to offset funding shortfalls resulted in the creation of a de facto private university operating within the public university structure, but at considerable variance with rules governing the formal structure. While successfully creating a private income stream that helps to ensure the university's survival, the special evening programs inadvertently distort the allocation of instructor time and motivation and undercut equity considerations in admissions. In responding to the financial crisis, the university essentially lost its control over faculty members' time and energy. However, the alternative was to lose the faculty members themselves to better paying jobs in the private sector.

BROADER IMPLICATIONS—LESSONS THAT TRAVEL

The tug on organizations to meet competing, and sometimes conflicting, demands is hardly new. In the Lao case, efforts to strengthen the financing of the university, seen as a necessary step in strengthening the quality of the institution, had quite the opposite effect and eventually served to undercut the very ends that the institution was trying to promote. The creation of special evening courses represents a creative adaptive response by NUOL to a difficult financial situation. Moreover, these private programs provide a useful response to market demand since the programs are only offered in subject areas in which a sufficient number of students are willing to pay a substantial private tuition.

The Laos example illustrates the risks of approaching the improvement of the core functions of higher education as a largely technical fix to a development problem. The needs of the university to serve a symbolic function got in the way of the need to serve a technical function (e.g., expanding the pool of highly trained personnel). Efforts to strengthen the financing of the university, seen as a necessary step in strengthening the quality of the institution, had quite the opposite effect and eventually served to undercut the very core functions that the institution was trying to promote.

The tensions higher education institutions can encounter in trying to fulfill both their symbolic and technical (e.g., development support) roles and the impact such conflicts can have on the operation of the university are not unique to Laos. The interwoven and largely unanticipated cross-impacts in the Lao case illustrate a set of issues common to universities in many developing countries. Resolving those conflicts will require a fundamental re-examination of the relationships of the university to the national government, and of university employees to their institution.

Reexamining the Relationship of the University to Government

The Lao example highlights the tensions that can arise between the national symbolism vested in a country's major universities and the operational needs of keeping the institutions running. National policies of free tuition and equitable access are not always linked to government funding decisions that would make such policies viable.

The problems of misalignment between national goals and university budgets is likely to get worse. Across the developing world, higher education faces stiff new competition for public funds, as governments address urgent problems of pollution, HIV/AIDS, and continued urbanization (Chapman, 2000; Lewin, 1996, 1998). It is not that higher education is viewed as unimportant, but that other issues have taken on greater urgency. The need to develop new (or at least more robust) funding streams to help support higher education is becoming acute.

Reexamining the Relationship of Faculty to the University

The pattern of underpaying university faculty while allowing (and encouraging) them to supplement their income through private consulting has been a rather common way of subsidizing higher education across the developing world. In most instances, everyone (with the possible exception of the students) wins. Instructors gain the prestige of having an academic title and affiliation that serve them well in their entrepreneurial ventures. Colleges and universities can boast of a distinguished faculty at a very low price. As long as instructors meet their classes and perhaps maintain minimal office hours, they are largely free to supplement their income through such activities as tutoring, consulting, and operating small businesses. Overall, it is generally a functional system of mutual benefits.

However, one consequence of low academic salaries in developing country institutions is that institutional administrators have little control over faculty time. Initiatives to channel faculty time to improving instruction, conducting research, or providing service is often lost to faculty members' struggles to maximize their income. Faculty salaries, then, frequently emerge as a central constraint on institutions' efforts to improve the quality of instruction.

This is well illustrated in Laos. While the special evening programs represent a creative, adaptive response to a difficult financial problem, the operation of the special evening courses at NUOL distorts faculty allocation of their time in ways that undercut the quality of the regular academic program of the university.

THE SEARCH FOR SOLUTIONS

Typically, the most promising way of recapturing academic staff time is to raise salaries to a level that allows them to work more fully through the university and then restrict the amount of consulting they can do outside of university channels. The university can then sell the teaching and research activities of their faculty to public and private enterprises wishing to purchase these services. The dilemma in Laos is that the country does not yet have a private sector robust enough to pay NUOL for research and other services.

Another possible source of funds to offset the financial shortfall is for NUOL to charge students a modest tuition. Indeed, governments in many countries are expecting students to pay more of the costs of their own higher education. This shift is propelled both by economic pressures on governments to reduce public funding of higher education and by growing pressure from international agencies. These agencies argue that the long-term benefits of public investment in higher education accrue primarily to the individual and that those who benefit most should pay the most.

In Laos, tuition and fees to the regular academic programs of NUOL are currently free for all students and board is provided for quota students. While the MOE is moving toward the introduction of a modest tuition, the plan is to introduce it in gradual phases and eventually level off at about 50,000 Kip per year. MOE officials express concern that this move will be widely unpopular with students and their families. They fear that a sudden introduction of a tuition charge could spark protests that could be disruptive to the university and embarrassing to the government. This position is ironic, however, since there already is clear evidence from the evening program that many students are willing to pay very substantial tuition rates for programs they think are worthwhile and relevant.

Formally instituting tuition, while it would have helped alleviate the financial plight of the university, would violate the symbolic message of government about open and inclusive opportunity for all citizens. The evening program, then, offers a means of charging students for the cost of their instruction without appearing to charge. It creates a needed funding stream, but at a remarkably high cost to the core functions of the institution.

In Summary

The dilemma faced by the National University of Laos in negotiating a path among competing goals illustrates a problem faced by higher education institutions in many developing countries. While the details vary from country to country, the essential problem arises from the university's need to serve several masters, each focused on a slightly different goal. As the Lao case illustrates, the pressures on the university to serve the national interest, galvanize public support, ensure adequate institutional funding, and improve instructional quality can easily converge in ways that undermine the very outcomes being sought. The thesis of this chapter is that the resolution to some of these conflicts and the continued strengthening of higher education in the developing world will require a re-examination of both the relationship of faculty to the university and of the university to government.

REFERENCES

Asian Development Bank. (1989). *Education sector study*. Manila: Asian Development Bank; Vientiane: Lao Ministry of Education.

Asian Development Bank. (1999). *Laos education sector study and education investment plan (1999)*. Manila: Asian Development Bank; Vientiane: Lao Ministry of Education.

Chapman, D. W. (1991). The rise and fall of an education management information system in Liberia. *Journal of Education Policy, 6*(2), 133–143.

Chapman, D. W. (2000). Trends in educational administration in developing Asia. *Educational Administration Quarterly, 36*(2), 283–308.

Deal, T. E., & Celotti, L. D. (1980). How much influence can (and do) educational administrators have on classrooms? *Phi Delta Kappan, 61*(7), 471–473.

Firestone, W. A. (1985). The study of loose couplings: Problems, progress, and prospects. In A. Kerckhoff (Ed.), *Research in sociology of education and socialization* (Vol. 5, pp. 3–30). Greenwich, CT: JAI Press.

Heyneman, S. P. (2000). *From the party/state to multi-ethnic democracy: Education and social cohesion in Europe and Central Asia*. Arlington, VA: International Management and Consulting Group Ltd.

Lewin, K. M. (1996). *Access to education in emerging Asia: Trends, challenges and policy options*. Manila: Asian Development Bank.

Lewin, K. M. (1998). Education in emerging Asia: Patterns, policies, and futures into the 21st century. *International Journal of Educational Development, 18*(2), 81–118.

Meyer, J. W., & Rowan, B. (1977). Institutionalized organizations: Formal structure as myth and ceremony. *American Journal of Sociology, 83*, 340–363.

Mingat, A. (1998). *Assessment of some basic education policy issues in Lao PDR from a cost and financing analysis*. Institute for Research in the Economics of Education (IREDU): CNRS & University of Dijion, France.

Nagel, J., & Snyder, C. W., Jr. (1989). International funding of education development: External agendas and internal adaptations—The case of Liberia. *Comparative Education Review, 33*, 3–20.

Weick, K. W. (1976). Educational organizations as loosely coupled systems. *Administrative Science Quarterly, 21*, 1–19.

Weidman, J. C. (1997). Laos. In G. A. Postiglione and G.C.L. Mak (Eds.), *Higher education in Asia: An international handbook and reference guide* (pp. 165–172). Westport, CT: Greenwood Press.

Weidman, J. C. (1999). Restructuring the university pedagogical institute of Laos: An outsider's view. In P.L.W. Sabloff (Ed.), *Higher education in the post-communist world: Case studies of eleven universities* (pp. 269–287). New York: Garland.

Part III

Coping with the Challenges of Greater Autonomy

Chapter 6

Current Challenges and Future Possibilities for the Revitilization of Higher Education in Africa

Jairam Reddy

Higher education institutions in developing countries face the highly important task of creating human capital for sustainable development. Yet, complex and challenging problems confront these institutions as they approach this task. This chapter begins by discussing several important issues affecting higher education institutions in developing countries. Then the chapter presents descriptions of the higher education situation in a number of African countries with emphasis on the possibilities for transformation. The chapter ends with suggested strategies for rejuvenating African higher education in light of emerging global changes and African realities.

IMPORTANT TRENDS AND CONTEXTUAL FEATURES

Several important trends influence the current circumstances and the future possibilities for higher education institutions in Africa.

Massification

The preeminent global tendency during the last few decades has been significant increase in enrollments in higher education, a process often called "massification." In 1960 world enrollment was 13 million; in 1970 it rose to 28 million; in 1980 it stood at 51 million; and in 1995 it had reached 82 million (UNESCO, 1998). This increase is the result of several interconnected factors: demographic growth, wider provision of secondary schooling, increased retention rates, rising social mobility, higher expectations, economic and labor market needs, the demand for multiskilling and reskilling, and the need for an informed and critical citizenry in an information and knowledge-dominated society. This rapid growth has created major challenges for higher education systems in many areas around the globe, particularly with respect to access, finance, quality of programs, curriculum restructuring, teaching and research, governance and autonomy, and organizational arrangement of complex systems.

In Martin Trow's (1973) terminology, the rapid expansion in higher education has resulted in the shift from "elite" systems (with up to 15% of the 20–24 year olds enrolled), to "mass" systems (enrolling between 15 and 40%) and "universal systems" (enrolling more than 40%). A major challenge facing the higher education sector is to cope with this expansion at a time of dwindling state funding.

Privatization

Private higher education is one of the fastest growing segments of post-secondary education at the turn of the twenty-first century. Nevertheless, the literature about this phenomenon is sparse, and its implications are poorly understood (Altbach, 1999). Key reasons for the growth of the private sector are the unprecedented demand for higher education and the unwillingness or inability of governments to provide for this demand. The ideology of the market and the idea of the academic degree as a private good have contributed to this growth. Private higher education is the fastest growing sector of education in Kenya, Zimbabwe, and South Africa. In most countries there is uncontrolled growth of this sector while its quality varies widely.

As already mentioned, in South Africa, the state is attempting to regulate the establishment of private higher education institutions in a manner that would not stifle their growth but would protect the public from unscrupulous providers. A system of registration of private providers with quality checks has been introduced. While there is considerable diversity in the range of program offerings, much of the expansion is in the lower end of the higher education system—in certificates, diplomas, and bachelor's degrees, many in the business, computer, and secretarial fields. One wonders how socially responsible these private institutions are. Do they balance the private and public goods of higher education? Are they providing social mobility for students by making higher education affordable? Are they protecting the autonomy of faculty members to pursue interests such as research and scholarship? Are they providing the infrastructure for quality higher education, such as an adequate library?

The rapid growth of private higher education in Africa, especially in the for-profit sector, raises some crucial questions: Why has the growth been predominantly in developing countries, including the former communist bloc countries? What regulation measures should governments impose, especially in terms of financial accountability and quality control? Should private institutions receive any government support (e.g., student bursaries and research grants)? What should be the relationship between private and public higher education institutions?

Globalization

Globalization, the second contextual trend discussed here, is a code word for a new socioeconomic system that is sweeping the world (Castells, 1998). Its core characteristics are a phenomenal increase in the size, complexity, and speed of global financial transactions. Science and technology, critical components of globalization, are concentrated in the leading economies of the world. The Internet, for example, is only accessible to 3 percent of the world's population. Globalization is heavily dependent on highly skilled workers and the formation of networks between companies across borders, between companies and nongovernmental agencies, and between companies and government. It is both an exclusionary and an inclusive phenomenon; as the standard of living has increased for some, for 80 percent of the world's population it has deteriorated.

Critics note that the implications of globalization for higher education are that managerialism gradually comes to dominate the organization of teaching and research, and research endeavors are increasingly applied to the requirements of government or industrial demands (Carnoy, 1998; Castells, 1998; Halsey, 1992; Slaughter, 1998). Additionally, the don or professor becomes a salaried or even a piece-work laborer in the service of an expanding middle class of administration and technologists. Corporate managerialism replaces elected deans and marginalizes faculty senates and academic councils, leading to a decline in collegiality. Other aspects of globalization include the commercialization of research, the commodification of knowledge, and the internationalization of higher education. Selling education to overseas students at full cost, selling intellectual work to industry, and outsourcing many services to create leaner structures are all part of the impact of globalization on higher education (Halsey, 1992; Slaughter, 1998).

Changing Government-University Relationships

Changing government-university relationships is a third important contextual trend. University autonomy (the capacity of self-government) must be balanced with the obligation of a higher education institution to be accountable to society by fulfilling its mission. Academic freedom and university autonomy imply that academics have an obligation to excellence and that institutions have an obligation to the advancement of knowledge. With massification, globalization, privatization, decentralization, and expectations for quality assurance, universities face a more complex relationship with society than in the past. Academic freedom and university autonomy must be tempered by accountability and responsiveness to external interests (Neave, 1998). The challenge for African higher education institutions is to negotiate this delicate balance in the context of two factors: the historical postcolonial subversion of traditional university freedoms, often by military dictatorships, and the emergence of pluralist democracies committed to the socioeconomic development of nation states.

Three basic positions have emerged in the policy contestations between governments and universities in Africa (National Commission on Higher Education, 1996). The first position asserts the autonomy of higher education institutions against any form of state interference and is captured in the recommendations of the Ashby Commission in Nigeria in the 1960s. The second position, expressed by the African Association of Universities at the Accra workshop in 1972, declared that the university in Africa occupies too important a position to be left alone to determine its own priorities and should therefore accept the hegemony of government (Yesufu, 1973). The third position sees higher education as a key agent of social change and mobility that must play an important role in promoting equity, both within education and in the broader society.

Moja, Muller, and Cloete (1996) have proposed three models that characterize government-higher education relationships.

- In the state control model, the system is created by and almost completely funded by the state, with key aspects controlled either by the bureaucracy or the politicians. Such a model is operative in Western democracies such as France, in Eastern countries such as Malaysia and Singapore, and in a number of African countries.
- In the state supervision model, the state sees its task as supervising the higher education system to ensure academic quality and maintain a level of accountability. Governments provide the framework within which the administrative leaders of the institutions are expected to produce the outputs the government wants. Variations of the model are found in the United States, Canada, Australia, the United Kingdom, and the Netherlands.
- When higher education institutions become sites of opposition to the state's development path, the state interference model aims to exert political or bureaucratic control while autonomy remains the official policy. Examples are Zimbabwe and South Africa during the apartheid era. In this scenario, the hegemony of government is not established. Rather, the key features are a weak civil society, a weak bureaucracy, and lack of mediating mechanisms between government and institutions.

The first and third models have largely characterized university-government interrelationships in Africa. The tendency of politicians to intervene in higher education has left many institutions hostage to factional policies, with decisions on student selection, faculty appointments and promotions, curriculum design, and other matters made on political grounds rather than on merit.

Additional Challenges Facing Higher Education in Developing Countries

With half of today's higher education students living in developing countries, their higher education systems are under great strain, because they are underfunded while facing escalating demand. Faculty members are often underqualified, lacking in motivation, and poorly rewarded. Students are poorly taught and curricula underdeveloped. Many students with poor primary and secondary schooling are unprepared for higher education studies. Lack of remedial education exacerbates the problem. The difficulties facing higher education institutions in developing countries have their roots in a lack of resources. Far less per student is spent in developing countries than in developed countries. Tuition revenues as a contribution to institutional income are either negligible or nonexistent. Budgets are approved by government officials who have little understanding of the goals and capabilities of particular universities. Large amounts of funding are spent on personnel and student costs, leaving little for building maintenance or for research. Thus higher education institutions in developing countries are confronted with deteriorating buildings, inadequate libraries, and scientific equipment that cannot be used because of lack of supplies.

The North-South scientific gap is large and growing (World Bank, 2000). On a per capita basis, industrialized countries have ten times as many research and development scientists and technicians as developing countries. Industrialized countries account for 84 percent of scientific articles published and 97 percent of patents registered. While the rate of scientific publications has grown phenomenally in the past two decades, the ranking of publications per capita does not include a single developing country among the top fifteen.

The need for updated books and computers and broader access to the Internet is urgent in developing countries. Since 1996, industrial countries have had about 20 times as many personal computers per capita as middle-income countries and more than 100 times as many Internet hosts. The rapid and chaotic expansion of higher education in developing countries has led to the underfunding of the public sector, while the private sector is having difficulty offering quality programs that address other than short-term market needs.

POSTINDEPENDENCE HIGHER EDUCATION DEVELOPMENTS IN AFRICA

The tradition of higher education as exemplified by the universities at Al Azar in Cairo, Kairouine in Fez, Debre Damo of Axum, and Sankore of

Timbuktu is indeed a proud one in Africa. Fourah Bay College was established in Freetown in 1827. Over a hundred years later there followed the University of Gold Coast in Ghana in 1947, the University of Ibadan in 1948, University College of Addis Abba in 1950, and Makerere in Uganda in 1950. Later universities were established in Nairobi, Kenya, Dar-Es-Salaam, Tanzania, and Sheick Ante Diop, Senegal (Mehrutu & Ogundimu, 1999). During the 1960s and 1970s, characterized as the golden era, higher education enjoyed political support and a generous flow of resources (Oniang & Eicher, 1999). Universities provided countries with high-level skilled personnel for public service, the professions, business, industry, commerce, and agriculture. The number of universities in Africa increased from around 20 in 1960 to 160 by 1996, while the number of students increased from 12,000 to over 2,000,000 during the same period (Beintema, Pardey, & Roseboom, 1998).

A workshop held by the Association of African Universities (AAU) in Accra in 1972 on "Creating the African University" highlighted two main purposes: (1) establishing identity and links with the past, and (2) addressing practical needs of high-level manpower, the production of knowledge and skills to create wealth, and the modernization of African societies.

As more countries became independent during the period from the 1960s to the 1980s, the number of universities, student enrollments, and courses offered expanded considerably. The 1962 Tananarive Conference on the "Development of Higher Education in Africa" proposed an idealistic and ambitious mission. Universities were viewed as key instruments for national development.

At the end of colonial rule there were a few scattered universities across Africa, with the exception of the Arab north and South Africa. Much of the development of higher education has been a postindependence achievement in Africa. For example, while at the establishment of independence Nigeria had one university with a thousand students, in 1991 it had 31 universities with 141,000 students.

Whatever their shortcomings, African universities during the period from the 1960s to the 1980s succeeded in providing high-level personnel for the civil service, for the schools, and in the applied sciences of medicine, agriculture, and the social sciences. However, the collapse of African economies, diminishing support from governments, corruption, mismanagement, and government intrusion into university matters eroded institutional autonomy and led to the precipitous decline of African universities. Thus, by the 1980s, they were in a state of crisis. The decay of physical facilities, with many of them in need of maintenance and refurbishment, the lack of modern electronic and technological infrastructure, and poorly stocked and managed libraries are widespread features of current African higher education. Most of Africa's universities are "indeed a mere shadow of their earlier glory drained of teaching staff, lacking in equipment and teaching materials, housed in degenerated infrastructure, surrounded by an air of demoralisation and incipient decay. They are at the same time besieged with a growing demand for high quality service and public accountability" (Sutherland-Addy, 1993).

Most devastating of all is the massive brain drain of well-trained and skilled academic staff, mainly to Western Europe and the United States. The World Bank estimates that some 23,000 qualified academic staff are emigrating from Africa each year in search of better working conditions (Blair & Jordan, 1994). Rising student enrollments, declining state funding, poor salaries, and the intrusion of politicians subverting academic freedom and institutional autonomy have collectively contributed to the loss of this intellectual talent.

The following section discusses developments that led to decline and crisis in higher education across a number of African countries, including Uganda, Sudan, Nigeria, and the Democratic Republic of the Congo, and countries in Francophone Africa.

Uganda

By the 1960s the University of Makerere had a proud record of achievement and standards in research, in graduating students, and in attracting quality academic staff. In the late 1960s, Milton Obote, the president of the country, appointed the secretary of his cabinet as vice-chancellor of the university. "General Idi Amin who replaced him in 1971 as Chancellor of the University did not even have the benefit of complete elementary education and proved to be a capricious ruthless tyrant" (Ade Ajayi, Goma, & Ampah-Johnson, 1996, p. 120). When the vice-chancellor referred his request for an honorary doctorate for a decision by the Senate and council, he was kidnapped and disappeared. Successive corrupt regimes crippled the once flourishing university until a recovery began in 1986 with the accession to power by Musoveni, the restoration of democracy, and the rejuvenation of the economy.

The Sudan

In the Sudan there were two traditions of higher education—the Islamic, modeled after Al Azar, and the British. In order to curb the growing opposition of students to his regime, General Aloud appointed himself as chancellor in 1963 and placed the council of the university under the minister of education. A succession of coups led to the seizure of power by General Bashir, reportedly with the aid of teachers and intellectuals. The new regime emphasized the Arabic languages and Islamic studies with direct control by the Government National Commission on Higher Education. The attempt to impose "Arabicization" over all the peoples of the country, including the non-Arabic, non-Islamic peoples of the south, led to political instability and civil strife.

Nigeria

The Asby Report of 1960 led to the establishment of three regional and two federal universities in Nigeria. Spurred on by oil revenues, the National Universities Commission established many universities but without any planning considerations. Another round of universities was established with the granting of concurrent powers to federal and state governments to establish universities. "The Head of State was known to announce off the cuff the establishment of universities which were not even mentioned in the prepared speeches" (Ade Ajayi, Goma, & Ampah-Johnson, 1996, p. 141). It was therefore uncertain just how many universities had actually been put into operation. Student enrollments increased from 14,500 in 1970 to 200,000 in 1992. The Lomge Commission in 1992 pointed to the severe problems created by this rapid expansion: declining research output, fewer books and less equipment, poor staffing, and declining quality. The heads of state became chancellors, who in turn appointed vice-chancellors, resulting in tension between students and government. Student violence, bouts of drinking, secret cults, and gang warfare on and off campus were the consequences.

Democratic Republic of the Congo (DRC)

On achieving independence from Belgium in 1960, the DRC, with a population of 47 million, had only two universities, both established in the mid-1950s. They had a total enrollment of 2,000 students. The government has since established several pedagogical institutes designed to produce secondary school teachers. Further pressures led to the establishment of several three-year institutes as well as private universities offering, among others, degrees in medicine, the sciences and economics, international relations, law, politics, communications, humanities, and philosophy. Acute shortages in technology, the sciences, and medicine prevail. The DRC has one doctor per 14,000 inhabitants. The country continues to have a very low proportion of its citizens enrolled in higher education. Most universities lack the basic infrastructure to provide quality higher education. Students have no textbooks. The majority have no libraries, no telephones, and no computers. As the faculty is poorly paid, many choose to teach in several universities to make ends meet or to move to corporations for higher pay. These factors have led to corruption and subjective assessments of students' work. There are few faculty members with graduate level training. A further problem is that all students are registered full-time and it is rarely possible to study part-time. Failing to pass any course cancels all grades for that year. The lack of managerial and financial autonomy is not conducive to good governance. These pervasive problems are undermining the country's ability to capture the benefits of higher education.

National Higher Education Systems in Francophone Africa

Attempts were made in the 1960s to establish higher education institutions in the Republic of Mali, Cote d'Ivoire, Benin, Togo, Congo-Brazzaville, Gabon, Chad, and the Central African Republic. These efforts met with varying degrees of success, but they raised two main issues: first, the question of national identity in view of the continuing predominance of French cultural influence and financial support, and second, the problem of organizing universities in small countries with limited financial resources.

Cameroon

Cameroon was not typical of the Francophone countries in that it had both German and English influences arising from their territorial rights. Under the influence of the UNESCO Commission, an all-embracing bilingual institution was established in 1962 to include all the postsecondary institutions in the country. In the French tradition, higher education had to be under the control of the minister of education while the British tradition indicated the need for an intermediary body between the university and government. A compromise was effected whereby a chancellor who represented the government presided over the university council. The vice-chancellor/rector, as the chief executive officer, was responsible to the council and the chancellor. In 1972 a unitary republic was declared and the name of the university was changed to the University of Yaounde. The university grew rapidly from 676 students in 1964 to 14,000 in 1984–1985. In order to accommodate this expansion, university centers for vocational training were established in languages and interpretation, business adminstration, agriculture and forestry, and science and technology. In 1977 these centers were granted autonomy and were responsible directly to the minister. The specialist centers, schools and institutes for training specialists (Health Sciences, Journalism, International Relations, Advanced Teachers College, etc.) remained under the chancellor. The Centre for Health Sciences became well reputed for its innovative and exemplary approach to medical education in Africa.

Guinea

Guinea rejected the option of being part of the French community in 1958. It was joined in this by Mali, which sought a Russian or Vietnamese rather than a French approach to the establishment of higher education for development. Guinea developed a State Research Agency to administer the National Archives and National Library and Museum, to conduct research in the social and natural sciences, and to supervise the Pasteur Institute and two agricultural research stations. The main higher education institution was the Conarky Polytechnic—built, financed and equipped by the USSR to train engineers and teachers at the professional and auxiliary levels.

Mali

With financial and advisory support from the USSR, Mali established a number of vocational institutes teaching at different levels from upper secondary to subprofessional, and through the master's level. The government created advanced teacher training, a rural polytechnic, and national schools of engineering, public administration, and medicine. These schools, together with the Institute for Advanced Training and Applied Research, were then incorporated into the University of Mali in 1986.

Thus, Mali and Guinea were able to experiment with a different national model of development-oriented higher education influenced by the Soviet system of higher education.

Senegal

The University of Dakar was developed as the University of Senegal, retaining the French structure with faculties open to holders of baccalaureates, and a number of grand ecoles and institutes for specialist professional studies. The university was renamed *Cheikh Anta Diop* in 1987 in honor of the famous Senegalese physicist and philosopher. Student numbers rose sharply, reaching 14,789 in 1988. It was against this background that a second university, the University of St. Louis, was opened in 1990.

Cote d'Ivoire

Student numbers at the University of Abidjan, which included among other disciplines agronomy, public works, statistics, administration, and teacher training, rose dramatically from 6,000 in 1972–1973 to 21,356 in 1993. The students in Abidjan became a political force whenever they allied with the Union of Teachers and other workers. In 1991 the government reorganized the university and changed its name to the National University of Cote d'Ivoire with the faculties and institutes shared among the three campuses—Cocody, Abobo-Adjame, and Bouake.

The continent will have to be cognizant of emerging new realities as it sets about transforming its higher education systems to meet the challenges of the new millennium. These challenges include the end of the East-West Conflict and the ensuing cold war, the collapse of communism and the disintegration of the former Soviet Union into many smaller states in Eastern Europe, and ethnic and national upheavals not least in Africa (the Rwandan crisis, the continuing conflicts in Algeria, the Sudan, Ethiopia/Eritrea, the Congo Republic, and Angola). Other issues are the powerful forces unleashed in favor of market economies and political pluralism, the emergence of global markets creating a competitive world economic system characterized by rapid knowledge generation and technological innovation, the downsizing of the civil service, and increased privitization leading to under- and unemployment of graduates. The disjuncture of the types of graduates produced and those required by the information and knowledge economy—especially in science, technology, engineering, and computer skills—poses a challenge. Economic advantage is now based not on raw materials but on technology-relevant management efficiency and on national human resource capacities to manage these increasingly complex systems.

REJUVENATION OF HIGHER EDUCATION IN AFRICA

Despite immense challenges, some developments in Africa signal important rejuvenation. Three examples are described here.

South Africa

The new democratic government appointed a National Commission on Higher Education (NCHE) in 1995 to provide a framework for transforming the higher education system, which was devised during the apartheid era. Its proposals were largely encapsulated in the White Paper on Higher Education (1997) and the Higher Education Act of 1997. The NCHE found that it had to transform a system highly fragmented along the axes of race, gender, and academic/technical/vocational studies. This system was characterized by a large university sector and a much smaller technical/vocational sector, a gross discrepancy in the participation rates of White and Black students (i.e., 12% for Africans and nearly 70% for Whites), a disjuncture between the kinds of graduates produced and what commerce and industry needed.

In 1955, there were some 21 universities with 364,000 students and 16 technikons with 174,000 students, all under the jurisdiction of the national ministry of education. Under the responsibility of the provincial ministries of education were some 100 colleges of education with 150,000 students and the further education sector with approximately 175,000 students. Among these students were 50,000 who were registered for higher education programs. Nursing, agricultural, and police and military colleges were under the respective provincial ministries. There were over 100 private colleges enrolling several hundred thousand students and offering diploma and certificate programs of varying quality.

In the new dispensation, the ministry's vision is of a transformed, democratic, nonracial and nonsexist system of higher education that is located within the government's broader view of a future where all South Africans will enjoy an improved and sustainable quality of life, participate in a growing economy, and share in a democratic culture. Several principles guide the framework for transforming the higher education system: *equity, democratization, development, quality, effectiveness and efficiency, academic freedom and institutional autonomy, public accountability*. Three general features are to underpin the system: increased participation, greater responsiveness to societal interests and needs, and increased cooperation and partnerships.

The main recommendations contained in the White Paper and Higher Education Act of 1997 included a single coordinated system comprising universities, technikons, and colleges; a National Qualifications Framework (NQF); a Higher Education Quality Committee (HEQC) for quality assurance; three-year rolling plans; a regulatory framework for private higher education institutions; rationalization of teacher education colleges; growth of the higher education sector; research funding to be dispersed for competitive research projects and new niche areas, and to develop research capacity; a model of cooperative governance with a branch of higher education called a Council on Higher Education (CHE); academic freedom and institutional autonomy entrenched in a context of increased accountability; a formula funding component that will generate block grants for institutions offering approved higher education programs; an earmarked funding component for redress and development; and a National Student Financial Aid Scheme.

Challenges continue, however, within the higher education sector in South Africa. Since 1997, enrollments in the historically disadvantaged institutions have decreased sharply, with a flight of excellent students and staff to the advantaged institutions. The disadvantaged institutions also have been beset with management and financial problems to the extent that their viability is now in question. While the percentage and numbers of Black students have risen considerably, there has been mission drift, a failure to shift enrollments to the areas of science and technology, no increase in the numbers of postgraduate students, and little meaningful regional cooperation between institutions. Given these developments, the Council on Higher Education (2000), at the request of the minister of education, has proposed a differentiated and diverse higher education system. It also has suggested a net reduction in the number of institutions through a process of combinations and mergers.

Makerere University—The Quiet Revolution in Uganda

There has been a remarkable turnaround and rejuvenation of Makerere University in Uganda in the last seven to eight years (Court, 1999; Mwiria, 1999). In the face of declining state support, the student numbers have doubled and a semester system has been instituted with new courses, new degrees, new departments, and new faculties. Also noteworthy is sweeping and fundamental financial and administrative reform. Restructuring at Makerere has involved three key interrelated thrusts: alternative financial strategies, demand-driven courses, and new management structures.

Alternative Financial Strategies

Private fee-paying students have been admitted to certain faculties, as well as law and commerce in evening classes. Within three years, private students exceeded the number of state-supported students. Private students now account for over half of the total of 15,000 students admitted. A number of operations within the university were privatized, including the bookshop, bakery, and printing. The university established a consultancy bureau with 51 percent of shares owned by Makerere staff and 49 percent by the university. Consultancy services are widely provided to the private sector, governments, foundations, and other agencies, such as water, sanitation, and public health.

Demand-Driven Courses

Makerere decided to offer courses that private students are willing to pay for, such as new degrees and diplomas in business administration, nursing, tourism, urban planning, and laboratory technology, and specializations in drama, music, and dance. These courses are offered in day, evening, and weekend classes. The income in government subsidy in 1989 accounted for 69 percent of the budget and private funding constituted 31 percent. Staff salaries were increased from $30 a month to $1300 a month. This stemmed the tide of the loss of academic staff, brought about library enrichment, faculty development, and building maintenance and construction.

New Management Structures

A comprehensive strategic plan was formulated to bring about academic development by use of the best institutional structure and organizational opportunities, academic development, research planning, staffing, and rational use of space.

Autonomy

Institutional autonomy is now much greater, and the council is widely representative, with students, academics, and administrative staff. The management is devolved, with faculties managing their own budgets. A weekly newspaper keeps the campus informed of all major activities. Trimonthly meetings are held between deans, directors, and administrators.

The external examiner system is being expanded so that there is no fall in standards. However, the dropout rate in some faculties is still high, research is donor-dependent, and science graduates are in short supply.

With sustained economic growth of 6 to 8 percent during the past decade, entrepreneurial activity in Uganda has flourished. Real incomes have grown, and there is more to spend on education. With the accession to power of Musoveni in 1992, there has been unprecedented political stability. He supports greater autonomy for the university but with greater responsibility for funds.

The commitment, energy, and imagination of university management has been responsible for much of the reform. The Makerere University reform process has become a model for the region's public universities. A number of Kenyan universities have introduced parallel training programs for fee-paying students as a means of expanding access and supplementing financial resources. The main achievements of the Makerere reform program have been increased access, more institutional autonomy, enhanced internal governance and management efficiency, and the acceptance of cost sharing between government and students. The reform has also been marked by improvement in terms and conditions of work for university academics, improved university learning and assessment mechanisms, university education more responsive to national needs, and improvement of relations between the administration, staff, and students.

Despite the apparent success of the rejuvenation at Makerere University, serious concerns have been expressed about the transformations occurring there. Problems include overcrowded facilities, overworked staff, de-emphasis of the research role of the university, and unequal development of academic programs with the sciences receiving little support. Observers also note the high rate of student dropouts and worry about students' abilities to pay fees. The concession by government to greater institutional autonomy is applauded, even as concerns are raised about government financial support. This general trend in Africa of greater autonomy coupled with lower funding should be carefully monitored.

Despite the concerns expressed, the history of Makerere University in Uganda offers a ray of hope for the rejuvenation of the higher education sector in Africa (Court, 1999). It emerged as a pre-eminent institution in the 1950s, and then deteriorated with the collapse of democracy. With the emergence of a democratic culture and growing economy, it experienced a subsequent rejuvenation through effective management, innovation, and private-public partnerships.

Nigeria

There are currently 43 higher education institutions in Nigeria: 29 federal, 11 state, and 3 recently approved private universities. Five of the federal universities have enrollments of between 16,000 and 30,000 students, and eight have enrollments of less than 10,000 students. The total enrollments number nearly 400,000 students, with a participation rate of 395 per 100,000 persons, about half the average for developing countries. During the 1990s, enrollments have grown faster than budgets, resulting in a reduction in expenditure per student from US$700 in 1991 to US$362 in 1998. This has resulted in the deterioration of staff salaries, the brain drain of staff, and recruiting difficulties. Demand for access is higher than the system's capacity to accommodate students. In 1998, 35,000 new students were admitted from some 400,000 applicants. Three parallel strategies are being pursued in order to expand access: (1) the National Universities Commission is planning to establish a VSAT network for use in distance education, academic networking, and research collaboration, (2) the establishment of good quality private universities is being encouraged, and (3) plans are being made to expand all university enrollments to a maximum of 30,000 students.

The government provides 95 percent of university funding through a funding formula based on full-time equivalent students. Ten percent of the budget is earmarked for library development and 5 percent for research. Funding has been insufficient to maintain the high standards set for program accreditation. The government is considering a block grant approach combined with a deregulation of student fees. It is assumed that universities will be able to generate 30 percent of their income needs.

Frequent changes in government policies during the past two decades have introduced instability into the system. Future policies will emphasize strategic planning, development of comparative advantage into more specialized academic capacities, deregulation of student fees, and the decentralization of management responsibilities to university councils.

The nation's 43 teacher training colleges are operating at 35 percent capacity, enrolling 105,000 students in facilities that could accommodate 300,000 students. Teachers receive poor salaries, and teaching is regarded as a low status profession. The National Board for Technical Education oversees 125 technical training institutions. These include 49 polytechnics (17 federal, 27 state, and 5 private), 36 colleges of agriculture, and 12 specialized training institutes (petroleum engineering, health, etc.). Although government policy requires 70 percent of enrollments to focus on science and engineering, only 40 percent of them do. This is largely due to the lack of adequate science education in schools. Academic planning needs to increase the relevance of training programs to current labor market needs (Court, 1999; Mwiria, 1999).

REVITALIZING UNIVERSITIES IN AFRICA

The role of universities in Africa in research, evaluation, teaching, information transfer, and technology development is critical to national social progress and economic growth. Yet the quality of university education has declined significantly as a result of dwindling resources during a period of growing enrollments. Poor national economic performance, inappropriate governing structures, political interference, weak internal management, and campus instability have all contributed to this decline. How are African higher education systems to respond to the demands of their impoverished populations and the advent of globalization as we enter the new millenium? Can they be the "engines of development" as argued by Castells (1993)?

In light of these developments, the Association of African Universities, the World Bank, African organizations with an interest in higher education, and the Working Group on Higher Education have proposed strategic guidelines for the revitalization of universities in Africa. Highlights from these guidelines as well as additional suggestions for the revitalization of higher education in Africa are presented below (ADEA, 1999).

- Strategic planning provides university leaders and stakeholders with the means to analyze conditions, express a vision, and formulate goals, thereby promoting the advancement of the institution in a systematic manner. Among critical issues discussed at institutions should be the budget allocation process, management, institutional autonomy, and accountability to government and the public.
- State of the art management information systems are powerful instruments to assist managers in making informed decisions and in facilitating evaluation and monitoring. Instructional technology also is useful as both a strategic and a cognitive tool. If colleges and universities are to become contemporary and effective organizations, their strategic academic technology agenda should be focused on the production of intelligence rather than on the storage and recall of random and quickly outmoded information (Privateer, 1999).
- Comprehensive quality assurance mechanisms should be developed to ensure that teaching and research capacity meet international standards. At a minimum, comprehensive quality systems should include an institutional audit, program accreditation, and evaluation of teaching and learning. Evaluation should be accompanied by plans for improving quality.
- Management training courses should be available for university managers and administrative staff, including deans and department heads.
- Governments facing enormous pressures for socioeconomic development on a number of fronts are in a quandary about how to provide adequate funding for universities. Public funding accounts for more than 90 percent of funding for African higher education institutions. About 70 percent of revenue should come from government, 20 percent from private sources including tuition fees, and 10 percent from other income-generating activities, such as contract research or renting university facilities. As a general rule, a country should spend about 15 to 25 percent of its education budget on higher education. Overall, the education budget should represent about 7 percent of the GDP. Unit cost is one indicator of quality and, should it fall below $1,000 per student, institutions will find it difficult to provide adequate educational quality. Methods to diversify funding should be considered, and might include such options as tuition fees, continuing education, contract services to business and industry, renting university facilities, and donor funding.
- While institutions must be accountable and responsive to external interests, governments also should respect institutional management autonomy, initiative, and

academic freedom. Any cost savings and funds generated by the institution should be regarded as supplemental funding. The performance of institutions should be evaluated and their financial records audited.

- Historical events resulted in a system of British education and standards that were transplanted in Africa, even though they were out of context for actual needs. For example, medical schools tended to focus on advanced surgical techniques with meager resources devoted to primary care. Mamdani (1994, p. 4) noted, "Ironically, a decontextualised notion of standards stifled creativity and undermined independence of thought." Mamdani further emphasized the importance of highly contextualizing research and teaching agendas.
- Private institutions are a reality in the developing world and could make a positive contribution in meeting the increasing demand for higher education. The challenge for public higher education and governments is to create enabling environments for the establishment of private tertiary education institutions, including measures to ensure quality and relevance to the development goals of the country.
- Institutional diversity should be a priority in reconfiguring higher education systems for both educational and financial reasons. Different types of institutions at different cost levels are needed to meet diverse student needs. The comprehensive research university has been the "gold standard" which every country in Africa aspires to establish. Alternatives to the research university, such as predominantly teaching institutions, polytechnics, and community/technical colleges, should be considered.
- International experience has demonstrated enormous potential for regional collaboration in the sharing of expertise, expensive equipment, exchange of staff and students, and research collaboration. Such consortia could be either intracountry or across countries. In particular, the construction of expensive professional faculties such as medicine, engineering, and architecture will not be feasible in the smaller countries. The Association of African Universities is an appropriate forum for a discussion of the establishment of regional professional schools as well as "centres of excellence" in key academic areas.
- Donor agencies have historically operated individually and not always with the priorities of African higher education in mind. They should recognize the importance of investment in higher education for social and economic development and support such activities as strategic planning, assistance for library development, management information systems and communication technologies, institutional linkages, and management training.

The challenges confronting African universities are great. Those leading these institutions should be inspired and supported by knowing that their work is critically important. An efficient, reinvigorated, and transformed higher education system can make a difference to the African continent by providing the research, the technical and professional skills, and an educated citizenry necessary to cope with a rapidly changing and complex world.

REFERENCES

Ade Ajayi, J. F., Goma, L.K.H., & Ampah-Johnson, G. (1996). *The African experience with higher education*. The Association of African Universities, Accra in association with London: James Currey and Athens: Ohio University Press.

ADEA (Association for the Development of Education in Africa). (1999, December). *ADEA Working Group on Higher Education Report*. Abuja, Nigeria.

Altbach, P. G. (1999). Private higher education: Themes and variations in comparative perspective. In P. G. Altbach (Ed.), *Private prometheus: Private higher education and development in the 21st century* (pp. 1–15). Westport, CT: Greenwood Press.

Beintema, N. M., Pardey, P. G., & Roseboom, J. (1998). *Educating agricultural researchers: A review of the role of African universities* (Discussion Paper No. 36). Environmental Production and Technology Division. Washington, DC: International Food Policy Research Institute.

Blair, R., & Jordan, J. (1994). *Staff loss and retention at selected African universities: A synthesis report* (AFTHR Technical Note 18). Washington, DC: The World Bank.

Carnoy, M. (1998). *Sustainable flexibility: Work, family and community in the information age*. New York: Cambridge University Press.

Castells, M. (1993). The university system: Engine of development in the new world economy. In A. Ransom, S. M. Khoo, & A. M. Selvaratnam (Eds.), *Improving higher education in developing countries*. Washington, DC: The World Bank.

Castells, M. (1998, June). *Possibilities for development in the Information Age*. Paper prepared for the United Nations Research Institute for Social Development, Geneva, Switzerland.

Council on Higher Education, South Africa. (2000). *Towards a new higher education landscape*. Pretoria, South Africa: Council on Higher Education.

Court, D. (1999). *Financing higher education in Africa: Makerere, the quiet revolution*. Unpublished Paper. Washingon, DC: The World Bank.

Griffith, M., & Connor, A. (1994). *Democracy's open door*. Portsmouth, NH: Boynton/Cook Publishers.

Halsey, A. H. (1992). *The decline of donnish dominion*. Oxford: Oxford University Press.

Higher Education Act. (1997). Department of Education, Government of South Africa, Pretoria.

Mamdani, M. (1994, July). *A reflection on higher education in Equatorial Africa: Some lessons for South Africa*. Paper presented at the conference entitled "The Future Role of Universities in the South African Tertiary Education System," Columbia University, New York.

Mehrutu, A., & Ogundimu, F. (1999). *Revitalizing the African university and the challenge of the future*. Background paper presented at Michigan State University African Studies Center, East Lansing, Michigan.

Moja, T., Muller, J., & Cloete, N. (1996). Towards new forms of regulation in higher education: The case of South Africa. *Higher Education, 32*(2), 129–156.

Mwiria, K. (1999). Case II: Makerere University, Uganda. In S. Bjarnson & H. Lund (Eds.), *Government/university relationships*. Commonwealth Higher Education Management Service. London: Association of Commonwealth Universities.

National Commission on Higher Education. (1996). *Final report*. South Africa: Ministry of Education.

Neave, G. R. (1998, October 5–9). *Autonomy, social responsibility and academic freedom*. Paper presented at the World Conference on Higher Education in the Twenty First Century: Vision and Action, UNESCO, Paris.

Oniang'o, R., & Eicher, C. (1998, October 19–23). *Universities and agricultural development in Africa: Insights from Kenya*. Paper presented at the "Transforming the Agricultural Research System in Kenya: Lessons for Africa" conference, Bellagio, Italy.

Privateer, P. M. (1999). Academic technology and the future of higher education. *Journal of Higher Education, 70*, 60–79.

Slaughter, S. (1998). National higher education policies in a global economy. In J. Currie & J. Newson (Eds.), *Universities and globalization* (pp. 45–70). Thousand Oaks, CA and London: Sage Publications.

Sutherland-Addy, E. (1993). *Revolt and renewal: Reflections on the creation of a system of tertiary education in Ghana* (AFTHR Technical Note No. 10). Washington, DC: The World Bank.

Trow, M. (1973). *Problems in the transition from elite to mass higher education*. Berkeley, CA: Carnegie Commission on Higher Education.

UNESCO (1998, October). *World Statistical Outlook on Higher Education: 1980–1995*. Paper presented at the World Conference on Higher Education, Paris.

White Paper on Higher Education. (1997). Department of Education, Government of South Africa, Pretoria.

World Bank. (2000). *Higher education in developing countries—Peril and promise*. Washington, DC: The Task Force on Higher Education and Society.

World Development Report. (1999). *Knowledge for development*. New York: Oxford University Press.

Yesufu, T. M. (Ed.). (1973). *Creating the African university—Emerging issues of the 1970s*. Oxford: Oxford University Press.

Chapter 7

Higher Education and the State in Mongolia: Dilemmas of Democratic Transition

John C. Weidman and Regsurengiin Bat-Erdene

This chapter uses the example of Mongolia, a country closely aligned with the former Soviet Union, to illustrate the dynamics of higher education reform in countries undergoing the transition from a command to a market economy and from a socialist to a democratic government. While there are unique aspects of the Mongolian context, there are also similarities to the larger experience of higher education reform in the Newly Independent States of Eastern Europe and Central Asia.

The changing relationship between the national government and higher education with respect to institutional vitality and autonomy in the areas of finance, student admission, governance, and accreditation is the focus of this chapter. Specifically, it traces the tensions between the central government and Mongolian higher education arising from legislation intended to provide institutions with greater administrative autonomy. As higher education institutions achieved new levels of autonomy, not all groups with an interest in the operation of the national higher education system shared a common understanding of what the changes meant in practice. Policies to address individual facets of university management (e.g., finance, student admissions, governance, accreditation) were enacted without sufficient attention to the larger consequences of those policies on other aspects of university operations. This led to contradictions and misalignments in policy and uncertainties about what some of the new rules and regulations meant. While, in some cases, leaders exploited this ambiguity for their own purposes, often these misalignments were a product of well-intentioned individuals and groups moving at different speeds and from different perspectives on what they were trying to accomplish. This chapter illustrates the systemic nature of higher educational reform and the costs of not anticipating these misalignments in the process of granting (and accepting) greater institutional autonomy.

Relationships between government and university are products of their context and history. To understand the current tension, it is necessary to understand key aspects of the contemporary Mongolian situation. To that end, data are provided on demographic characteristics of the population as well as on funding and enrollment patterns in the entire Mongolian educational system. An assessment of the characteristics of political, social, economic, and educational transitions now underway is used to identify salient issues that affect the higher education sector. The chapter concludes with the development of a general conceptual model of underlying processes, including implications for understanding higher education reform in a global perspective.

THE MONGOLIAN CONTEXT

Mongolia is a landlocked country sandwiched between Russia and China, each of which also has an ethnic Mongolian population (.5 and 3.5 million, respectively). In 1998, the country had 2.42 million inhabitants who lived in an area of 1.56 million square kilometers, making it one of the least densely populated nations in the world. Just over one-third (35.6%) of the population were aged 15 or younger. The capital city of Ulaanbaatar (Ulan Bator in common English spelling) has a population of 668,800 (27.7% of the country's total). Provincial (*aimag*) centers have another 21.3 percent of the population. Most of the remaining half of the population are nomadic (*Mongolian Statistical Yearbook, 1998*, pp. 17, 22, 25, 29).

Its 1998 per capita gross domestic product (GDP) of US$437 places Mongolia among the poorest countries in the world (Bray, Davaa, Spaulding, & Weidman, 1994; *Mongolian Statistical Yearbook, 1998*, pp. 22, 54). An annual growth in GDP of 3.5 percent was reported for 1998. Almost half (48.7%) of the 809,500 people employed in Mongolia in 1998 worked in agriculture, primarily breeding and tending 33 million livestock (*Mongolian Statistical Yearbook, 1998*, pp. 45, 51, 55, 56, 84).

In 1921, a Buddhist religious ruler was deposed and the People's Government of Mongolia was founded. Three years later, the Mongolian People's Republic was established as the world's second communist country and a single-party government held power until 1990. Mongolia maintained close political and economic ties with the USSR, but was never one of its constituent republics. At the peak of this alliance, almost a third of Mongolia's gross domestic product (GDP) was provided by the Soviet Union. This included significant support (e.g., books, equipment, training of teachers and researchers) for Mongolian higher education (Bray, Davaa, Spaulding, & Weidman, 1994).

ONGOING POLITICAL, SOCIAL, AND ECONOMIC TRANSITIONS

The period since 1991 in Mongolia has been characterized by rapid political, social, and economic transition (Weidman, Bat-Erdene, Gerel, & Badarch, 1997; Weidman, Bat-Erdene, Yeager, Sukhbaatar, Jargalmaa, & Davaa, 1998; Yeager & Weidman, 1999). The government has shifted from a position of strong ideological monitoring by a single political party to a tolerance of pluralism under a multiparty democracy. There has been a gradual change from centralized government control of the country to more decentralized management at the provincial (*aimag*) level. Restrictions on entry into the country have been greatly relaxed and Mongolian citizens may travel outside the country. In 1999, it became possible for foreign visitors to get 30-day tourist visas at major border points.

The first democratic constitution was ratified in 1992 and an election for the unicameral parliament (Great Khural) held the same year. The Mongolian People's Revolutionary Party (MPRP, composed primarily of members of the former Communist Party) won 72 of the 76 seats and moved ahead with the passage of legislation for governing the fledgling democracy, welcoming foreign aid, and working with donors to fund a variety of projects.

The second parliamentary election in 1996 resulted in a complete shift of power, with a coalition of five democratic parties winning two-thirds of the seats. Interestingly, there were few dramatic policy shifts, and agreements made under the MPRP regime were, for the most part, honored. By 1997, however, the coalition began to unravel with the election of a president from the MPRP, a corruption scandal, and the untimely deaths of democratic coalition members. There was also serious instability at the prime minister and cabinet levels resulting in the appointment of three different sets of ministers during the course of 1998. The struggling democracy was shaken by lack of compromise and cooperation, not only among opposing party members but even within the majority coalition. The parliamentary election in June of 2000 resulted in another dramatic shift of power, with the MPRP again winning all but four of the seats.

During the past decade, the fundamental social transitions have involved changes from a collectivist society to one in which individuals are expected to assume increasing responsibility for themselves. This includes a gradual shifting of responsibility for social welfare from the government to the individual, largely through "cost sharing," in which individuals pay varying amounts for services that were previously provided at no cost by the government. Greater emphasis is being placed on personal achievement and individual as opposed to collective well-being, including the change from notions of a "classless" to a "class-based" society (Weidman et al., 1998).

Mongolia continues to move forward in its transition from a centrally planned (command) economy in which the state owned all property and enterprises. Pressures on the government to change to a market-oriented economy have come from a variety of donors, development banks, and the International Monetary Fund (IMF). One significant consequence of the pressure by donors on developing countries to change their economic situation has been the imposition of so-called "structural adjustment" policies as a condition of obtaining grants and loans (Weidman et al., 1998). According to Carnoy (1995, p. 653), "structural adjustment is normally associated with the correction of imbalances in foreign accounts and domestic consumption (including government deficits) and the deregulation and privatization of the economy." This tends to be identified with public sector austerity and consequently, in many countries, with growing poverty and an increasingly unequal distribution of income (Carnoy, 1995).

Mongolia is no exception to this pattern as it continues to undergo a rapid shift in the distribution of income. The ratio of the income share of the highest 20 percent of the Mongolian population to the lowest 20 percent has risen from 1.6 in 1992 to 5.6 in 1995 (*Human Development Report Mongolia 1997*, p. 64). State-owned enterprises are slowly being privatized and ownership of property transferred to individuals, though members of parliament from the MPRP were among the most resistant to total divestiture of government assets. State controls on prices of goods and services have been greatly reduced in favor of market-driven pricing. A system of taxation on personal income and private enterprises has also been introduced, but collection mechanisms are not fully functional.

ONGOING EDUCATIONAL TRANSITIONS

Transitions in the education sector have been fueled by pressures similar to those mentioned for the political, social, and economic sectors. The education sector is also influenced by structural adjustment policies that tend to place increasing emphasis on improving efficiency and effectiveness of education at all levels through rationalization and decentralization. This has led to a gradual shifting of the burden of payment from the sole responsibility of the central government to the shared responsibility of local governments, as well as students and their families (Weidman et al., 1998). In Mongolia, among the most important responses to multilateral donor pressure are what Carnoy (1995) terms finance-driven reforms (e.g., shifting public funding from higher to lower levels of education, privatization of higher education, and reduction of cost per student at all school levels).

Prior to 1992, higher education in Mongolia was totally controlled by the state. The government owned, financed, and operated all of its higher education institutions. Government officials appointed the vice-chancellors, and the ministry dictated degree requirements and curricula (Task Force, 2000, p. 53).

Since 1990, there has been a relaxation of state control over curriculum in Mongolia with efforts at diversification based on local community needs. This includes eliminating the ideological content that had been prevalent, especially in social science and humanities disciplines, and shifting from a teacher-centered to a more student-centered curriculum. Administration of schools at all levels has been decentralized and less reliance placed on national planning approaches to the allocation of spaces for students in various types of curricula. The government has introduced measures aimed at cost sharing with parents and students so that the share of education funded by the central government can be reduced, especially at the higher education level. Legislation also has been passed allowing private sector provision of education at all levels. Finally, there has been an ongoing change from a highly specialized and compartmentalized system of education based on the Russian model to a more flexible system. Four-year bachelor's degree programs that include common foundational components are now the norm in higher education, though some three-year diploma programs remain in certain vocational areas and primary school teaching.

While academic programs are becoming more flexible, both public and private higher education institutions remain specialized. The National University of Mongolia is the closest to a comprehensive university, containing several traditional arts and sciences departments as well as law. Virtually within walking distance of each other in Ulaanbaatar, however, are specialized public universities (each with its own rector and administrative structure) for medicine, engineering, and culture. The Agricultural University is located on the outskirts of the city.

The basic education system providing the foundation for admission to higher education in Mongolia is ten years (four years of primary, four years of intermediate, and two years of secondary or specialized vocational education). About 20 percent of the 18 to 24 year-old age cohort attend higher education. Table 7.1 shows basic indicators for the entire Mongolian education system in the four years from 1995 through 1999. Government spending on education during that period stayed around 15 percent of the total expenditure budget and 5.5 percent of GDP. Since 1991, enrollments in private schools (including postsecondary education) have increased from zero to 29 percent of the total. Postsecondary enrollment in both the public and private sectors has been increasing rapidly. The country reports a very low school drop-out rate. Historically, Mongolia has had one of the highest literacy rates in Asia (more than 85%), largely because the communist government provided all schooling free of charge, including schools for children with special needs and boarding schools for children from nomadic families (Weidman et al., 1998).

Table 7.2 shows the enrollment patterns by level for the past two decades. Enrollments in general primary and secondary schools declined in the immediate post-transition years of 1992 through 1994, but have been in-

Table 7.1
Basic Indicators for the Education Sector, 1995–1998

Indicator		1995–1996	1996–1997	1997–1998	1998–1999
1.	State Expenditure Budget for education sector (million tugrugs, current prices)	23,525.3	31,188.4	42,161.0	47,815.5
2.	Education sector as percentage of total State Expenditure Budget	15.8	14.8	14.7	14.7
	Education sector as percentage of GDP	5.5	5.3	5.6	5.5
3.	Percentage of students in public and private schools				
	- Public schools	78.0	74.0	72.0	70.8
	- Private schools	22.0	26.0	28.0	29.2
4.	Investment (million tugrugs)				
	- in building reconstruction and vocational and technical schools	64.3	74.5	167.0	205.0
	- in equipment and training facilities	20.0	32.5	97.0	135.0
5.	Number of public universities, institutes and colleges	29	29	29	33
	- number of students in all public postsecondary programs*	29,167	31,391	35,229	46,185
	- numbers of teachers	2,693	2,683	2,799	3,261

6.	Number of private universities, institutes and colleges	41	51	57	71
	- number of students in all private postsecondary programs*	8,930	11,861	14,405	19,087
	- number of teachers	383	522	617	925
7.	Technical and vocational secondary schools	34	33	38	38
	- number of students	7,987	11,308	12,320	11,650
	- number of teachers	495	767	742	656
8.	Number of primary and secondary schools	664	658	645	630
	- primary schools (Grades 1–4)	83	79	89	96
	- lower secondary schools (Grades 1–8)	232	208	219	214
	- general secondary schools (Grades 1–10)	349	371	337	320
	Number of students in primary and secondary schools	403,847	418,293	435,061	447,121
	Number of teachers in primary and secondary schools	19,411	20,090	18,511	18,118
9.	Percentage of drop-outs	4.29	3.53	3.92	2.50
10.	Number of kindergartens	660	667	660	658
	- number of children in kindergartens	64,086	67,972	70,035	73,955
	- number of teachers in kindergartens	2,004	2,998	2,985	3,015

Note:* Data combine enrollments in postsecondary vocational (diploma), bachelor's degree, and postgraduate degree programs.

Sources: Ministry of Science, Technology, Education and Culture (1999), Table 1.1; National Statistical Office of Mongolia (1999), Tables 5.1 and 8.3.

Table 7.2
Growth of Enrollment by Level Since 1980–1981

Level	*General Primary and Secondary Education (Grades 1–10)*		*Technical and Vocational Education (Grades 9–10)*		*Specialized Vocational Education (Postsecondary Diploma)*		*Higher Education (Bachelor's or Equivalent Degree Only)*	
Academic Year	**Total**	**Growth Rate (From Previous Year)**	**Total**	**Growth Rate (From Previous Year)**	**Total**	**Growth Rate (From Previous Year)**	**Total**	**Growth Rate (From Previous Year)**
1980–1981	372,618	–	18,651	–	17,391	–	17,152	–
1981–1982	379,444	1.83	19,464	4.36	18,518	6.48	17,731	3.38
1982–1983	387,997	2.25	19,409	–0.28	19,492	5.26	18,705	5.49
1983–1984	397,991	2.58	19,458	0.25	20,063	2.93	19,692	5.28
1984–1985	406,283	2.08	21,553	10.77	20,426	1.81	19,152	–2.74
1985–1986	415,726	2.32	23,236	7.81	21,612	5.81	18,487	–3.47
1986–1987	424,110	2.02	25,036	7.75	21,714	0.47	17,358	–6.11
1987–1988	430,540	1.52	28,269	12.91	22,336	2.86	16,482	–5.05
1988–1989	438,152	1.77	30,574	8.15	21,248	–4.87	15,074	–8.54
1989–1990	446,665	1.94	31,194	2.03	19,223	–9.53	14,101	–6.45
1990–1991	440,986	–1.27	26,431	–15.27	17,609	–8.40	13,825	–1.96
1991–1992	411,696	–6.64	17,961	–32.05	14,986	–14.90	13,223	–4.35
1992–1993	384,069	–6.71	11,491	–36.02	8,116	–45.84	16,917	27.94
1993–1994	370,302	–3.58	8,317	–27.62	5,566	–31.42	22,135	30.84
1994–1995	381,204	2.94	7,555	–9.16	5,849	5.08	26,490	19.67
1995–1996	403,847	5.94	7,987	5.72	5,584	–4.53	32,241	21.71
1996–1997	418,293	3.58	11,308	41.58	3,730	–33.20	39,157	21.45
1997–1998	435,061	4.01	12,320	8.95	4,426	18.66	44,864	14.57
1998–1999	447,121	2.77	11,650	–5.44	4,094	–7.50	59,444	32.50

Source: Ministry of Science, Technology, Education and Culture, Mongolia.

creasing steadily to reach by 1998–1999 the pretransition peak of 1988–1989. Speculations are that the post-transition privatization of herds and introduction of fees for the boarding schools traditionally serving children from nomadic families led to a pattern of keeping children (especially boys) home to work with the herds instead of sending them to school.

Enrollments in technical and vocational education and training programs at both the secondary and postsecondary diploma levels also dropped dramatically, in large part because there was no longer a command economy with national manpower planning that determined not only the specific types of jobs that would be available for graduates but also guaranteed them employment. At the bachelor's degree level, enrollments hit a low of just over 13,000 in 1991–1992 but then exploded to almost 60,000 in 1998–1999, largely in response to strong student demand for advanced training and credentials for prospective employment in the rapidly changing economy.

Table 7.3 shows recent enrollment patterns by public or private control, level, and gender. Private sector higher education expanded rapidly from the opening of the first private institutions in 1990, reaching 29 percent of Mongolia's total enrollment at that level by 1999. As is the case in many developing countries (Altbach, 1999), private higher education institutions in Mongolia are highly specialized and market driven, providing instruction in fields with high student demand that cannot be met by public sector institutions (e.g., market economics and business, law, foreign languages, computer-related areas).

Mongolia is unique among Asian countries in the proportion of females enrolled in the highest levels of education. More than 60 percent of students in bachelor's degree programs in public institutions and more than 70 percent of students in private institutions are females. Even at the postgraduate level, females outnumber males by almost 2 to 1. Table 7.4 shows the distribution of students by public or private control, gender, and field of study. This table indicates that "computing" is the sole field in which there are substantially more male than female bachelor's degree students, and then only in public higher education institutions.

Despite the rapid expansion of postsecondary education in Mongolia, there have been continuing tensions between the government and higher education institutions over control of resources and decision making. The next section of this chapter places the Mongolian higher education system in global context and addresses some of the unresolved issues that reflect dilemmas of democratic transition for the higher education sector in Mongolia.

Table 7.3
Enrollment by Level, Type of Control, and Gender, 1997–1998 and 1998–1999

Level	1997–1998						1998–1999					
	Public			Private			Public			Private		
	Schools	Total Enrolled	% Female	Schools	Total Enrolled	% Female	Schools	Total Enrolled	% Female	Schools	Total Enrolled	% Female
General Primary and Secondary Schools	628	434,310	53.3	17	751	53.0	609	445,851	52.5	21	1,270	51.6
[Workers' Programs–Evening]	[87]	4,018	47.5				[107]	5,287	47.1			
Technical and Vocational Schools	34	11,990	51.5	4	330	67.3	34	11,461	55.3	4	189	71.4
Higher Education Institutions	29			57			33			71		
Postsecondary Technical (Diploma)		4,011	77.9		415	27.0		3,764	71.4		330	53.9
Bachelor's Degree		31,218	66.5		13,646	71.5		40,696	61.9		18,748	70.4
Postgraduate Degrees (M.A., Ph.D.)		1,657	61.9		14	85.7		1,725	64.1		9	77.8

Source: Ministry of Science, Technology, Education and Culture, Mongolia.

Table 7.4
Enrollment for "First University Degree or Equivalent Qualification" (ISCED Level 5) in Higher Education Institutions by Field of Study and Gender, 1992–1993 and 1998–1999*

UNESCO Field of Study **		Public 1998–1999		Private 1998–1999		Public 1992–1993	
		Total	% Female	Total	% Female	Total	% Female
1	Education and Teacher Training	6,048	79.3	3,635	76.0	4,775	73.8
2	Fine and Applied Arts	962	49.5	539	51.8	412	49.0
3	Humanities, Religion, Theology	3,776	77.3	3,060	79.6	1,679	73.6
4	Social and Behavioral Science	2,774	65.0	2,451	75.3	255	65.9
5	Journalism and Information	641	73.6			86	69.8
6	Commerce and Business Administration	5,710	68.9	4,091	70.7	1,705	59.2
7	Law	999	61.4	2,539	65.3	282	46.5
8	Life Sciences	725	82.5	68	79.4	**	**
9	Physical sciences	1,286	47.2			727	54.3
10	Mathematics and Statistics	777	63.8			**	**
11	Computing	644	30.3	229	50.2	455	41.1
12	Engineering and Engineering Trades	1,819	77.2	30	90.0	1,973	40.3
13	Manufacturing and Processing	7,432	41.0	296	65.2	241	49.0
14	Architecture and Building	167	45.5			38	26.3
15	Agriculture, Forestry, and Fishery	1,926	67.0	55	60.0	956	54.1
16	Veterinary						
17	Health	2,295	83.7	90	75.6	2,748	79.3
18	Social Services						
19	Personal Services	275	66.5	1,173	44.9	116	75.9
20	Others	2,440	15.2	492	63.4		
TOTAL		40,696	61.9	18,748	70.4	16,917	63.8

Notes:
* ISCED = International Standard Classification of Education, program leading "to the awarding of a first university degree or equivalent qualification," Level 6 in 1992 was the same as Level 5 in 1998.
** In 1992, the category "Natural Sciences" included BOTH "Life Sciences" and "Physical Sciences," and the category "Mathematics and Computer Science" included BOTH "Mathematics and Statistics" and "Computing."

Source: Ministry of Science, Technology, Education, and Culture, Mongolia.

THE TRANSITION FROM TOTAL STATE CONTROL TO SYSTEM AUTONOMY

A recent World Bank report (Task Force on Higher Education and Society, 2000) identifies several "desirable features" of higher education systems in developing countries: adequate and stable long-term finance, including system-wide resources; competition; immunity from political manipulation; supportive legal and regulatory structure; well-defined standards; and flexibility. For countries like Mongolia and the Newly Independent States, these desirable features must be developed at the same time as the broader social, economic, political, and educational transitions outlined earlier in this chapter are occurring. Institutions and systems of higher education in such countries are clamoring for greater autonomy in accordance with the overall movement toward democratization and economic transition, but they often encounter tensions in various forms of resistance from national governments. Governments often have well-established patterns of reluctance to relax controls. The following sections use the Mongolian experience to illustrate tensions in four areas that are also problematic in the higher education systems of many other developing countries in the world: finance, student admission, governance, and accreditation.

Finance

A student fee structure was introduced in 1993, but unlike most other countries, student fees in Mongolia are expected to cover the full cost of faculty salaries, instructional costs, and other expenses (Bray et al., 1994). Initially, the government provided funds for utilities as well as building maintenance and upkeep, but since 1997 only heat, water, and electricity costs are covered. Despite these shifts, the 1997 annual tuition cost remained at the same inflation-adjusted level as when the fee structure was first introduced, about four months' salary of a university senior lecturer or senior government employee (Weidman et al., 1998).

In financial terms, Mongolian public higher education institutions were effectively privatized in 1993. The government has, however, limited institutional autonomy with respect to finance in several ways. Despite a pattern of reductions in state allocations, public higher education institutions have not been allowed to raise their fees to the levels necessary to offset increased costs. Institutions propose a fee structure each year, but the Ministry of Science, Technology, Education and Culture (MOSTEC) usually reduces the proposed amounts. MOSTEC has, however, permitted institutions to vary fees by academic major. In Mongolia, the fee structure was originally based on overall instructional costs but is also now tied to student demand (the higher the demand, the higher the fee) in fields such as law and business. Institutions must compete for students because of their dependence on the revenue from student fees for operating expenses, including salaries of academic, administrative, and support staff.

The government continues to treat all institutional income and assets (including computers, furniture, laboratory equipment, etc.) as state property. Consequently, public higher education institutions are not able to sell outdated equipment and use the proceeds for purchasing replacements without formal permission from the State Property Committee. Not until financial instability of government banks made the security of deposits uncertain were higher education institutions permitted to put revenues from student fees and other sources into private bank accounts. Most higher education institutions have begun to diversify their sources of revenue through operation of various types of enterprises (e.g., shops, printing houses, guest houses, livestock herds, etc.), but they have had to repulse government efforts to claim a significant portion of these funds (Weidman, 1995).

There are continuing problems with payment of government obligations for such things as student loans and scholarships. Funds for students on mandated government scholarships have either not been paid at all or not paid in a timely fashion to higher education institutions. Examples of such scholarships include students selected to fill provincial enrollment quotas, one eligible child of any government employee, children from poor herdsmen's families, and students with disabilities.

Student Admission

Before 1992, the State Planning Board, in consultation with the Ministry of Education, set admissions quotas by academic field for all public higher education institutions based on projected employment needs in the command economy. The government has continued to set quotas for admission to public higher education institutions by province and major field, now primarily to establish the eligibility of students for government scholarships and loans but also to make certain that space limitations due to the distribution of instructional faculty by major field are not exceeded. Setting quotas by major field is quite problematic because, under a market economy, there has been no systematic study of the emerging labor market to provide data upon which to project demand for highly educated employees. While individual higher education institutions have been able to increase the numbers of spaces available for those students who can pay their own fees, they have not been allowed to increase admissions to levels that would be justifiable in terms of student demand.

In order to generate additional revenue, the National University of Mongolia has also instituted an obligatory admission contribution that is determined by the applicants' admissions test scores (the lower the score, the higher the fee!). These one-time charges, payable upon initial enrollment, are based on the fees for each major field and can be an amount up to quadruple the normal annual fee. Hence, students whose scores do not qualify them for government financial aid or regular admission may be admitted if they can pay the sliding fee.

Governance

Higher education institutions are managed by a rector appointed by MOSTEC and an administrative structure established by the rector. Faculty participation in governance varies by institution, but tends to be limited. The 1998 Amendments to the Education Law required the establishment of governing boards for all institutions of higher education. In the case of public institutions, while the boards elect their officers, most boards have a chair who is a member of Parliament. Each board is also required to have a faculty member and a student elected by their respective constituencies. While this type of structure maintains a strong state presence in institutional governance, it also provides avenues for increased participation of faculty and students.

Public higher education institutions have also been accorded increasing autonomy with respect to the management of revenue from student fees and other nongovernment sources, including responsibility for payment of staff salaries. In fact, academic staff in public higher education institutions have continued to receive salaries even when there have been problems with payment of teachers at the primary and general secondary level who receive their salaries directly from the government. This is a significant factor in the relatively high levels of enthusiasm exhibited by higher education faculty, staff, and administrators for their work.

Accreditation

In accordance with provisions in the 1995 Education Law, a national body for higher education accreditation was established in 1998. There were concerns that the relatively unregulated rapid expansion of private sector higher education had resulted in the establishment of institutions of questionable quality. In addition, it was hoped that the accreditation process might cast some light on the relative quality of institutions, both within Mongolia as well as in the international higher education community. While all higher education institutions were required to undergo accreditation, there was a phase-in period with most of the public and only a few of the leading private institutions participating in the first year. Only those institutions which passed the accreditation process were to be eligible to receive government funds. For the first time, students attending accredited private institutions were also eligible for government loans.

The 1995 Education Law specified that the national higher education accreditation agency was to become a nongovernmental entity. However, the first chair of the board appointed by MOSTEC was the state secretary of education. Further, the person appointed to be the executive director of the National Council for Higher Education Accreditation (NCHEA) was a senior MOSTEC official also responsible for overseeing the assessment of applications for the initial license for a higher education institution to operate. A majority of the board members were, however, rectors of participating higher education institutions and there is some indication of the intention to make the NCHEA an autonomous and self-financing body. The primary source of revenue is the fees charged to institutions for accreditation reviews.

Funds from an Asian Development Bank loan supported the establishment of the NCHEA, including training of board members and executive staff and workshops for representatives of institutions undergoing accreditation. The first group of institutions was accredited in 1999. One unanticipated consequence of this process carried out initially at the *institutional* (as opposed to *program*) level was that several of the newly accredited institutions took approval as a blanket authorization to begin offering graduate degree programs even though there was no effective mechanism in the accreditation process for quality assurance at the graduate level. Because this is one of the few areas in which MOSTEC seemed unable to exercise control through formal inspection/evaluation procedures, accredited institutions were relatively free to increase the level of their degree offerings. The models embraced in the establishment of the NCHEA were drawn from American regional accreditation agencies that emphasize more formative approaches to quality assurance based on characteristics of individual higher education institutions rather than summative approaches based on fixed standards and criteria. Since this was the first time accreditation had been implemented, part of the process involved developing standards appropriate for the Mongolian context on the basis of data collected in the institutional self-studies and visits of the accreditation teams.

The establishment of nongovernmental oversight bodies is a difficult process in countries accustomed to state control of all public entities. Mongolia is, however, making progress along these lines in the higher education sector. Both the institutional boards and the National Council for Higher Education are fledgling examples of "buffer mechanisms" aimed at

> balancing the state's responsibility to protect and promote the public's interest with an individual institution's need for academic freedom. . . . Buffer mechanisms generally consist of statutory bodies that include representatives of the government, institutions of higher education, the private sector, and other important stakeholders. (Task Force on Higher Education and Society, 2000, ch. 3)

Figure 7.1
Higher Education in the New Millennium: Social, Economic, Political, and Educational Influences

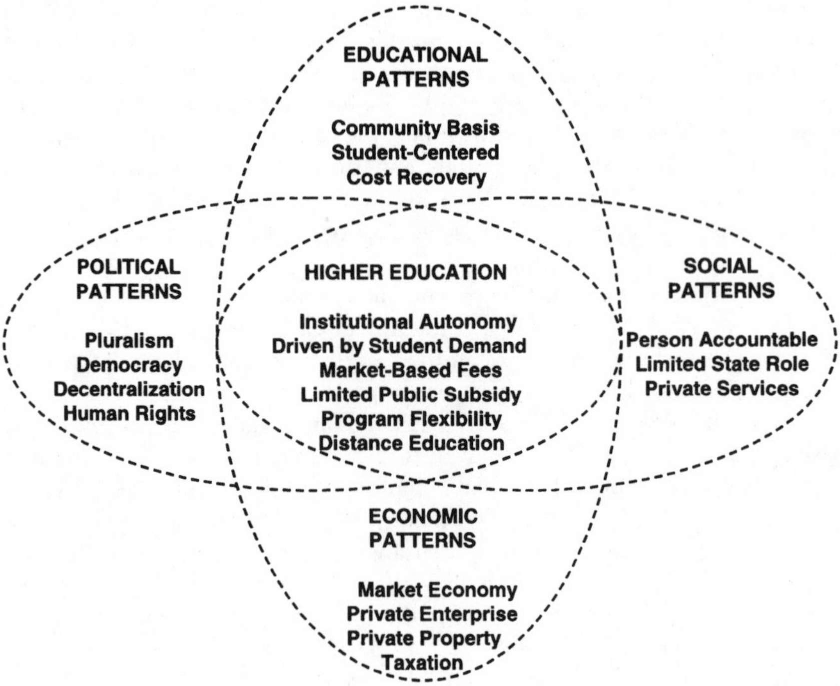

HIGHER EDUCATION IN THE NEW MILLENNIUM: A FRAMEWORK

Reform of higher education in response to political, social, and economic change is not just characteristic of Mongolia but of educational systems throughout the world. As has been suggested in the foregoing discussion, democratization and economic transition are key drivers of higher education reform in Mongolia.

Taking these key international drivers and the particular Mongolian context into consideration, Figure 7.1 presents a framework for characterizing influences on higher education in the new millennium. *Higher Education* forms the central ellipse in Figure 7.1 which suggests that the selected emerging patterns (institutional autonomy, driven by student demand, fees based on market, limited public subsidy) are a function of four sets of patterns (*Political, Educational, Economic, Social*) represented in the surrounding bubbles. The ellipses have broken rather than solid lines to suggest that the underlying processes are nonlinear, interactive, and interdependent.

With respect to the *Political Patterns* shown in the left side of Figure 7.1, underlying notions of transition based on democratic principles emphasize accepting pluralism of interests and human rights accompanied by general reduction of state control over citizens. This includes decentralization of authority and citizens gaining an increasing voice through such means as civil society organizations, community groups, local chambers of commerce, religious organizations, and parents' associations (World Bank, 1999). As a result of reduced state involvement in Mongolia, education is becoming increasingly more decentralized, with greater community influence. Efforts are being made to develop curriculum that is more student-centered and flexible. At the higher education level in Mongolia, this is reflected in greater institutional autonomy, even though it is a source of continuing tension.

The top section of Figure 7.1 shows basic *Educational Patterns* that reflect an emphasis on reducing centralization of education and increasing involvement at the community level. This includes tailoring curriculum to local needs and moving from teacher-centered to student-centered models of instruction. There is also increased pressure for cost sharing through such things as fees for books and laboratory use, and donations by parents toward payment of school utilities and maintenance (e.g., the high cost of heating schools in Mongolia). Since 1996, however, school textbooks in Mongolia have been free.

Despite concern about reaching remote areas of the country, both public and private sector higher education institutions are concentrated in Ulaanbaatar. Even though enrollment in public higher education institutions located in provincial (aimag) centers (virtually all of which have become branch campuses of universities in Ulaanbaatar) has increased by 67 percent since 1993–1994, the vast majority (88%) of public sector students and virtually all private sector students attend institutions located in Ulaanbaatar (Weidman et al., 1998).

The bottom section of Figure 7.1 suggests several important *Economic Patterns*. Underlying this section of the framework is an emphasis on transition to a market economy, including encouragement of private sector development, privatization of state enterprises, and cost recovery from beneficiaries through fees and taxes. As the World Bank (1999) points out, market economies now prevail in countries accounting for over 80 percent of the world's population, up from under 30 percent a decade ago. Where other (mainly centrally planned) systems used to provide fewer opportunities but more certainty, market systems now reward risk-taking, skill, and agility, but offer less security and a constantly changing environment.

Privatization goes hand in hand with market economies, in large part because it is believed to generate competition leading to increased rationalization and efficiency of economic activity. There tend to be, however, transitional periods during which governments relinquish increasing shares of state-owned enterprises. This may stimulate initiative by motivating individual higher education institutions to seek investment from nongovernmental sources. It may also lead to the blurring of distinctions between public and private sector entities, thereby posing dilemmas for countries like Mongolia that are emerging from many decades of total state control of the economy.

The right side of Figure 7.1 shows *Social Patterns* appearing throughout the world that reflect pressures on national governments to reduce the involvement of the state, particularly in terms of finance, in provision of goods and services to citizens. This includes greater emphasis on making individuals accountable for their own well-being rather than relying on the state. Limiting the role of the state is also reflected in such shifts as contracting with private providers for a variety of services rather than having government agencies provide them directly.

The center of Figure 7.1, *Higher Education*, reflects political, economic, educational, and social influences generated within its own national, international, regional, and local contexts. Institutional autonomy is an area of contention throughout the world, as countries attempt to balance national with private interests. The expansion of private sector higher education in Mongolia as well as in many other countries is driven largely by the inability of public institutions to meet the excess demand from students clamoring for access to training and skills necessary for rapidly changing economic conditions (James, 1991). Even public higher education institutions, partly in response to increased private sector competition, have begun offering part-time programs in high demand areas. Several foreign universities have also begun offering degree programs in Mongolia.

Fees for students in higher education in Mongolia are increasingly market-based, despite state controls imposed on public institutions. The admission "donation" charged by the National University to admit students who do not meet regular admission standards is a prime example. Part-time business programs in both public and private higher education institutions are also charging market-based fees. In Mongolia, state subsidies for public higher education were radically reduced in 1993 by shifting from direct appropriations to institutions to aid to students in the form of scholarships and loans at a much lower level of aggregate government expenditure: just over half of the students admitted under government quotas for 1998–1999 actually received loans (Weidman et al., 1998).

Conditions are being created in Mongolian higher education institutions to enable more individualized academic programs in which students are expected to read and study independently rather than relying solely on didactic instruction and copious note-taking. This will encourage greater flexibility both within and among institutions. There will be more comprehensive preparation of teachers with greater emphasis upon enhancing subject area competence and encouraging independent work (Weidman et al., 1998). Efforts are also underway at the Technical University and other higher education institutions to develop distance education programs that will reach students in provincial centers far from Ulaanbaatar. This may stimulate more cooperation among institutions because of the need to share available technological resources such as Internet connections. Of course, distance education programs originating from foreign universities are also becoming available in Mongolia.

HIGHER EDUCATION REFORM IN TRANSITIONAL COUNTRIES

Over the past decade, Mongolia has embraced the reform agenda delineated by the World Bank and Asian Development Bank and been the recipient of significant donor funds for implementation. It also has managed to use the donor funding to achieve demonstrable accomplishments in each of the three key areas identified by the World Bank as critical for systemic reform: standards, curriculum, and achievement assessment; governance and decentralization; and provision and finance of education by nongovernmental sources (World Bank, 1999). What has been learned from the Mongolia experience can be used to inform efforts at systemic reform of higher education in other emerging market economies, keeping in mind that each country has its own set of peculiarities that make adaptation of successful approaches to reform perilous.

As has been the case in Mongolia, emerging market economies must grapple continuously with the dynamics of rapid transition, with different elements of the society changing at different speeds. They must resist external pressures from donors to change along lines that are not congruent with their national interests while also finding avenues for accommodation in order to obtain donor funds necessary for sustaining and improving their educational systems. Significant tensions between state education authorities and individual institutions of higher education will continue to permeate the landscapes of transitional economies. While there are many internal and external pressures on the government to "democratize" higher education by extending greater autonomy to institutions, vestiges of political and social tension continue to hinder reform efforts, particularly in countries whose people are accustomed to strong government control of all major social sector institutions. With the recent re-ascendance of former Communist Party members in the governments of several Newly Independent States in addition to Mongolia, it remains to be seen if these governments will continue to embrace the ongoing transitions to more democratic and market-oriented institutions that have had limited success.

NOTE

Most of the data on education in Mongolia in this chapter are drawn from projects funded by the Asian Development Bank. However, the opinions presented are those of the authors and do not represent official policy of the Asian Development Bank or the government of Mongolia.

REFERENCES

Altbach, P. G. (1999). Comparative perspective on private higher education. In P. G. Altbach (Ed.), *Private prometheus: Private higher education and development in the 21st century* (pp. 1–14). Westport, CT: Greenwood Press.

Bray, M., Davaa, S., Spaulding, S. S., & Weidman, J. C. (1994). Transition from socialism and the financing of higher education: The case of Mongolia. *Higher Education Policy, 7*(4), 36–42.

Carnoy, M. (1995). Structural adjustment and the changing face of education. *International Labour Review, 134*(6), 653–673.

Human development report Mongolia 1997. Ulaanbaatar, Mongolia: United Nations Development Programme.

James, E. (1991). *Private finance and management of education in developing countries: Major policy and research issues.* Issues and Methodologies in Education Development: An IIEP Series for Orientation and Training, No. 5. Paris: International Institute for Educational Planning (UNESCO).

Ministry of Science, Technology and Culture. (1999). *Analysis of 1998 education sector statistical data.* Ulaanbaatar, Mongolia: Ministry of Science, Technology and Culture.

National Statistical Office of Mongolia. (1999). *Mongolian statistical yearbook, 1998.* Ulaanbaatar, Mongolia: National Statistical Office of Mongolia.

Task Force on Higher Education and Society. (2000). *Higher education in developing countries: Peril and promise.* Washington, DC: The World Bank.

Weidman, J. C. (1995). Diversifying finance of higher education systems in the third world: The cases of Kenya and Mongolia. *Education Policy Analysis Archives, 3*(5). http://olam.ed.asu.edu/epaa/v3n5.html.

Weidman, J. C., Bat-Erdene, R., Gerel, O., & Badarch, D. (1997). Mongolia. In G. A. Postiglione & G.C.L. Mak (Eds.), *Asian higher education: An international handbook and reference guide.* Westport, CT: Greenwood Press.

Weidman, J. C., Bat-Erdene, R., Yeager, J. L., Sukhbaatar, J., Jargalmaa, T., & Davaa, S. (1998). Mongolian higher education in transition: Responding under conditions of rapid change. *Tertium Comparationis, 4*(2), 75–90.

World Bank, Human Development Network. (1999). *Education sector strategy.* Washington, DC: The World Bank.

Yeager, J. L., & Weidman, J. C. (1999, Spring). Higher education planning in transitional countries. *Planning for Higher Education, 27*, 1–8.

Chapter 8

Chinese Higher Education for the Twenty-First Century: Expansion, Consolidation, and Globalization

Gerard A. Postiglione

This chapter examines selected social and economic aspects of the reform and development of Chinese higher education. Like other countries that are experiencing a rapid expansion of higher education, China's main challenge is to boost quality at low cost (Task Force, 2000). This is especially true in its nonelite institutions, provincial universities, western region colleges, and the growing number of popularly run (*minban*) colleges and universities (Green Paper, 2000). China's membership in the World Trade Organization (WTO) makes improving higher education a top priority and will probably lead to more cooperation with foreign universities, including increased trade of educational and training services, potentially resulting in further improvement of teaching and scholarship (Zhang, 1999). This chapter will review the past development, reforms, expansion, consolidation, and global dimensions of Chinese higher education, focusing on the potential role of academic staff in university development.

A HALF CENTURY OF REFORM: FROM A PLANNED TO A MARKET ECONOMY

China's higher education system has experienced momentous change over the past half century (Pepper, 1996). After the revolution in 1949, when Chairman Mao Zedong and Premier Zhou Enlai took a leading role, universities were nationalized and all forms of private higher education ceased to exist. The Soviet Union had a major influence in the 1950s when higher education was expected to ensure a close link between education and labor, as well as broad access for peasant and worker children. Higher education also provided ideological support for socialist construction and emphasized specialization rather than broad liberal education. Student fees were abolished and graduates were allocated to work positions according to the state plan.

Colleges and universities came to be run by various ministries of the central government and by provincial authorities. The basic unit of social life was the *danwei*, providing all with an "iron rice bowl," which included salary, accommodations, meals, health care, and other benefits guaranteed for life. It also controlled all aspects of organizational life including staff appointments and the form and content of educational institutions. Most academic exchange occurred with the socialist block nations. Teaching methods were traditional, and socialist ideology penetrated classroom life. Professors mainly relied on a unified national curriculum and textbooks, with a strong emphasis placed on science and technology (Hayhoe, 1996). When cooperation with the Soviet Union soured in the late 1950s, the structure of higher education remained intact, except that the pace of expansion quickened during the Great Leap Forward (1958–1962) period.

Higher education was thrown into chaos beginning in 1966 during the period known as the Cultural Revolution. Enrollments shrank, professors were criticized, standards were ignored, and teaching and research became judged by erratic political trends. University staff and students were sent off to work in rural areas and much talent was lost. Higher education was left in a weakened state, though China's system of basic education provided an attractive model for the developing world. As China exited the Cultural Revolution, Deng Xiaoping's economic reforms and opening to the outside world had an enormously positive effect on higher education.

The shift away from a planned economy brought unprecedented change. Students and professors were sent to study in many overseas countries, and academic exchanges flourished (Hayhoe, 1989). China's higher education system moved back to an emphasis on examination standards and academic achievement. To strengthen the enterprise, the Ministry of Education was upgraded to a commission from 1985 to 1998, during which time major reforms occurred in higher education (Chinese Communist Party Central Committee, 1985). Universities were granted more autonomy and began to charge tuition to a portion of their students which was extended to most students in 1994 and later became a key consideration in the decision of 1999 to embark upon the largest expansion in this century of the higher education system.

In short, after a period of conservative expansion of higher education due to concern for social stability and the cost in comparison with higher yield investment in basic education, China has embarked on a breakneck-paced expansion. The university mission has shifted from emphasizing class struggle within a planned economy to a mission shaped by economic reforms and the opening to the outside world (Min, 1997). The new mission, while recognizing the goals of the revolution, has embraced market forces.

Moreover, universities are being compelled to react to the growing demand for higher education, particularly among residents of urban China, where an increasing number now attend school for twelve years. There is also an urgent need in the information age for high-level scientific and technical specialists called for by the national framework developed under Deng Xiaoping and continued under Jiang Zemin.

EXPANSION: FINANCE, PRIVATIZATION, AND THE BANKING SECTOR

This section will look at the development of China's expanding system of colleges and universities. China educates one-quarter of the world's students on one percent of the world's education budget (Zhang, 1999). The proportion of GNP dedicated to education rose from 2.49 percent in 1997 to 2.79 percent in 1999 (*National Report*, 2000). This is far lower than the aim of 4.0 percent, which would be expected for a developing country like China. The total percent of government-budgeted expenditure on education is less than for most developing countries, with only about 13 percent of it allocated to colleges and universities (Hu & Shi, 1999, p. 12).

Between 1978 and 1994, the number of regular universities and colleges in China grew from 598 to 1080, and enrollment increased from 0.86 to 2.8 million (World Bank, 1996). In 1997, China had 1,020 regular colleges and universities, with 3.17 million students, which constituted about 4 percent of the relevant age group (Cai & Tian, 1999). At the time, there were also 1,017 adult institutions of higher education with 2.73 million students. In its regular institutions of higher education, only 52 percent of students were in undergraduate degree programs, 44 percent in short-cycle nondegree programs, and 4 percent in graduate studies. In adult institutions of higher education, only 33 percent of the students were in a program of undergraduate degree studies.

In 1999, China's higher education system admitted 2.8 million new students of which 1.6 million were admitted into regular institutions of higher education (47.4% of all students in higher education) and the rest to adult institutions of higher education. The proportion of students who took the national entrance examination and were admitted to higher education was 49 percent, up 13 percent from the previous year. The enrollment rate in colleges and universities in 1999 was 10.5 percent (Li, 2000).

China now allows adults over the age of 25 to enter undergraduate degree programs. Previously people who were over 25 or married were eligible only for special adult education programs. Starting this year, however, age limits have been lifted from the entrance examination used for colleges. The changes are part of a set of reforms designed to make higher education more accessible to the masses. Another reason for opening regular higher education to adults may be that such students are less of a drain on universities' resources, which lately have been strained by increasing enrollments and dwindling support from the central government. Adult students may be better able to afford tuition and less likely to require dormitory space. In 1999, 4,367,700 students were in regular higher education programs and 3,054,900 in adult education institutes.

In 2000, there were 2 million new students admitted to regular institutions of higher education. The decision to expand was due in part to the pressure from below resulting from the increase in students graduating from secondary school. The government's decision to expand aimed also at getting families to spend more of their savings in an effort to stimulate the economy in the aftermath of the Asian economic crisis (and to keep more students in school during a period of rising unemployment). Savings for education is the fastest growing sector of consumer spending by urban residents and is increasing at an average rate of about 20 percent annually. An average of 10 percent of savings goes to education which is higher than the seven percent put aside for housing (Hu & Shi, 1999). For example, a survey of 1,200 households in Wuxi city near Shanghai found that the average education expenditure from kindergarten to university was 63,000 yuan (almost US$8,000). The average expenditure per student per term was 1,540 yuan (almost US$200). The average expenditure per college student per term was 3,949 yuan (almost US$400) (*Wuxi Daily*, 2000).

The globalization of the Chinese economy is compelling universities to adapt and compete like never before. As the certainty of a planned economy has given way to the uncertainty of market forces, Chinese higher education has moved toward reforms similar to those in other parts of the world, including a proliferation of nongovernment institutions of higher education. Popularly run (*minban*) colleges and universities are entering the scene for the first time since 1949, and their numbers are increasing rapidly. One source put the number of *minban* colleges and universities at 1,800 (Minban, 1998). The government identifies over 1,000, enrolling close to one million (950,000) students. However, quality is a problem and only 37 of these colleges and universities have approval to issue standard credentials. Of these 37, only four issue a standard undergraduate degree (Li, 2000).

The universities run by the Ministry of Education remain in a favored position and still attract the best students. Even so, most are compelled to increase operational efficiency as state allocations fail to keep pace with the expansion. University administrators are looking beyond the state for assistance, and banks are beginning to find that colleges and universities are attractive investment targets. According to Cai and Tian (1999):

> Education is a domain still unexplored by banks, and investing in higher education will help higher education open up a new line of business. In circumstances where new commodities have entered a buyer's market, higher education, as a scarce com-

modity with enormous demand, has a typical seller's market, and will naturally become the future target of competition among banks. (pp. 16–17)

They argue that, along with developments in the market economy, the industrialization of higher education is an inevitable trend. In their view, there will be no need to worry about demand. As long as the supply of higher education institutions exists, investments in such institutions will be a very profitable business. Operating higher education as a kind of industry, they believe, will solve many problems for participating banks (Cai & Tian, 1999).

Thus, higher education is viewed as a new and scarce commodity in a buyer's market with enormous demand, and many enterprises are investing in higher education in order to make a profit (Ji, 2000). In this environment, the mission and core functions of the university need to remain in focus.

Given the enormous power of market forces being unleashed in the Chinese economy, there is little else that colleges and universities can do but respond by expanding and increasing the price for their services. Costs are increasingly being passed on to consumers. Yet, parents seldom make demands on the university for quality improvement, as their main interest is acquisition of credentials leading to lucrative employment. As parental education levels rise, demand for quality may increase. In the meantime, quality assurance will be up to a professoriate that is severely underpaid, a college and university administration that is focused on financing the expansion, and a government education apparatus that has transferred much autonomy and responsibility to individual institutions. Although academic accreditation of university programs remains under government control, the process by which program quality is maintained occurs within the walls of the university and external reviews are rare.

CONSOLIDATION: ECONOMIES OF SCALE, EFFICIENCY, AFFORDABILITY, AND LOANS

China's universities have responded to changes around them in a number of ways, including shifting to formula funding, generating more of their own revenue, running enterprises, cooperating with industry and banks, charging higher student fees, admitting adult learners into continuing education programs, permitting regular students to choose their own jobs after graduation, and consolidating small institutions to attain economies of scale.

While the Ministry of Education is maintaining its direct control over the 3 to 4 percent of China's state universities that compose the Ivy League of Chinese higher education, most of the other ministries of the central government have surrendered their universities to local provincial or municipal control. Over 400 institutions of higher education formerly under the authority of various central government ministries have been transferred to provincial or local education bureaus.

This has occurred as a result of the national policy to slim down state-owned enterprises and the central government bureaucracy. This action has led many provinces to consider ways to strengthen their university systems through consolidation with other institutions. There are many examples throughout China of this process of consolidation of colleges and universities. In line with the 1993 decision to establish 100 world-class universities, the so-called 211 project, universities are aiming for higher standards and economies of scale.

The average number of students in regular institutions of higher education was 3,112 in 1997, up from 1,919 in 1990, when about 80 percent of China's universities had less than 4,000 students, and about 60 percent had less than 3,000 students (*China Education Yearbook*, 1990). By the year 2000, 612 colleges and universities were consolidated into 250 (Li, 2000). Yet, some contend that economies of scale will not in themselves ensure quality, especially if the institutions that are being combined are themselves overstaffed with redundant personnel. As Pan (1999) notes:

> Colleges and universities have subsequently been swept up in a fad for combining faculties and disciplines into grand academies (*da xueyuan*), calling this "merging tracks internationally." Are these actions beneficial to higher education? I seriously doubt it. . . . Such universities may be the largest in the world, but they are certainly not among the world's first rate universities. The basis for becoming one of the world's first rate universities is a first rate management system. (pp. 6–7)

Most agree that a first-rate management system is necessary to ensure that the universities' core mission and functions are being carried out with an emphasis on quality. Consolidation is one step in a process to improve China's universities. It may be that the next step will be for the newly consolidated institutions to institutionalize a comprehensive set of reforms to make departments accountable for optimum delivery of the core functions of teaching, research, and service.

The national framework of reform and opening has also challenged the universities to ensure equal access and equity. China's domestic market reforms have accentuated regional disparities. After decades of struggling to develop its own model of socialist higher education with Chinese characteristics, their system has taken on some of the basic characteristics of higher education in Western societies. For example, expansion of higher education may benefit urban residents more than their poorer rural counterparts since without sufficient dormitory rooms, universities must admit more commuters, who coincidentally, can pay fees more easily. Students from urban Beijing, for example, can be admitted to universities in China with lower scores than rural students, despite the fact that rural students attend schools far less equipped in terms of learning resources and qualified teachers. Yet, poor rural families have not been forgotten. The Commercial Bank of China will provide student loans to university students with a 5 percent interest subsidy by government. Likewise, the Bank of China has introduced loan schemes and will lend funds to families for children's education from primary to higher education, including overseas study. The Pudong Development Bank in Shanghai has even launched an overseas study loan scheme, with a maximum loan of 500,000 renminbi and six years repayment. There are also proposals for "education banks," in which parents would deposit early savings for their children's education and the bank would make use of the resources to strengthen university development. Nevertheless, urban students increasingly hold the edge in access over their rural counterparts.

THE NEW SUB-DEGREE SECTOR: COMMUNITY COLLEGES FOR ECONOMIC DEVELOPMENT AND SOCIAL OPPORTUNITY

Among the other major changes occurring in Chinese higher education is the transformation of the sub-degree sector, which, not unlike U.S. community colleges, constitutes about half of the tertiary sector. China's secondary school graduates who do not score high enough to attend a university often gain entrance to what were formerly called upper level specialized technical colleges (*dazhuan*), with a two- or three-year program leading to a diploma, and the new tertiary vocational-technical colleges (*gaodeng zhiye jišhu xueyuan*). However, the most dynamic development in the tertiary sub-degree sector is the expansion of community colleges (*shequ xueyuan*), which are sprouting up as China scrambles to meet the needs of a changing economy with a growing number of urban unemployed, including secondary school graduates, most of whom were not able to gain entrance to the university. Their transfer function is being touted, and therefore universities can expect to be recruiting more community college graduates in the years to come. New options are needed for the increasing number of secondary school graduates. By focusing on the first two years of higher education, community colleges have a better chance of ensuring a quality program of study.

China's interest in community colleges spans several decades. Cooperation between the United States and China dates back almost 20 years, when the World Bank supported selected Chinese institutions to carry out a program of learning about American community colleges. In the late 1980s, more cooperation followed, this time with Canadian community colleges. However, sustained community college development only took off at the beginning of the twenty-first century, a time when the Ford Foundation was already supporting an array of community college development activities in at least four parts of China. By December 2000, the minister of education announced that the establishment of community colleges should be encouraged across China in district level cities and that transfer of community college graduates to university degree programs should be a future option. It is clear that China, like an increasing number of countries including Mexico, Brazil, South Africa, and elsewhere, has adapted community college models to produce an alternative form of tertiary education for the growing number of secondary school graduates. They mesh with China's emphasis on community development, its focus on vocational-technical education, its preparation for membership in the WTO, the opening of its western regions, and its search for alternative forms of tertiary education during the transition from elite to mass higher education.

In fact, almost half (3 million plus) of the total enrollments of institutions of higher learning in China are students in two- or three-year programs. The postgraduation employment rate for undergraduates from four-year programs is around 70 percent, but for graduates of two- or three-year programs, the postgraduation employment rate is only around 40 percent. The reason is that the programs in two- or three-year institutions of higher learning are not closely related to the needs of the economy. Due to swift economic change, many students leave postsecondary school without long-term marketable skills. *China Education Daily* reported recently that post-secondary vocational education "has been disappointing." The difficulty of predicting what job skills will be needed has led educators to question the current form of secondary and postsecondary vocational-technical education.

Within China, community colleges can be found in both Hong Kong and Taiwan. This not only means that they may be well suited for Chinese societies, but also that these institutions survive well in the rough and tumble East Asian economic environment.

In the coming decade, *minban* colleges and universities will take up much of the demand for higher education, though the quality of their programs remains a major issue. There are already over 1,400 *minban* colleges and universities serving over one million students. Converting some of these to community colleges may help to consolidate their programs and improve quality.

As China embarks on mass higher education in 2015, what types of institutions will be suitable to make the transition to a community college? These will include the traditional higher specialized colleges (*dazhuan*) and their more recent counterpart, vocational technical colleges (*gaodeng zhiye jishu xueyuan*). Other educational institutions may also adopt community college characteristics, including *minban* colleges and adult/continuing divisions of universities (*daxue chengren jishu jiaoyu*), as well as some secondary institutions in the process of being upgraded such as middle level specialized colleges (*zhongzhuan*) and upper secondary vocational schools (*zhiye jishu gaozhong*).

Community colleges are finding their way in China and can now be found in large cities like Beijing and Shanghai, provincial-level cities like Taiyuan, prefectural cities like Nakchu, and county-level cities like Shaoxing. It still remains to be seen, however, to what extent they become institutions of access and equity for the poor, unemployed, migrants, and ethnic minorities.

THE CORE FUNCTIONS: THE COST OF THEIR PRESERVATION AND VITALITY

There is no lack of vision about the core functions of higher education in China. There is a consensus among the authorities that higher education must provide the scientific know-how to advance China's economy and make it a leader in scientific research. The importance of teaching, research, and service are recognized; however, there is yet to be a notion of scholarship that combines teaching, research, and service.

While there is no dearth of intellectual leadership about the functions of the modern university, problems remain. Without adequate salaries, the incentive for teachers to be committed to institutional reforms is much less than it might be. The market economy offers a plethora of opportunities to academics to supplement their salaries. The most talented can spend time consulting outside of the university and taking on other teaching opportunities. The dilemma at Beijing University is similar to that in other higher education institutions in China in that the expanding and self-financed adult education division of the institution is staffed by many professors from the regular university who, since they earn as much in the adult division, tend to give less attention to their regular undergraduate teaching duties. Special funds to maintain academic teaching staff of superior talent, such as the Changjiang project, are helping to keep top professors in the academy. University faculty can also earn subsidies by publishing in top-notch academic journals.

Reforms to teaching are driven by a number of factors. There is a recognition that problems exist in university teaching. Scholarly papers, government reports, and popular newspapers make note of the fact that teaching methods are still traditional and content/examination-oriented and that modern society needs innovative thinkers. Returning overseas students are especially aware of this. Regular scholarly conferences discuss ideas about teaching from different parts of the world. There is now wider recognition, for example, that teaching and learning are separate activities and that they need to be analyzed differently, though, as part of a process. Government agencies and university presidents are gaining an understanding of the constraints and obstacles in the way of good teaching. The "quality education" movement has led to the formation of committees to improve higher education.

Student approaches to learning are changing as they become influenced by new ideas from home and abroad. The knowledge-centered approach to teaching is being replaced by learning as a social activity. A comment by a fourth year student at a major university typifies a common problem:

> the greatest problem with university teaching in China is that students are not taught to think for themselves; it is a shame that the 'stuffed duck approach' is still used. Many students do not know how to even pose questions; not to say they have the ability to solve problems, it is an educational loss.

The fact that the problem is recognized and articulated is positive in itself, and more effective methods to address the problem are still being developed.

The nature of academic relationships does affect both teaching and research. As Hong Shen (2000) noted, in China, academic relationships are not as close as personal relationships. In recent years, contacts on a personal level have started to appear in academia. Up to a point, professors have the right to deal with problems related to student learning. Students may attempt to influence their grades by extracurricular activities. However, Shen found that students' friends and even senior officials and administrators may also attempt to influence student grades by discussing them with the professors involved. Such a situation is not easy for faculty to contend with. Shen also found that while scholars are free to submit their research projects to appropriate bodies, the network of personal relations influences even the peer review and approval procedures except in some of the larger national institutions. Many faculty do not believe there is real freedom for projects (Shen, 2000).

Extra funds have been allocated to promote world-class university research. Project 211 was launched in 1995 to turn 100 universities in China into high-level research institutions. To date, 96 universities have arranged 602 research programs covering a variety of fields, including humanities, economics, politics, environmental and natural sciences, industry, and agriculture. For example, Tsinghua University has developed a radiation imaging technology system and has promoted educational cooperation between China and Britain. Projects will be further developed during the 10th Five Year Plan (2001–2005). Over 100 universities will be equipped with advanced research facilities and high speed computer networks for teaching and research to help universities improve academic standards (Cui, 2000).

As part of university efforts to raise revenue for research, many have created new businesses to generate revenue for their research, though some are coming to question whether universities should be running businesses. With better intellectual property rights legislation and enforcement, universities could move toward selling off their businesses and having their research staff develop their own relationship with the market. The market, however, is a source of grave concern. It is often the case that the stronger the market force, the less the sense of academic duty. Many professors become part-time company managers or hold other posts in business. Much time is spent at their second or even third jobs.

The service links between the university and industry have brought new sources of revenue, breaking the insularity of university life. Commercialization can also have negative effects on the core mission of the university if the best university professors have been lost to the market where salaries are higher. In some cases, notable professors are being attracted to join new and wealthier institutions, usually in the more prosperous southern regions of the country.

In China, the service function of the universities is now often referred to as mainly running the campus companies. This relates little to academic affairs in the traditional sense of the word. For the most part, Chinese academics seldom use their intellectual powers to protect their right to influence national policy-making. In a survey conducted by Hong Shen (1999) of Central University of Science and Technology, 67 percent of the staff respondents "thought that their research results could have no effect on policy making at a national, or even a university level. Furthermore, 16 percent of those questioned said that such results should not affect policy making."

In short, administrative efforts to implement measures to improve the quality of higher education confront an academic staff that is not well paid and even encouraged to supplement their income by taking second jobs. Despite that fact, assessment measures are increasingly common. For example, East China Normal University in Shanghai conducted an assessment of 570 professors and associate professors. The unqualified were given a period of time to work harder to improve themselves, otherwise, their academic title would be revoked. The university asked professors to report on their journal publications, research projects and grants, and their professional awards and to submit an oral report of their work within their particular academic unit after which the assessment committee classified professors and associate professors as either excellent, qualified, or unqualified (Wenhui, 2000).

ACADEMIC STAFF IN TWO CITIES

Illustrative comparisons can be made from data collected in surveys of members of the faculty of top universities in Shanghai (STU) and Beijing (BTU) (Postiglione, 2001). These cities are arguably the most international cities of China, and therefore we might expect that this has affected the view of academic staff. The survey was based on an adaptation of the Carnegie Foundation for the Advancement of Higher Education's International Survey of the Academic Profession (see Boyer, Altbach, & Whitelaw, 1994). In Shanghai, 276 academic staff across five departments of three major universities were sampled. In Beijing, 278 academic staff from a top university were sampled.

The contemporary concept of scholarship in most Western countries make little or no distinction between the activities of teaching and research. Yet, staff assessment at universities in China's two systems divides these two activities. Academic departments of top-tier universities in Hong Kong, for example, are allocated government resources on the basis of their research productivity, procurement of outside research funds, and number of postgraduate students completing their degree. In mainland China, universities are increasingly being told by government to take their wares to the marketplace in an effort to raise funds for their universities. Low- and no-budget research is still the norm, and under these conditions government funding remains the largest source for research and, therefore, has a major influence on the direction and scope of research. Most research journals and books are based at universities or research institutes rather than tied to associations as is the case in the West. Nevertheless, there are more similarities with regard to views concerning research than in all other areas surveyed. Over half of the STU and BTU faculties say their interests lean toward or lie primarily in research rather than teaching, not unexpected since they are all top-tier research universities.

Nearly equal numbers of STU and BTU faculty would agree that a strong record of successful research is important in staff evaluation at their institution, and that it is difficult for a person to achieve tenure if he or she does not publish. When asked if publications used for promotion are just counted and not qualitatively evaluated, less than 10 percent of STU and 14 percent of BTU faculty disagree. (At Hong Kong's top research universities, 23% disagreed with that statement; however, this figure was still lower compared to most countries in a recent international survey, except Russia [Postiglione, 1997].)

When it comes to the pressure to do research and how much is expected, STU and BTU faculty see themselves as more challenged than their counterparts at universities in other countries. On the international survey, only Chilean academics (38%) and Hong Kong academics (26%) felt under more pressure. Forty-four percent of BTU and almost 50 percent of STU faculty agreed that they frequently feel under pressure to do more research than they would actually like to do. This finding may partly be due to the difficulty of conducting research with scarce resources but also to pressure on staff to find ways to supplement their income that takes precious time away from doing research. They may not be expected to do regular research activity by their authorities, but when it comes to promotion, a lack of research publications will stifle their upward mobility, creating pressure on individual scholars.

While a large number of BTU and STU staff believe that regular research activity is expected of them, they see a shortage of research funds and facilities as a key constraint. Only about 17 percent of BTU and 10 percent of STU faculty agree that research funding is easier to get now than it was five years ago. Moreover, their rating of the quality of their research equipment and computer facilities contrasts sharply with places like Hong Kong where staff are near or at the top of the international ratings. Ratings of the quality of research facilities by STU and BTU staff were at or near the bottom of the countries in the international comparison.

Less than half of the Chinese faculty members agree that it is an especially creative and productive time in their fields. More than half of their counterparts in the other 14 countries surveyed had the opposite view. It should again be stressed that the mainland China universities surveyed were all top-tier institutions while the survey results were drawn from a more heterogeneous grouping of institutions. The situation is particularly acute in Shanghai where over half of STU staff agreed that if they had to do it all over, they would become an academic again, but only 42 percent indicated that their affiliation with their academic discipline is important to them. Despite the market economy, universities in China remain iron rice bowls. Only about 5 percent of STU staff have held regular academic appointments at more than two institutions (less than any of their international counterparts).

THE GLOBAL DIMENSIONS: STAFF PERSPECTIVES, TRADE OF SERVICES, TRANSNATIONAL MOBILITY, AND PARTNERSHIPS

There are many forms of globally linked academic activity, and some universities excel more than others. Indicators of these linkages include the number of foreign students and scholars that flow back and forth between university systems, the global character of the curriculum, and cross-national scholarly publishing in other languages (Postiglione, 1998).

Nearly 60 percent of BTU staff and 78 percent of STU academics reported that foreign students are enrolled frequently or occasionally at their institutions, a figure higher than reported by the more globally minded academics at Hong Kong's top three universities (32%). However, when the flow of students and scholars in the other direction is examined, the picture is quite different. STU and BTU staff reported that only about 42 percent of their students have studied abroad. This is understandable given the high cost of overseas study. When it comes to academic staff traveling abroad to study or do research, only 10 percent of those sampled said they had studied overseas for one or more months over the last three years. About 75 percent of the academics surveyed believe that the curriculum needs to be more international in its focus than it is at present.

When it comes to linking up to others in the global academy, most STU and BTU faculty indicated that connections with overseas scholars were very important to their professional work. For example, STU academics (95%) and BTU academics (57%) reported that international connections are important in faculty evaluations at their institutions. Finally, about 90 percent of STU academics and 87 percent of BTU academics indicated that they must read books and journals published overseas in order to keep up with developments in their fields.

China's universities are increasingly affected by global economic integration, domestic market reforms, and the stepped up academic exchanges with the global academy. There is growing interest in joint degree programs. The joint law degree offered by Temple University and the China Politics and Law University is one example. More global academic exchange may occur if a proposal to establish a special educational zone is supported (Shen, 2000). The motivation for such a zone, which is based on the success of China's four special economic and two special administrative zones, would be to stem the outflow of talent by permitting foreign universities to set up in China. This is especially important in the lead up to China's participation in the WTO. Joint projects with reputable foreign universities could also create competition that would increase the quality of teaching and scholarship (Hu & Shi, 1999).

CHINESE HIGHER EDUCATION FOR THE TWENTY-FIRST CENTURY: GLOBAL ARCHITECTURE WITH NATIONAL BRICKS AND MORTAR

China's higher education system is experiencing more change than it has since the Cultural Revolution when universities were turned into arenas of class struggle. The driving forces are domestic economic reforms, administrative decentralization, and globalization. The rapid expansion of higher education is at once a product of national conditions—human resource needs for economic development and social demand of a more educated populace—and a product of global circumstances—an interdependent global economy, entry into the World Trade Organization, the need to remain globally engaged and attract foreign investment, and rising world education standards. In an effort to establish "world class universities," the government has chosen to focus its resources on a limited number of institutions and let the rest fend largely for themselves. The central government-sponsored universities not only are getting more funds, attention, and special treatment, but they are also becoming globally networked. For example, Peking, Qinghua, and Fudan universities have joined the consortium *Universitas 21*, a group of international universities that is preparing to launch an Internet degree program.

China's higher education system is reacting to globalization in ways common to other countries. It has expanded its enrollments, rationalized its administrative structure, consolidated to achieve economies of scale, and encouraged the development of private colleges and universities. Further, it has broadened the curriculum to accommodate a diverse market of demands. It has introduced tuition fees and student loans and encouraged universities to raise more of their own revenue through joint ventures with other organizations. The government has provided more autonomy to innovate, demanded more accountability, propagated a series of laws governing higher education, and raised the qualifications of staff. Globally minded universities have increased the number of academic exchanges, developed telecommunications and the Internet capacity, become a member of international university consortia, introduced incentives and assessment practices for good teaching, made more research funds, and maintained a commitment to service.

However, a number of factors, including national development, academic traditions, state-university relations, and engagement in the international order, account for how these reactions have manifested themselves and are in some ways similar to situations in other developing countries. The central government maintains a strong sense of control over higher education. When autonomy is provided, universities do not always take advantage of it, partly due to the added responsibilities it incurs to the surrounding society. Consolidated universities have been constrained by old-fashioned politics so that they operate less efficiently than expected, private institutions have been plagued by low standards and profit motives, and measures to encourage good teaching have been hampered by opportunities for staff to engage in second jobs. There are other difficulties. Development of the social sciences has been stifled by lack of finances and organizational will at a time when such fields as gender and women's studies, anthropology, and environmental studies are necessary to meet emerging social development challenges. Expansion has led to more access; however, the proportion of poor, women, and minorities has not increased.

Many difficulties faced by Chinese higher education are shared by other developing countries. The global economy and international agreements, such as the WTO, may soon overtake universities in China. It is becoming clear to the government in China that globalization means that it is hardly possible for even their top universities to catch up to their global counterparts under current funding arrangements. This may leave little choice but to acquiesce in the business model of higher education. For-profit subsidiaries of major universities are symptomatic of what is to come. The commercialization of knowledge will continue to increase. The selling of knowledge products, partnership with corporations, education companies, increases in student fees, and the proliferation of private universities will be tempting ways for Chinese higher education to deal with future financial challenges. This can lead to significant altering and weakening of the university's mission to serve the public good.

In the market economies of East Asia, including Hong Kong and now mainland China, the leaders of the business community, many of whom have earned their degrees in top Western universities, will have less commitment to provide financial aid to their local universities without a profit motive, especially as the bulk of the business community has not fully recovered from the Asian economic crisis. In this environment, emerging academic systems face large obstacles. Teaming up in an effective way with universities in other parts of Asia, including Singapore, Malaysia, South Korea, and Thailand, to strengthen each other's efforts to build a knowledge economy will take many years if not decades (Postiglione & Mak, 1997). The top Chinese universities instead prefer to link up with Western universities while other universities in their national system are left struggling to survive. Also of special relevance to Chinese higher education is the fact that globalization has resulted in a change in the linkages that bind people and places and has changed the way that identities are moored. Chinese professors and research students increasingly move back and forth within the global academy, including mainland China, Hong Kong, Taiwan, Singapore, and many other developed economies around the globe. The way in which universities react to these scholars will affect their national identities within the new architecture of the global academy.

REFERENCES

Boyer, E. L., Altbach, P. A., & Whitelaw, M. J. (1994). *The academic profession in international perspective.* Princeton, NJ: Carnegie Foundation for the Advancement of Teaching.

Cai Bin & Tian Yong. (1999, April 5). Gaodeng jiaoyu: zhongguo jingji zengzhang de liang dian [Higher education: The bright spot in China's economic growth]. *Gaige neican* [*Internal Reference Materials on Reform*], no. 7, pp. 15–19. Quoted from *Chinese Education and Society, 33*(1) (2000), 53–60. New York: M.E. Sharpe.

China Education Yearbook. (1990). Beijing: People's Education Press.

Chinese Communist Party Central Committee. (1985). *Reform of China's educational structure.* Beijing: Foreign Language Press.

Cui Yu. (2000, December 7). Extra funds promote university research. *China Daily,* p. 2.

Green paper on education in China 2000. (2000). Beijing: Education Science Press.

Hayhoe, R. (1989). *China's universities and the open door.* Armonk, NY: M.E. Sharpe.

Hayhoe, R. (1996). *China's universities: A century of cultural conflict.* New York: Garland Publishers.

Hu Angang & Shi Zulin. (1999, January 20). Jiakuai fazhan jiasubiange woguo gaodeng jiaoyu [Heighten the development and reform of Chinese higher education]. *Neibu Canyue* [*Internal Reference Reading*], no. 4, pp. 11–16. Quoted from *Chinese Education and Society, 33*(1) (2000), 53–60. New York: M.E. Sharpe.

Ji Baocheng. (2000, December 22). Education must be reformed. *China Daily*, p. 4.

Li Jingwen. (2001). Jiaoyu xingzhi de bianhuan: Jiaoyu ji shi shiye you shichanye—jiaoyu zai ershiyi shijide fazhan chushi jiqi zhanlue sikao (xia) [The transformation of the nature of education: Education is both an undertaking (shiye) and an industry (chanye)—Development trends of 21st century education and its strategic considerations]. *Lingdao canyue* [*Leadership Reference Reading*], no. 11, pp. 16–18. Reprinted in *Chinese Education and Society 33*(1) (2000), 53–60. New York: M.E. Sharpe.

Li Lanqing. (2000). Guanyu shishi kejiao xingguo zhanlue gongzuo qingkuang de baogao [Report concerning the implementation of work strategies for the invigoration of the nation through science and technology]. *Zhongguo renmin gongheguo quanguo renmin daibiao dahui changwu weiyuanhui gongbao* [*Gazette of the Standing Committee of the National People's Congress of the People's Republic of China*], no. 5, pp. 533–543.

Min Weifang. (1997). China. In Gerard A. Postiglione and Grace C. L. Mak (Eds.), *Asian higher education* (pp. 37–55). Westport, CT: Greenwood Press.

Minban. (2000, November 20). Minban daxue mianlin de wenti [Problems facing Minban colleges and universities]. *Gaige neican* [Internal Reference Materials on Reform], pp. 39–40. Reprinted in *Chinese Education and Society, 33*(1) (2000), 53–60. New York: M.E. Sharpe.

National Report for Education for All: 2000 Assessment. (2000). Beijing: Ministry of Education and National Commission for UNESCO.

Pan Wei. (1999, March 20 & April 5). "Yi da er gong" bu yingshi gao jiao de gaige fangxiang (shang, xia) ["Large in size with a high degree of government administration" should not be the direction of higher education]. *Gaige neican* [*Internal Reference Materials on Reform*], no. 6, pp. 6–10, & no. 7, pp. 12–15. Reprinted in *Chinese Education and Society, 33*(1) (2000), pp. 53–60. New York: M.E. Sharpe.

Pepper, Suzanne. (1996). *Radicalism and educational reform in 20th century education.* New York: Cambridge University Press.

Postiglione, Gerard A. (1997). The academic profession in Hong Kong higher education within a period of profound change. In Philip Altbach (Ed.), *The academic profession: Studies from 14 countries* (pp. 193–230). Princeton, NJ: Carnegie Foundation for the Advancement of Teaching.

Postiglione, Gerard A. (1998, February). Maintaining global engagement in the face of national integration. *Comparative Education Review, 42*(1), 30–45.

Postiglione, Gerard A. (in press). Globalization and professional autonomy: The academy in three Chinese cities. *Education and Society.*

Postiglione, Gerard A., & Mak, Grace C. L. (Eds.). (1997). *Asian higher education.* Westport, CT: Greenwood Press.

Shen Hong. (2000). Academic freedom and academic responsibility in Chinese universities. In Organization for Economic Cooperation and Development (OECD) (Ed.), *Current issues in Chinese higher education* (pp. 21–35). Paris: OECD.

Shen Ronghua. (2000). Special education zone urged. *International Herald Tribune*,

July 25. Based on an article by Kazer, W. (2000). Shanghai advised to open field to foreigners to stop flood of talent heading overseas. *South China Morning Post*, July 25.

Task Force on Higher Education and Society. (2000). *Higher education in developing countries: Peril and promise*. Washington, DC: The World Bank.

Wenhui Daily. (2000, December 6). As summarized in the China Education News Archive, http://www.hku.hk/chinaed/chinaed_news/chinaednews_index_highered.htm.

World Bank (1996). *China higher education reform*. Washington, DC: The World Bank.

Wuxi Daily. (2000, June 13). As summarized in the China Education News Archive, http://www.hku.hk/chinaed/chinaed_news/chinaednews_index_ed_and_finance.htm.

Zhang Baoqing. (1999). Zhonggong zhongyang dangxiao—Baogao xuan [Party school of the Chinese Communist Party—selected reports], no. 1, January 10, pp. 2–17. Reprinted in *Chinese Education and Society, 33*(1) (2000), pp. 53–60. New York: M.E. Sharpe.

Part IV

Achieving Equity While Managing Expansion

Chapter 9

Equity Effects of Higher Education in Developing Countries: Access, Choice, and Persistence

Darrell R. Lewis and Halil Dundar

Almost all of higher education is in trouble but nowhere more so than in the developing world. Demand for higher education in the developing world has grown as more students complete secondary education and as national economies grow. At the same time, demand for public resources has been directed away from higher education to other pressing public needs. As a consequence, enrollments in most of the public universities have risen while financial resources per student have fallen dramatically. Across the developing world the number of students has more than tripled over the past 20 years while the amount of recurring public resources allocated to higher education has only increased in real terms by about 15 to 20 percent (World Bank, 1995). It has been estimated that real expenditures per student have declined by over 50 percent across most of the developing world (e.g., Albrecht & Ziderman, 1992; Winkler, 1990).

These dramatic financial declines in per student support have led to major concerns about diminished quality. At the same time there is little evidence of increased efficiency. In spite of the dramatic expansion of higher education across most developing countries, little has been said about the equity effects resulting from the recent transformations taking place in the higher education systems of most developing and transition countries. We first give an overview of the likely effects of the expansion on equity. Second, we briefly review the various strategies employed for expanding access. Third, we examine the problematic issues involved in improving equity through expanding access, providing greater student choice, and encouraging student persistence and degree completion. Finally, we conclude by reviewing the unresolved issues related to achieving equity via supply and demand policies.

EFFECTS OF EXPANSION ON EQUITY

Higher education expansion strategies in most developing countries have led to an unprecedented growth in student numbers. The average annual growth rate in student enrollment has been between 4 and 6 percent in most developing countries. Over the past 20 to 30 years this expansion has tripled student enrollments and in doing so undoubtedly provided extra places for students who come from traditionally underrepresented groups. Without adequate numbers of student places, it is impossible to provide greater equality of opportunities in higher education admissions. Such expansion policies, however, are a necessary but not a sufficient condition for the provision of greater equity in access to higher education. Other conditions, factors, and understandings about equity also must be present.

Almost everyone has some notion about the nature of equity. Most people believe that it refers to a dimension of "fairness" in the distribution of some good, service, or cost. But seldom do they have a conceptual understanding about what constitutes such fairness or how one might measure it. Does it mean, for example, "equal treatment of equals" whereby people are grouped and everyone within the group is treated the same? This line of argument is often used to support the "fairness" of national examinations for university admission or for arguing against tuition. However, even within small groups there will be individual differences. This results in equal treatment for unequal participants and this, in turn, can lead to counterproductive equity effects. Most people use equity to mean that unequal groups (or individuals) should have unequal treatment and that differential assistance should be given to less advantaged groups or individuals. Two problems arise here: The groups or individuals in need of differential treatment must be defined, and the differential treatment must be determined.

To address these problems, the equity effects that are likely to result from both the supply and demand sides of these issues must be systematically examined. It has been generally assumed that the expansion of national systems of higher education would contribute to greater equity in access through increased participation of traditionally disadvantaged groups such as women and students from lower socioeconomic status (SES) or from rural and developing regions. In many countries expansion was intentionally aimed at these results. Trow (1974) identified this process of change in higher education as movement from an "elite" to a "mass access" system.

In many cases, such supply side expansion policies certainly have helped to increase the number of students accessing higher education. But expanding access has not necessarily led to "mass access" systems in most developing countries, nor has it necessarily led to greater equality of opportunity. Only in a few countries, such as in Uruguay and Honduras, has there been any attempt to provide "open access" for all secondary graduates. In both of these cases there are still important equity issues relating to limited access for historically disadvantaged students (largely due to bottlenecks created by inadequate secondary schools).

Major equity problems in access, choice, and persistence in higher education continue to persist in most developing countries. There also are still serious questions about the demand side negative effects of various factors on students' secondary academic achievement, and on their access, choice, and graduation rates in higher education. Concerns about inequalities of participation and the persistence in higher education of traditionally disadvantaged groups continue to persist.

Students from these groups in most developing countries have been historically underrepresented in both applications and admissions to university-level education. In countries where the demand for higher education exceeds the supply, seats in higher education are often distributed by competitive examinations without any consideration to its equity effects. Even if an admissions examination is used, the probability of applicants from lower socioeconomic status passing the competitive exams has been estimated to be about three times lower than applicants from higher income groups in some countries (Ozgediz, 1980). Moreover, the possibilities for private tutoring and for attending higher quality private or public secondary schools have reinforced the fact that students from higher income groups are much more likely to pass the admissions exams and have more options for attending higher quality institutions than students from lower socioeconomic backgrounds.

Supply side policies to reduce social pressure for higher education often have been criticized as resulting in a deterioration of quality (see, for example, Castro & Levy, 1997; Williamson, 1987). The majority of universities, particularly those that have been newly established outside large metropolitan cities, often have been characterized as having low quality educational services. While many new institutions frequently lack the minimum level of educational resources for teaching and research, they are also frequently characterized as having "very high average costs" due to small size with diseconomies of scale and inefficient deployment of resources (Lewis & Dundar, 1995). The issue here has historically been whether there is, indeed, a natural trade-off between quality and efficiency. An equally important question is whether there is a trade-off between equity and efficiency, along with declining quality. More specifically, do expansion strategies provide greater access for disadvantaged groups? Or do they simply both increase inefficiency within the system and perpetuate existing inequities in access? Unfortunately, the effects of such "supply-side policies" have not yet been systematically examined or reported in most developing countries.

Historically, public policy makers in most developing countries have paid little attention to the "demand side" of the problem. In spite of an unprecedented growth of higher education during the past two to three decades, most developing countries' systems have not provided access to more than one-third of all applicants each year. Public policies often ignore the factors affecting student demand for higher education and assume that low cost-recovery with low to no tuition and fees and low financial aid policies (along with the availability of a large number of financial concessions to *all* students in the forms of subsidized food, housing, books, health care, and the like) will provide greater equity and equal access to a larger segment of the population who are coming from lower-middle or lower-income socioeconomic status.

Unfortunately, several studies in the economics of higher education indicate that, in the case of strong private demand and limited supply, such funding policies are likely to contribute to greater social *inequality*. In short, most observers of higher education in both developed (Hansen & Weisbrod, 1969) and developing (Brunner, 1996; Carlson, 1992; Psacharopoulos, 1980; World Bank, 1994) countries have argued that heavy subsidization of students in higher education means that poorer families who lack access to higher education support the more privileged. Democratized access fueled by public subsidies has not materially improved the participation of low-income students (Ziderman & Albrecht, 1995).

Another aspect of equality in access to higher education in most developing countries is that considerable underinvestment and low quality exists in many of their secondary levels (World Bank, 1990, 1993, 1995). Declines in the quality of primary and secondary education have had negative effects on equal access to higher education, especially in the context of very competitive university entrance examinations (e.g., Baloglu, 1990; TUGIAD, 1993). A recent Higher Education Council study in Turkey (YOK, 1990) reported, for example, that about 45 percent of all secondary school graduates in that country did not have "the required minimum academic knowledge" to pass the first stage of the entrance examination for study at the university level. This was attributed largely to a limited supply and decline in the quality of secondary education across the country. In order to compensate for the low quality of secondary education, more students have been attending private tutoring courses wherein the cost is often higher than the cost of attending higher education.

Most public institutions and politicians in the developing world have mistakenly argued that low or no tuition and fees have provided greater equality of educational opportunity through providing greater access to historically underserved populations. Such reasoning is incorrect. A rising tide in public higher education in developing countries does not necessarily raise all ships. To be sure, some additional low-income students have gained access to higher education through the enrollment expansions of the past 20 years, but the overwhelming public subsidy has accrued and continues to accrue primarily to students from middle- and high-income families.

Research has consistently shown that proportionate access to higher education by lower income groups is not materially improved by "no-tuition" policies. In fact, no-tuition systems usually lead to a regressive redistribution of income—i.e., poorer citizens who lack access to higher education support the more privileged (Brunner, 1996; Psacharopoulos, 1980; World Bank, 1994; Ziderman & Albrecht, 1995). Both the World Bank and the regional development banks have consistently pointed out that in most developing countries the middle and highest income groups overwhelmingly gain the most subsidy and subsequent benefits resulting from higher education.

This regressive effect of the subsidy results from several factors. First, many students from lower SES and disadvantaged families either drop out before graduating from high school, attend weak secondary schools, or fail competitive admission examinations. This results from the cumulative disadvantages of growing up in culturally disadvantaged families and communities and from attending weak secondary schooling. Even in those countries with open admission policies to their public universities (e.g., Honduras and Uruguay), well over half of all lower SES students drop out prior to graduation. Second, most of the private costs of higher education do not result from tuition and fees, but from transportation, food, and housing. Since most public universities are located in urban centers, these costs are more pronounced for low-income students coming from rural areas outside the main cities. And finally, the opportunity cost of attending higher education (i.e., foregone earnings) is also a material detriment for many students coming from low SES families.

Raising Tuition and Fees to Pay for the Expansion

Several commentators on higher education in developing countries (e.g., Carlson, 1992; Ziderman & Albrecht, 1995) have noted that high SES students are relatively price inelastic or insensitive to increases in tuition and fees. Evidence indicates that many of these middle- and higher-income students have both the ability and willingness to pay for higher tuition and fees. Most observers recommend increases in such private costs of up to 20 or 25 percent of their direct instructional costs.

But what would be the effect of such increases on low-income students? Given that most low-income students in both developing and developed countries are highly sensitive (or price elastic) to such price increases, it is likely that, without effective scholarship grant and loan programs in place, major losses would take place. Targeted grant and loan programs for low-income students with increased tuition and fees would not only generate more revenue for the institution and contribute to greater quality, but it would also contribute materially to enhanced access for low-income students with high abilities (Johnstone, 1998). This proposition is assuming, of course, that such loans and aid are widely publicized and implemented in fair and accurate ways and that there is an available and functioning capital market for any loan program.

In spite of these arguments in support of greater instructional cost recovery through expanded student fees, it is important to note that the total outcomes of higher education do not accrue solely to the individual students but to the larger society as well. There is a continuing need for public subsidy of higher education for the external effects resulting from many of these social benefits. The research and development work product coming from higher education in many developing countries is also important. It has been estimated by Castro and Levy (1997, p. 5) that higher education in Latin America contributes "roughly 80 percent of the research undertaken and a major share of the national science and technology effort." Equally important, many advocates for public higher education in developing countries (e.g., Birdsall, 1996; Castro & Levy, 1997; Tunnermann, 1996) have noted that the public university often plays a critical role in producing and disseminating national culture and in building a national identity. Nevertheless, the greatest beneficiaries of university instruction are the students themselves. Rates of both private and public returns have generally remained positive into the 1990s for most developing countries (Birdsall, 1996), even according to estimates given by critics of public higher education (World Bank, 1995).

Although Castro and Levy (1997) have noted that changes in policies on supply subsidization typically encounter severe political constraints in most developing countries, several countries have shown considerable progress in cost recovery through raising tuition and fees. In Chile, for example, only one-third of all funding for higher education comes from the government. Nearly 40 percent of all Latin American students are in private institutions, usually receiving no public funds or very little public support.

A major problem in several of the countries in transition has been the probable negative equity effect of their efforts in seeking alternative sources of instructional funding. In Poland, for example, higher education institutions have made remarkable progress with respect to the mobilization of alternative sources of funding to complement decreasing governmental allocations. They have been charging all students in extramural (i.e., evening or weekend) programs tuition and fees, while at the same time providing education with no tuition or fees to their regular day students. Today, over 50 percent of all students have been defined as being in such programs. It appears that the quality of education offered to extramural students is not on par with the programs offered to regular day students, except when "extramural" students are permitted to attend regular day classes. It appears that most universities have become dependent on these fee payments and that the fee-paying students are subsidizing regular day students.

Similarly, in most countries in transition student fees have been introduced even in the public higher education institutions. Although in most of these countries "constitutional provisions" prohibit universities from charging tuition and fees, many universities have nevertheless developed ruses for charging such fees. Many public institutions now are accepting an increasing proportion of their students on a fee-paying basis. As a rule, government-assisted places are supposed to be allocated to students with no fees on the basis of university entrance examinations. On the other hand, by the mid-1990s, it had been estimated that about 45 to 50 percent of all students entering state universities in Azerbaijan and Poland, about 30 percent of all students in the Kyrgyz Republic, and about 10 to 15 percent of all students entering state institutions in Russia, Belarus, and Hungary (based on personal conversations with key university administrators; Johnstone, 1998; Rysalieva & Ibraeva, 1999) were fee-paying students. Again, we know nothing about the equity effects of such cross-subsidies. Although data do not exist, it is highly probable that most of the fee-paying students have lower socioeconomic status backgrounds than most of those students found within the regular day school—resulting in strong regressive transfers of subsidy to higher-income families.

Other differences in family costs resulting from corruption in transition countries have also resulted in likely negative equity effects. It is reported (Balzer, 1998) that considerable corruption and bribery have been taking place in most of the economies in transition, particularly those from the former Soviet Union. For example, parents often have to pay informal fees (i.e., bribes) to get their children into university, either in a lump sum or in the form of high hourly rates paid to whoever authors the entrance examinations to "tutor" their child for the examinations. In Azerbaijan it is alleged that students at university also can pay their teachers for good grades, a top mark in an examination is supposed to cost between US$100 and $125. In Moldova bribes are alleged to vary in amount, depending on whether a degree in a particular field of study is expected to yield a high income. Having family wealth in these countries obviously helps getting your children admitted to university.

EXPANDING UNIVERSITY ENROLLMENTS DRIVEN BY EQUITY CONCERNS

Discussions about equity in the higher education of most developing countries have been largely hortative or only generalized as an important social goal of public policy. Seldom have measurable results been reported in the literature. To the extent that policy discussions about equity have occurred, concerns have focused on access and expanding enrollments with very little discussion concerning the other aspects of equity such as choice or persistence to graduation. As a consequence, very little public or institutional policy has been directed to expanding student choice or reducing student dropouts. Unfortunately, the proposed "equity policies" in most developing countries have not necessarily led to their expected results. Often the results are just the opposite. It is the purpose of the remaining parts of this chapter to more carefully examine these propositions.

Most central governments have addressed the issue of equality of educational opportunity in higher education largely by responding to the supply side of the problem and paying little attention to the demand side. Expanding higher education places has simply been assumed to automatically improve access to higher education for all groups, including historically disadvantaged groups. As a result of restructuring efforts within transition economies during the 1990s, strategies to increase enrollments while at the same time enhancing equity have typically followed one (or more) of five tracks: (1) sharp increases in enrollments in the existing institutions, (2) establishment of new universities, particularly outside of the major cities, (3) expansion of two-year vocational colleges, (4) expansion of nonconventional approaches to higher education such as distance education and evening programs, and (5) development of private higher education institutions.

The trend has clearly been toward greater student participation in the private sector. In a good number of countries the share of enrollments in private institutions has risen to more than half of the total. Unfortunately, there is little useful empirical data to indicate the likely equity effects of these rather dramatic changes.

Although it has been historically argued that expanding private higher education in developing countries will *necessarily* lead to greater problems of unequal educational opportunities, recent evidence indicates just the opposite is probably taking place. Tan and Mingat (1992), for example, estimated that for several selected Asian countries there was an *inverse* correlation between the share of cumulative public spending on education received by the 10 percent best-educated within the population and the extent of private financing in higher education. They have argued further that there is a relatively high correlation between gross enrollment rates in higher education and the extent of private financing in higher education within their sample of eleven Asian countries. All of this gives further support to the argument that private financing helps mobilize resources thus augmenting public funds for expanding coverage. Similar results also appear to be taking place in the regions of Latin America, the Middle East, and the transition countries of the former Soviet Union where the private sectors of higher education have recently expanded as their respective economies have undertaken economic growth or transition initiatives.

CONTINUING PROBLEMATIC ISSUES RELATING TO EQUITY

In spite of these growing concerns and perceptions about the equity outcomes that are alleged to be resulting from the recent expansion initiatives (Castro & Levy, 1997; World Bank, 1994), only limited information exists about the efficacy of these efforts. Nevertheless, we know that equality of educational opportunity in higher education can be measured across several dimensions and notions relating to institutional *access*, institutional and program *choice*, and *persistence* to graduation. Although these dimensions are often interrelated, in most cases they are measurable and have separate recognizable identities.

Access to Higher Education

A number of models have been developed in the United States to explain why and how individuals make decisions about accessing higher education. A useful summary of these models can be found within Hossler, Braxton, and Coopersmith (1989). They included detailed econometric and sociological models, often with multiple decision stages, in order to give conceptual understanding to the process. Their discussion provides insight into the factors that might influence the decision process about whether to participate in postsecondary education. This and other studies focusing on educational attainment and access to higher education have categorized the main determinants of such access into several major groups. These categories of influence have included students' socioeconomic status, ascribed attributes such as ability and gender, community context such as rural or urban setting, educational background characteristics, and labor-market and wage-rate effects.

Socioeconomic Status

One of the best-established results of educational attainment research is that the student's SES (largely determined by family income, occupations, and educational levels) is strongly related to educational achievement (e.g., Bidwell & Griedkin, 1988; Sewell & Hauser, 1975; Stevenson & Baker, 1992) in both developed and developing countries. Yet little is known about the success of the recent expansion policies in higher education in *reducing* inequalities among different social and income groups. We do know, for example, that a recent study by the Student Selection and Placement Center in Turkey (OSYM, 1992) indicated that individuals from higher SES families (as measured by parents' education level and income) have higher chances and opportunities to access higher education. We also know from a few other studies in developing countries such as Brazil (Holsinger, 1975; Jallade, 1982), Israel (Neuman, 1991), Kenya and Tanzania

(Armitage & Sabot, 1987), Greece (Patrinos, 1995), and the Philippines (Smith & Cheung, 1986) with similar expanding systems of higher education that the influence of socioeconomic status has not weakened in determining educational access and achievement. Basically, it has been argued that such a system expansion will make additional positions for some groups that have been historically underrepresented—but will it reduce inequalities in educational opportunities?

Over the past two decades, several studies in developing countries have examined which income groups benefited the most from subsidies for higher education. In four developing country cases (Chile, Colombia, Indonesia, and Malaysia), Psacharopoulos and Woodhall (1985) reported that the highest income groups in each country were overwhelmingly the major beneficiaries of highly subsidized or free higher education. In Colombia, for example, the top 20 percent income group in the country received over 60 percent of all higher education subsidies, while the bottom 40 percent received only 6 percent. In Indonesia, the top 30 percent income group received over 83 percent of the subsidization to higher education. Moreover, other data from the Philippines confirm this tendency toward skewed high socioeconomic status. At the publicly funded University of the Philippines, the average salary of the fathers of all students was two and a half times that of the general population and 77 percent of these fathers were in a "professional" class of employment (Smith & Cheung, 1986).

Tan and Mingat (1992) have illustrated that the degree of social bias in the educational systems of a country can be assessed by comparing various socioeconomic groups' shares of enrollments (at various levels) to their shares in the general population. In Thailand, for example, they note that in university education the professional group's share of enrollments is over 36 percent compared with their population share of only 3 percent. The farmers' share of university enrollment is about 11 percent compared with their population share of 69 percent. They found similar results in their work in the Philippines and India. Their work illustrates that the bias against children whose parents are farmers begins with dropouts and inadequate primary schooling. For children of laborers the bias largely takes place in the transition to secondary education. Where primary education is universal in some developing countries, differences among socioeconomic groups occur mostly in access to subsequent levels of education. These patterns in access suggest that the families of professional and business groups continue to strengthen their advantage in the transition from secondary to higher education.

The problem of achieving proportional social representation in higher education is very difficult and was not solved even in the former Soviet Union. Although standardized and historical data are hard to uncover, it appears as if the nature of the population attending universities in Russia has not changed materially since the 1930s. University students with professional family backgrounds were 2.4 times overrepresented in 1939 and still 2.1 times overrepresented in 1970. Policies of deliberately putting students with "proletarian" backgrounds at an access advantage in the 1930s may have had a short-term positive equity effect whereby 1939 university students with manual labor backgrounds were overrepresented by 10 percent compared with their percentage within the population. Nevertheless, by 1964 they were again underrepresented by over 35 percent.

As we noted earlier, similar problems and concerns have arisen in the developed world. Most European countries, for example, have historically offered free higher education as a perceived means of expanding access to working-class students, at least prior to several efforts toward cost recovery in the late 1980s and the 1990s. Nevertheless, several earlier studies (in Sweden, Germany, and the United Kingdom) consistently found that participation rates among working-class students had not increased, and that most of the subsidies had been received largely by middle- and high-income students (Ziderman and Albrecht, 1995). In the United States, university students from professional backgrounds were 2.5 times overrepresented in 1957; similar students in the United Kingdom were overrepresented by 2.4 times in 1979 and in France they were 2.4 times overrepresented in 1965 (World Bank, 1995). Experience and studies have consistently shown that access to higher education by lower socioeconomic groups has not improved materially with low tuition and fees.

Gender

Do women and men with similar academic abilities and achievement have similar chances to succeed and access higher education? In most developing countries the answer to this question is still largely unknown, although Tan and Mingat (1992) have reported that there is a positive correlation between female share of enrollment in higher education and per capita GNP in selected Asian countries. Although women's access to higher education in Turkey, for example, has improved substantially over the past three decades, the proportion of female enrollments in higher education is still low compared to most developed countries (Baloglu, 1990; World Bank, 1993). The proportion of female students in higher education increased from 18.7 percent in the 1969–1970 academic year to 27.5 percent in 1981–1982, and to 35 percent in the 1991–1992 period (OSYM, 1992). As is common in most developed and developing countries, the majority of women students are studying in the general arts, social sciences, and humanities.

Evidence in many countries has indicated that participation of women in higher education is influenced by many factors, including educational, cultural, and economic influences (Subbarao, Raney, Dundar, & Haworth, 1993). Most important, disparities between men and women in higher education largely come from previous inequities in their education. A recent study by the World Bank (1993) on women in other developing countries noted that the bottleneck for women's access to higher education was largely at the transition from primary to secondary school.

Rural Location of Students

In many countries there are substantial differences in access to higher education by location as individuals from urban areas and developed regions of the countries have better access to secondary and higher education institutions. Many more high quality secondary schools are located in urban and developed regions of the country and students from those schools perform much better on university entrance examinations. Moreover, the absence of a nearby postsecondary school tends to discourage and restrict access to higher education for many individuals regardless of parental SES, as Smith and Cheung (1986) found in the Philippines.

Equally important, location can have a "double negative impact" for access on some historically disadvantaged groups. Women and students from lower SES family conditions in rural areas and developing regions may have two serious disadvantages for attending higher education due to (1) the probable low quality of their secondary education and (2) the limited possibility for attendance because of not having a nearby postsecondary school.

Moreover, there is clear evidence in the literature (e.g., Cuccaro-Alamin & Choy, 1998; Hearn, 1994) that the strongest economic influence on access is not tuition and fees but rather the other private costs of attendance; and staying at or near one's home would clearly minimize such additional costs. Several Polish studies found that in the case of full-time students living away from home, parental contributions were very high and they could even exceed a quarter of the family budget. "In kind" contributions by parents for students living at home, on the other hand, reduced the cost burden associated with university-level studies to around 6 percent of the family budget (Paszkowski, 1987).

The negative effects of such location-specific disparities in education in most developing countries have been long recognized, and major attempts have been made to reduce them. For example, one of the goals of both the 1982 and 1992 expansions of higher education in Turkey was to provide greater access to students outside the three large urban centers. In spite of the substantial expansion of higher education, often in rural areas of the country, there are still considerable regional disparities in Turkey today (Baloglu, 1990; Dundar & Lewis, 1999).

Educational Attributes of Students

The educational attributes of students can be best understood by examining several of their major components in the context of developing countries. These would include, first and most notably, the quality of the secondary educational experience. They would also relate to the nature (i.e., academic or vocational track and intensity) of such experiences. The quality and nature of educational provision at the secondary level are very important factors in access to higher education (e.g., Alexander, Holupka, & Pallas, 1987; Hearn, 1991). It is known, for example, that attending a university is more likely to be "a given" for students who attend elite private high schools than for students who attend public high schools (McDonough, 1997). Even after controlling for academic characteristics, socioeconomic background, and educational aspirations, students attending private high schools are more likely than their peers attending public high schools to enroll in four-year university training (Falsey & Heyns, 1984).

Assessing the age cohort participation rate in higher education does not tell the full story. For example, the enrollment rate for an age cohort of university students in Turkey has been estimated at only about 10 percent. However, since only 50 percent of that age cohort would have attended secondary school, the effective participation in higher education among those who actually completed secondary school was 20 percent (World Bank, 1999). The remaining half of that age cohort had already been eliminated from the opportunity of a higher education because of inadequate or unavailable secondary education. Similar stories exist throughout the developing world.

Psacharopoulos (1994) reviewed several studies in developing countries that compared "academic or general" secondary education to "technical or vocational" secondary education and found that, on average, rates of returns to general education were much higher (i.e., 16% compared to 11% for vocational education). Costs were the principal factor; vocational education is far more expensive to provide than more general academic programs. The higher economic benefits of academic programs parallel the equity benefits accruing from strong academic secondary programs, facilitating access to higher education as well. Many countries with strong upper secondary vocational training programs, such as in Poland, have disproportionately larger numbers of students with lower SES participate in these programs. In such cases, the secondary vocational tracking system effectively precludes many low SES students from success on the entrance examination for higher education.

Access to an Academic Curriculum

Adelman (1999) examined whether and how the nature of the secondary curriculum might influence attendance and persistence in the higher education system of the United States. Using data from a nationally stratified longitudinal sample called the High School and Beyond/Sophomore Cohort (from 1980 until the cohort was roughly age 30 in 1993), Adelman found that the nature of the high school curriculum had a profound effect on both access and completion in higher education. He found that the impact of a high school curriculum of high academic intensity and quality had the highest positive association with both access and completion, greater than any other single variable including socioeconomic status. It is highly likely that such circumstances exist in most developing countries as well.

Access to Private Tutoring

Private tutoring is a form of education outside of formal schooling employed to prepare students for the university entrance examination. This form of education is a type of "shadow education" and is commonly used to assist access to higher education in many countries (e.g., Japan, Taiwan, South Korea, Hong Kong, Turkey, Greece, and Russia and most of the other countries in transition) where the supply of spaces is limited and spaces are allocated through very competitive centrally administered examinations (Dundar & Lewis, 1999; Stevenson & Baker, 1992).

In several developing countries, the importance of this type of education has dramatically increased since the early 1970s as increasing numbers of students receive some private tutoring to prepare for university education. A report in Turkey (OSYM, 1992) indicated that students who took such private tutoring were, indeed, more successful in the university entrance examination than students who did not take such tutoring. However, without a causal modeling analysis, it is premature to arrive at such a conclusion since the majority of these students might have attended higher quality secondary schools or have come from higher SES families. Nevertheless, the private costs of such tutoring is often higher than attendance in many post-secondary institutions. And such cost burdens are frequently very high for low SES students.

Effects on Access of Changing Labor Markets

Changing labor markets have been found to have important effects on the enrollment patterns of higher education in most developed countries (e.g., Boesel & Fredland, 1999; Chressanthis, 1986; Corazzini, Dugan, & Grabowski, 1972; Hossler, 1984). It has been shown clearly that during periods of high unemployment, such as during the world recession of the late 1970s, students are more likely to attend a postsecondary institution rather than be unemployed. Economists have explained this effect as resulting from the materially reduced "opportunity cost" of earnings while being unemployed. Postsecondary attendance is much less expensive because earnings are not foregone.

It is highly probable that historically disadvantaged prospective students are also those individuals most likely to be unemployed in both developed and developing economies when aggregate unemployment increases. Thus, it appears that increases in national unemployment may induce larger numbers of low SES and other disadvantaged students to attend higher education. On the other hand, in most developing countries today, economic development and employment are rising. Such market conditions seem to be contributing to raising the opportunity costs for higher education. Beyond the other income and social demand effects (i.e., increased demand for access to higher education as well as for other social services) resulting from an expanding economy, it appears that all students who are or who have prospects for employment also will be experiencing rising opportunity costs for attendance.

Effect of Changing Wage Rates on Access

It is also important to recognize that wage rates have changed over time and across industries in both developed (Boesel & Fredland, 1999) and developing countries (Psacharopoulos, 1985) as their economies have experienced increases in both their national incomes and employment. In most developing countries the wage rates of university graduates are not only positive, but frequently very high (Bennell, 1995; Psacharopoulos, 1989, 1994). The net effect of such changes in most countries has resulted in an *increasing* "wage gap" between high school graduates and university graduates in the labor market (Psacharopoulos, 1994). Moreover, these wage gaps have increased over time when viewed across industries; those jobs that require higher levels of education have had both their productivity and wages increase at a faster rate. This has been particularly true in transition economies. Today thousands of students in these countries are attempting to access business schools and other applied social science fields because of their rising industry wage rates.

In summary, there have been increasing economic incentives for individuals in developing countries to access higher education, but we have limited evidence about the proportion of these new enrollees coming from historically disadvantaged populations. Lower SES students are more sensitive to price and cost changes, so as opportunity costs of foregone earnings might increase, one would expect that proportionately fewer low SES students would enroll. As the wage gap and rates of return increase on behalf of higher education graduates, this also will lead to greater variance in income patterns across the country's entire population (Psacharopoulos & Woodhall, 1985).

Choice Making within Higher Education

Consumer choices within higher education have often been neglected, but nowhere more so than in developing countries. The question of choice relates not only to which institution one attends, but also to the program and courses in which one actually participates. Young people's choices of what and where to study are often based on flimsy information. Information about programs and institutions, academic reputation, dropout rates, and labor market prospects are not easily available in most developing countries.

Financial aid offered to students either by reduced tuition or special grant has been an important institutional instrument used by many colleges and universities to recruit not only the best and brightest students but also for recruiting those student populations with priorities under affirmative action policies. Researchers (Lay and Maguire, 1980; Leslie et al., 1977) have generally concluded that among low-income students, both costs (i.e., levels of tuition and other private expenditures) and the availability of financial aid were among the most important reasons for selecting a particular institution. As one would expect, the largest proportion of low-income students were found at public two-year junior colleges and vocational schools where tuition was low and aid was high. In fact, a powerful argument can be made for a high-tuition and high-aid system in the higher education of both developed and developing nations because of its ability to not only ensure access for low-income students through high-aid, but also because it gives greater choice in selecting programs and institutions to high-ability students from lower income families. This has been particularly true in the private sector of developed countries wherein high tuition receipts from high-income students are often used for aid to low-income students. Although most of the "equity in choice literature" has been drawn from studies in developed countries, there is no reason to believe that similar circumstances in the majority of developing countries would necessarily result in different outcomes.

Others (e.g., Chapman & Jackson, 1987; Hearn, 1984) have found that with the most academically talented students the roles of financial aid and tuition are clearly not as important. They also found that most academically talented students come from middle and higher SES families. They concluded that for these students perceived quality and reputation has a greater impact on the choice of institution than does the net cost (i.e., high tuition with high aid). This was found to be true in Turkey as well. Recently when students were surveyed and asked if they would have been willing to pay much higher rates of tuition if they could have gotten into a higher choice (presumably a higher quality) university or program, a very large proportion indicated a willingness to pay larger sums of money in tuition and fees (Council on Higher Education, 1998). Again, it is instructive to remember that high SES students are not as price sensitive as low SES students.

Still others have demonstrated that location is an important criterion in choosing which postsecondary institution to attend. In some cases, particularly for low SES and low ability students, it has been argued (e.g., Cuccaro-Alamin & Choy, 1998; Hearn, 1994) that location overwhelms most other factors in choice of a postsecondary institution. Postsecondary vocational training programs and two-year colleges, for example, are often situated in rural areas so as to ensure equity in access for disadvantaged populations. But often overlooked in reviewing such settings are the major negative effects on equity in student choice and graduation.

There is a clear body of literature that indicates that student tracking takes place and very few of these students go on to four- and five-year degrees where the largest socioeconomic payoffs result. In reality, most developing countries have very inflexible courses of study. When a student either drops out of a program or even finishes it (particularly at most two-year schools), that student is required to start over again if undertaking a new program or set of courses in a four- or five-year program. The notion of transferring credits or courses both between and within universities is seldom permitted in most developing countries. This inflexibility in the curriculum is most pronounced in economies in transition. Thus, again we have a set of policies based on equity concerns, the net effect of which is largely negative with limited options (i.e., precluding choices for program and university degrees) for historically disadvantaged students.

Persistence and Completion in Higher Education

Persistence and degree completion in higher education is often a forgotten dimension of equity in both developed and developing countries. Nevertheless, the reasons for focusing on persistence and degree completion should relate principally to equity and not just efficiency issues. In the United States, for example, where over 75 percent of high school graduates are currently entering postsecondary institutions under an essentially open admissions system, their rates of completion are dramatically less than their rates of admission. While the "college access gap" between Whites and Blacks and Whites and Latinos in the United States has closed from the 11 to 15 percent range to 5 percent over the past two decades, the "degree completion gap" remains stubbornly high at over 20 percent (Smith, 1996). In the developing countries such gaps relating to differing subpopulations undoubtedly also exist, though the literature is very limited.

Over nearly two decades of research in the United States persistently demonstrated that the power of a student's prior academic background overwhelms the predictive power of demographic variables (e.g., gender, race, socioeconomic status) in relation to test performance (Alexander and Pallas, 1984), postsecondary access, and college completion (Alexander, Riordan, Fennessey, & Pallas, 1982). Surprisingly, few other researchers have paid much attention to this rich body of literature. Nevertheless, in his most recent study with the High School and Beyond cohort data set, Adelman (1999) found that the impact of a high school curriculum of high academic intensity and quality was indeed a very powerful predictor of college and university completion. He found that "academic resources" (the composite of high school curriculum, test scores, and class rank) produced a stronger association with a bachelor's degree completion than did socioeconomic status. "Students from the lowest two SES quintiles who are also in the highest academic resources quintile (at the secondary level) earn bachelor's degrees at a higher rate than a majority of students from the top SES quintile" (Adelman, 1999, vii). The impact of a high school curriculum of high academic intensity and quality on degree completion was even greater for African-American and Latino students than it was for White students.

Several developing countries recently have become concerned about their largely invisible dropout rates and are attempting to develop better accountability and reporting systems. In Chile, for example, over 60 percent of all secondary school graduates are going on to universities, but only about half are graduating. Some of these failures occur quite late in their regular university programs. *The Economist* recently (Dropping out, 1999) reported on a five-year accountability program being funded by a loan from the World Bank. Chile is attempting to develop a national accreditation system for its universities along with a strong publicity scheme for reporting on such statistics as dropout rates. Similarly, Turkey has developed public policy requirements as a part of their national reform initiatives for higher education, requiring all students in four-year programs to complete their programs within a six-year time period.

In addition to better and more public information about institutional dropouts, Chile is attempting to address another reason for its high level of dropouts—namely the inflexible nature of its higher education curriculum. Because midstream program changes are virtually impossible, a student who has chosen the wrong route must start over again, "a costly procedure for which few have the nerve or the resources" (Dropping out, 1999, p. 34). The nation's largest public university, the University of Chile, is trying to address this problem by introducing an initial two-year curriculum common to all students. Although it is expected that this may lengthen many of the university's programs to at least five or six years, they are hopeful that the results will be worthwhile, with more curricular options (especially for less informed low SES students), fewer dropouts, and more broadly educated students.

UNRESOLVED ISSUES RELATING TO EQUITY

It is clear that higher education in most developing countries continues to face a number of unresolved but crucial questions concerning issues of equity in access, choice, and persistence. What are the most likely factors determining access to higher education? Who goes where? Does the system of publicly funded higher education with free or nominal tuition schemes and substantial private concessions provide equity in opportunities such as access and choice-making between men and women, between rural and urban students, and between different socioeconomic groups? Who benefits from and who finances higher education? Have the recent expansions of higher education helped generate a greater number of students from traditionally disadvantaged groups? Are historically disadvantaged students given access, only to drop out before graduation? All of these questions are still largely unexamined in most developing countries.

After rapid growth during the past three decades, conditions of financial stringency have arisen that appear to be impairing further expansion and improvement of most systems. Most of the new types of postsecondary institutions and programs established with no to low fees were allegedly expanded to provide greater access to traditionally disadvantaged students who might not otherwise participate in higher education. But the fruits of these efforts have been largely unmeasured. Institutional fiscal constraints need not necessarily undermine or compromise greater student access, choice, and persistence.

There has been rapid, and in some cases dramatic growth in enrollments, programs, and institutions with only limited progress on equalizing educational opportunities for disadvantaged groups. The data in most developing countries indicate that educational opportunities for traditionally disadvantaged groups are yet to be improved in material ways and in some countries the situation has declined. Students from these groups have continued to be underrepresented among both the applicants and admitted students for university-level education. The probability of applicants from lower socioeconomic status passing competitive entrance examinations has been estimated in some countries (e.g., Turkey) to be about three times lower than applicants from higher income groups; this participation rate does not appear to have materially changed over the past two decades. Most students from lower SES and rural areas still have limited options and choices and are still found predominantly in two-year or less vocational schools or in high-tuition and fee-paying distance education or evening programs. Most of those low SES students who do get access are participating in lower quality programs and schools.

Even the funding policies and procedures of higher education in most developing countries contribute to *greater* social inequality. Even as an overwhelming majority of all students in higher education come from middle- and high-income families, there has been limited success in cost recovery through tuition or fees in most developing countries. Major public subsidies and postschool benefits are being directed to the highest SES students while a disproportionate number of low SES students are being denied access, limited in their choice of program or institution, not graduating, or paying high fees through evening programs. In addition, considerable underinvestment continues to exist in the secondary schools across most countries, especially in the rural areas of the developing world (World Bank, 1990). The need continues to be high for strong reforms in the financing of public higher education in most developing countries and the need to address the equity effects of current practices is urgent.

At the least, public policy attention needs to be focused on the major target areas of equity concern that we have reviewed throughout this chapter. Several specific initiatives to advance equity are identified in the following proposals relating to supply and demand policies in higher education.

Supply Policies

- Require each institution in postsecondary education to define its unique mission and goals in written and approved form so that it might better address its productivity with regard to instruction, research, outreach, and student equity concerns. Explicitly recognize that all such schools cannot aspire to becoming national and international class "universities" with major research and service missions. Many such institutions might become regional-class "universities" with major instructional and equity missions.
- Provide appropriate rules and regulations that would give each of the individual institutions in higher education greater accountability, incentives, and responsibility for using its resources flexibly in addressing its mission and goals. Such deregulation is necessary in most countries so as to increase the autonomy of universities in order to permit greater flexibility in designing curricula, programs of study, and alternative sources of revenue.
- Relax the barriers to moving between tracks, levels, and programs. Most of the educational systems in countries in transition from the former Soviet Union, as well as other developing countries, tend toward early and narrow specialization. This policy needs to be revisited. It conflicts with what almost all industrialized countries have come to understand as the preferred education for a modern economy and society. Each country, for example, needs to examine in what ways it might replace costly specialized secondary vocational education programs with less expensive training that integrates academic and vocational education and thus reduce the heavy tracking that often begins as early as the eighth and ninth grades.
- Encourage and urge all universities to develop relatively common curricula for the first two years of study so that students can avoid tracking systems and delay decisions on major courses of study.

Demand Policies

- Raise tuition and user fees at all public post-secondary institutions to approximately 20 or 30 percent of instructional costs and concurrently use some of the raised funds for means-tested qualifications for financial assistance. Address the possibility of lower tuition and fees for lower SES students. An important complication is that many countries—especially those from the former Soviet block—have constitutional provisions that guarantee free higher education. These countries must change or find ways to circumvent such provisions while at the same time providing access to qualified low-income students.
- Provide effective (i.e., highly visible) financial assistance via scholarship and loan programs to low SES students for food and housing, especially for those students

unable to live at home. An important key to a high-aid policy for low-income students is a strong information dissemination effort that is very visible.

- Target priority use of public resources on further developing and strengthening the secondary schools across the entire population so that every high school age student has access to a qualified general secondary school.
- Identify the top two graduates from each secondary school in the country for automatic admission into competitive universities with financial assistance through qualified means/incomes testing. This is essentially an affirmative action effort for historically disadvantaged but competitively qualified students.
- Adopt accreditation systems across each of the subsystems of higher education in each country so that students have better information about standards and choices and so that the public sector has some influence on institutional quality control.
- Develop common credits and courses across each system so that students might have the capacity for transfer and career changes.
- Modernize the entrance examination system. For those countries that do not have national systems of entrance examinations, attention needs to be given to standardizing both the examination and its process. To permit each university to write its own tests and administer them through oral interviews encourages the process to become both corrupt and discriminatory. Many such tests discriminate against the poor, are absent psychometric standards, and favor a privileged elite. Objective and fair examinations for entry into university are essential for equality of educational opportunities.

Although there are many other possible recommendations for policy changes in higher education that might relate to enhancing both the internal and external efficiency and efficacy of higher education, the above policy recommendations are those that most directly relate to the many equity concerns noted in this chapter. Given that many of the problems pertaining to equity in access, choice, and persistence relate to family circumstances of poverty, location, gender, and ethnicity, carefully developed policies of affirmative action are still possible. The need for such changes and reform is self-evident and urgent in most developing and transition countries.

REFERENCES

Adelman, C. (1999). *Answers in the tool box: Academic intensity, attendance patterns, and bachelor's degree attainment.* Washington, DC: Office of Educational Research and Improvement, U.S. Department of Education.

Albrecht, D., & Ziderman, A. (1992). *Funding mechanisms for higher education.* Washington, DC: The World Bank.

Alexander, K. L., Holupka, S., & Pallas, A. M. (1987). Social background and academic determinants of two-year versus four-year college attendance: Evidence from two cohorts a decade apart. *American Journal of Education,* 96, 56–80.

Alexander, K. L., & Pallas, A. M. (1984). Curriculum reform and school performance: An evaluation of the "new basics." *American Journal of Education, 92*, 391–420.

Alexander, K. L., Riordan, C., Fennessy, J., & Pallas, A. M. (1982). Social background, academic resources, and college graduation: Recent evidence from the National Longitudinal Survey. *American Journal of Education, 91*, 315–333.

Armitage, J., & Sabot, R. (1987). Socioeconomic background and the returns to schooling in two low-income economies. *Economica, 54*, 103–108.

Baloglu, Z. (1990). *Turkive'de egitim*. Istanbul: Turkiye Sanayicileri ve Isadamalari Dernegi.

Balzer, H. (1998). *Poverty, education, and white collar trends in post-communist transitions*. Unpublished manuscript prepared for workshop on transition countries at Georgetown University.

Bennell, P. (1995). *Using and abusing rates of return: A critique of the World Bank's 1995 education sector review* (Working Paper No. 22). London: Institute of Development Studies.

Bidwell, C., & Griedkin, N. (1988). The sociology of education. In N. J. Smelser (Ed.), *Handbook of sociology*. Newbury Park, CA: Sage Publications, pp. 449–471.

Birdsall, N. (1996). Public spending on higher education in developing countries: Too much or too little? *Economics of Education Review, 15*(4), 407–419.

Boesel, D., & Fredland, E. (1999). *College for all: Is there too much emphasis on getting a 4-year college degree?* Washington, DC: National Library of Education, U.S. Department of Education.

Brunner, J. J. (1996). Education in Latin America during the decade of 1980. In R. Kent (Ed.), *Los temas criticos de la educacion superior en America Latina*. Mexico City: FLACSO and Fondo de Cultura Economica.

Carlson, S. (1992). *Private financing of higher education in Latin America and the Caribbean*. Washington, DC: The World Bank.

Castro, C., & Levy, D. C. (1997). *Higher education in Latin America and the Caribbean: A strategy paper*. Washington, DC: Inter-American Development Bank.

Chapman, R. C., & Jackson, R. (1987). *College choices of academically able students: The influence of no-need financial aid and other factors* (Research Monograph No. 10). New York: The College Board.

Chressanthis, G. A. (1986). The impacts of tuition rate changes on college graduate head counts and credit hours over time and a case study. *Economics of Education, 5*(2), 205–217.

Corazzini, A. J., Dugan, D. J., & Grabowski, H. G. (1972). Determinants and distributional aspects of enrollment in U.S. higher education. *Journal of Human Resources, 7*, 26–38.

Council on Higher Education. (1998). *Parental income, educational expenditures, and finance and job expectations of university students*. Second Industrial Training Project, 2922-TU. Ankara: The Council of Higher Education, Republic of Turkey.

Cuccaro-Alamin, S., & Choy, S. (1998). *Postsecondary financing strategies: How undergraduates combine work, borrowing, and attendance*. Washington, DC: National Center for Education Statistics, U.S. Department of Education.

Dropping out. (1999, May 1). *The Economist*, pp. 34–35.

Dundar, H., & Lewis, D. R. (1999). Equity, quality and efficiency effects of reform in Turkish higher education. *Higher Education Policy, 4*(5), 1–24.

Falsey, B., & Heyns, B. (1984, April). The college channel: Private and public schools reconsidered. *Sociology of Education, 57*, 111–122.

Hansen, W. L., & Weisbrod, B. A. (1969). The distribution of the costs and benefits of public higher education: The case of California. *Journal of Human Resources, 4*(2), 176–191.

Hearn, J. C. (1984). The relative roles of academic, ascribed and socioeconomic characteristics in college destination. *Sociology of Education, 57*, 22–30.

Hearn, J. C. (1991). Academic and non-academic influence on the college destinations of 1980 high school graduates. *Sociology of Education, 64*, 158–171.

Hearn, J. C. (1994). Emerging variations in postsecondary attendance patterns: An investigation of part-time, delayed, and nondegree enrollment. *Research in Higher Education, 33*, 657–687.

Holsinger, D. B. (1975). Education and the occupational attainment process in Brazil. *Comparative Education Review, 19*, 267–275.

Hossler, D. (1984). *Enrollment management: An integrated approach*. New York: The College Board.

Hossler, D., Braxton, J., & Coopersmith, G. (1989). Understanding student college choice. In J. C. Smart (Ed.), *Higher education: Handbook of theory and research* (Vol. V). New York: Agathon Press.

Jallade, J. P. (1982). Basic education and income inequality in Brazil. *World Development, 10*, 187–197.

Johnstone, D. B. (1998). *The financing and management of higher education: A status report on worldwide reforms*. Washington, DC: The World Bank.

Lay, R., & MaGuire, J. (1980). Identify the competition in higher education. *College and University, 56*(1), 53–65.

Leslie, L. L., Johnson, G. P., & Carlson, J. (1977). The impact of need-based student aid upon the college attendance decision. *Journal of Education Finance, 2*, 269–286.

Lewis, D. R., & Dundar, H. (1995). Economies of scale and scope in Turkish universities. *Education Economics, 3*(2), 133–157.

McDonough, P. M. (1997). *Choosing colleges: How social class and schools structure opportunity*. Albany: State University of New York Press.

Neuman, S. (1991). Parental background, educational attainments and returns to schooling and to marriage: The case of Israel. *Applied Economics, 23*, 1325–1334.

OSYM. (1992). *1991 vuksekogretim ogrenci secme ve verlestirme sinavi: Adaylarin sosyo-ekonomik ozellikleri ve sinavdaki basarilari*. Ankara: Student Selection and Placement Center [OSYM].

Ozgediz, S. (1980). Education and income distribution in Turkey. In E. Ozbudun & A. Uluson (Eds.), *The political economy of income distribution in Turkey* (pp. 501–524). New York: Holmes & Meier.

Paszkowski, J. (1987). On the issue of individual costs of study. *Zycie Szkoly Wyzszej, 35*(2), 99–105.

Patrinos, H. A. (1995). Socioeconomic background, schooling, experience, ability and monetary rewards in Greece. *Economics of Education Review, 14*(1), 85–91.

Psacharopoulos, G. (1980). *Higher education in developing countries: A cost-benefit analysis* (Working Paper No. 440). Washington, DC: The World Bank.

Psacharopoulos, G. (1985). Returns to education: A further international update and implications. *The Journal of Human Resources, 20*(4), 584–604.

Psacharopoulos, G. (1989). Time trends of the returns to education: Cross-national evidence. *Economics of Education Review, 8*(3), 225–231.

Psacharopoulos, G. (1994). Returns to investment in education: A global update. *World Development, 22*(9), 1325–1343.

Psacharopoulos, G., & Woodhall, M. (1985). *Education for development*. London: Oxford University Press.

Rysalieva, S., & Ibraeva, G. (1999). *Educational financing in the Kyrgyz Republic*. Paris: International Institute for Educational Planning, UNESCO.

Sewell, W. H., & Hauser, R. (1975). *Education, occupation, and earnings: Achievement in the early career*. New York: Academic Press.

Smith, H. L., & Cheung, P.P.L. (1986). Trends in the effects of family background on educational attainment in the Philippines. *American Journal of Sociology, 91*(6), 1387–1408.

Stevenson, D. L., & Baker, D. P. (1992). Shadow education and allocation in formal schooling: Transition to university in Japan. *American Journal of Sociology, 97*(6), 1639–1657.

Subbarao, K., Raney, L., Dundar, H., & Haworth, J. (1993). *Women in higher education: Progress, constraints, and promising approaches*. Washington, DC: The World Bank, Education and Social Development Department.

Tan, J., & Mingat, A. (1992). *Education in Asia: A comparative study of cost and financing*. Washington, DC: The World Bank.

Trow, M. (1974). Problems in the transition from elite to mass higher education. In OECD (Ed.), *Policies for Higher Education* (pp. 51–101). Paris: OECD.

TUGIAD (Turkey Genc Isadamlari Dernegi). (1993). *2000 li yillara dogru Turkiye'nin onde gelen sorunlarina yaklasimlar: 2—Egitim*. Istanbul: TUGIAD.

Tunnermann, C. (1996). A new vision of higher education. *Higher Education Policy, 9*(1), 11–27.

Williamson, B. (1987). *Education and social change in Egypt and Turkey*. London: MacMillan Press.

Winkler, D. R. (1990). *Higher education in Latin America* (Discussion Paper 77). Washington, DC: The World Bank.

World Bank. (1990). *Republic of Turkey: Costs and financing of primary and secondary education* (Report No. 9097-TU). Washington, DC: The World Bank.

World Bank. (1993). *World development report 1993*. New York: Oxford University Press.

World Bank. (1994). *Higher education: The lessons of experience*. New York: Oxford University Press.

World Bank. (1995). *Priorities and strategies for education: A review*. New York: Oxford University Press.

World Bank. (1999). *Knowledge for development*. New York: Oxford University Press.

YOK (Yuksekogretim Kurulu). (1990). *Yeni universitelerin Kurulus yerlerinin seciminde uygulanacak olcultler: Ihtisas komisyonu raporu*. Unpublished Task Force Report. Ankara: Yuksekogretim Kurulu.

Ziderman, A., & Albrecht, D. (1995). *Financing universities in developing countries*. Washington, DC: The Falmer Press.

Part V

New Pressures and Forms of Accountability

Chapter 10

Quality Assurance for Higher Education: Shaping Effective Policy in Developing Countries

Elaine El-Khawas

Quality assurance, a term denoting a public responsibility to demonstrate high levels of performance, has been given major attention in recent policy debate on higher education. More than 50 countries have adopted mechanisms of quality assurance, many in the last five to ten years. International agencies have promoted the widespread adoption of quality assurance, especially in developing countries. The UNESCO *World Declaration on Higher Education*, issued in fall 1998, included a statement affirming the importance of greater attention to quality issues as higher education expands (UNESCO, 1998). The World Bank's 1994 publication, *Higher Education: The Lessons of Experience*, adopted a broadly similar theme about the necessity of greater attention to quality assurance.

As these and other documents have noted, the pressure for stronger mechanisms of quality assurance has emerged from several long-term trends (cf. El-Khawas, DePietro-Jurand, & Holm-Nielsen, 1998). Increasing enrollments and higher participation rates together comprise one such general trend. In many industrialized countries, participation rates for higher education study have risen to 35 percent or more of each year's cohort of school leavers. This, in turn, has increased spending pressures on governments, especially in countries where public funds almost totally subsidize higher education. As the recent World Bank and UNESCO report has emphasized, higher education expenditures expressed as a percentage of a country's gross domestic product have risen to unsustainable levels in many countries, especially when such spending is viewed against the demands of other education levels or other social needs (World Bank, 2000). Another significant trend, related to expanded enrollment, is a growing diversity in students: in their backgrounds, interests, circumstances, and reasons for pursuing advanced studies. Often, this has triggered increased differentiation in the types of institutions that offer higher education study.

Just as important is the impact on higher education of major global trends, from the fast pace of change in information technology, free trade policies, and the spread of multinational firms, to the steady shift toward what Gibbons, Limoges, Nowotny, Schwartzman, Scott, and Trow (1994) have called Mode 2 research. These trends have brought with them new pressures on universities and new expectations for the ways that universities should contribute to national and local needs.

One of the most significant policy responses to these pressures that emerged in the late 1980s and early 1990s was action to establish new mechanisms of quality control for higher education. Westerheijden, Brennan, and Maassen (1994), among others, have documented the way that various models developed in western Europe, including the introduction of different forms of external review in France, the Netherlands, and Denmark. The push to introduce quality assurance in many of these countries was part of government decisions to devolve authority and responsibility from the center (i.e., government ministries) to universities and their representatives (Neave & van Vught, 1991, 1994). These European developments, in turn, were part of a general trend in which governments have begun to take a more strategic position toward their systems of higher education (Neave, 1998). Around the world, this shift has produced greater governmental scrutiny of higher education on a number of policy matters: how universities should be funded, what level of administrative and financial oversight they require, and what role government and other external stakeholders should have in setting directions for university programs and services. Thus, in a context where governments are under pressure to rationalize their spending, new policies for quality assurance have emerged along with other initiatives aimed at higher education, including new funding models, changed governance structures, or greater differentiation of institutions by type or mission.

Similar pressures have been experienced in developing countries. Most countries in Eastern and Central Europe and in the newly independent states of the former Soviet Union adopted some form of accreditation or quality assurance as part of their transition to political freedom (Council of Europe, 1995). Several Latin American countries, among them Chile, Mexico, Brazil, and Argentina, have established accreditation councils or other forms of quality assurance, including agencies directed toward private institutions of higher education (Inter-American Development Bank, 1997b). South Africa is developing new mechanisms of quality assurance as part of its initiatives to set new directions for higher education in a postapartheid era.

For many developing countries, a special concern has emerged in recent years due to higher education's version of globalization, that is, the rapid expansion of overseas provision or "franchises" in which institutions from several industrialized countries are bringing their own educational programs to other countries often through electronic and other forms of distance education (Petersen, 1999; Swift & Morejele, 1996). Developing countries in southern Asia (for example, Thailand and Malaysia) have been the target of such initiatives.

As the broad trends of expanding enrollment and globalization continue to spread, the prospect is that still other countries around the world will need to formulate a new approach to quality assurance in the near future. What decisions will they make? How will they organize such an approach even as their higher education systems are experiencing rapid development?

In the past, some countries under pressure to develop quality assurance policies have adopted already established practices, especially those found in Western Europe. Yet, it is not obvious how and whether such practices could be usefully translated to a different setting. Indeed, many countries realize it may not be wise to adopt practices developed in specific national contexts, with distinctive circumstances and infrastructure, and with differing educational traditions. As reported recently with respect to Turkey, significant cultural, structural, political, and technical issues can affect any attempt to translate practices from one country to another (Billing & Thomas, 2000). A small country may wish to address certain quality issues immediately while paying attention to other aspects of quality assurance at a later time. Another country may wish to design an entirely different model attuned to its own traditions and realities. In many countries in Eastern and Central Europe, for example, quality assurance agencies were created with special sensitivity to issues of due process and democratic procedure and in recognition of the need to reintroduce indigenous languages in university-level teaching (Council of Europe, 1993).

As Figure 10.1 suggests, there is a wide variety of approaches to quality assurance, with considerable variation in how each approach is implemented. Although external review is a widely used mechanism for assessing quality, for example, quite different approaches have been developed (El-Khawas, 1993; Brennan, El-Khawas, & Shah, 1994). In Hong Kong and New Zealand, reviewers examine administrative processes that support quality (Massy, 1997), whereas in the Netherlands and in Portugal they visit and assess the strength of the educational and research accomplishments of specific academic departments (Amaral, 1995). The audits carried out under the voluntary program of the Association of European Universities (CRE) has a very broad approach; they examine an institution's strategic management processes, including its mission, policies, procedures, resources, and organizational structure (Association of European Universities, 1997). Even when external review is coordinated by a single national agency, as in France, Sweden, and Denmark, specific approaches still differ in many respects (Massaro, 1997; Staropoli, 1987). So too, approaches

Figure 10.1
Differing Models for Quality Assurance

Model	Country
Research assessment scores; teaching assessment	United Kingdom
Accreditation	United States, Hungary, Chile
National evaluation committee	France
Center for quality assurance	Denmark
External reviews of academic programs	The Netherlands, Portugal
Audits: reviews of quality processes within institutions	Hong Kong, New Zealand
Competitive fund for program improvement	Argentina, Sweden
Performance indicators	United Kingdom, United States
Performance contracting	France
External validation of degree awards	Ireland
Graduation examinations	Brazil, other countries
Licensing examinations in professional fields	Many countries

using performance indicators have been adopted at the state government level in the United States (Alstete, 1995), but at the national level in England, Scotland, and Wales (Schofield, 1998). Some countries, including Mexico, employ several mechanisms for quality assurance. Definitions of terms vary widely as well. In Croatia and other countries, accreditation is used to measure the initial, formal recognition given to a new institution. In other countries, comparable early-stage scrutiny is called licensing or authorization.

Many countries have changed their approach over time. Australia conducted national reviews of quality assurance for three years in the early 1990s, then had no formal mechanism for some years, but in early 2000 announced a new plan for quality assurance. In Chile, an accreditation council set up to monitor new, private institutions recently expanded its mandate to include reviews of academic disciplines. Bolivia took another approach, appointing a one-time assessment commission for private universities in 1997. In France, the National Evaluation Committee began with a focus on university-wide visits (Staropoli, 1987) but has recently added a program of discipline-focused visits. Sweden has changed the role of its "chancellor's office" several times during the last decade, but in each instance the role has included some form of quality oversight (National Agency for Higher Education, 1997; Stensaker, 1999). In the United States, regional accrediting agencies made major changes in their accrediting procedures in the late 1980s and early 1990s, but are also launching significant new directions at present (Council for Higher Education Accreditation, 1999; Dill, Massy, Williams, & Cook, 1996). Ireland is currently developing a new accreditation agency following years of relying on a national system for award validation.

Many countries that are new to quality assurance have adopted a gradualist or staged approach. They gain direct experience in this way, even as they work to build support for—and trust in—their quality assurance approaches. Indonesia began with a focus on evaluating and strengthening its teacher training programs. Poland began with an assessment of scientific research, and then gradually added an assessment of teaching programs. Similarly, both Argentina and Hungary began with evaluation of Ph.D. programs, then moved to other degree levels. In the Czech Republic, the initial focus of the national Accreditation Commission was on developing good recognition procedures, and later it turned to the introduction of evaluation and self-evaluation procedures (Council of Europe, 1993, 1995; El-Khawas et al., 1998).

Wherever possible, governments that wish to develop a quality assurance strategy (or change their initial strategy) would benefit from stepping back and developing a general approach to this broad policy arena. As the experience of many countries suggests, policy mechanisms for quality assurance are likely to become a regular, continuing feature of a country's overall system of higher education, so a long-term perspective and plan are warranted. Both short-term needs and long-term objectives should be identified and planned for, possibly calling for several different stages of development.

A staged approach may be especially valuable in countries that are undergoing rapid expansion of higher education enrollment. Staging may be appropriate, for example, where new institutions of different types are being developed and thus pose quite different quality issues than long-established institutions. In Romania, for example, the number of public institutions increased from 44 to 56 between 1988 and 1994, and 74 private institutions were added during that period (Council of Europe, 1995). Nonuniversity expansion is underway in many countries, for example in Egypt and in Estonia. Countries that undertake consolidations or mergers of several institutions face unique quality issues of their own.

Countries with extensive distance learning arrangements have found that quality issues can be somewhat different for distance education than for education in conventional settings (Farnes, 1997; Swift and Morejele, 1996). South Africa, for example, recently had to address special problems of poor administrative and tutorial support in its distance learning structures. Such issues are especially pertinent to developing countries that rely heavily on distance learning to expand educational opportunity. Already, the five largest programs of distance learning in the world are based in developing countries: Turkey, China, Indonesia, Thailand, and Korea (Task Force on Higher Education and Society, 2000).

Some countries have faced quality issues related to private institutions or to overseas providers (see Jamil Salmi's chapter in this book for further discussion). With new, for-profit private institutions, the concern is not so much with their status as private, profit-seeking entities but rather with questions of how the public interest will be served and how general consumer and academic purposes will be upheld while allowing free-market approaches to higher education provision. Some countries (for example, Romania) gave private institutions a special status within accreditation; others have established oversight rules outside of accreditation (Council of Europe, 1993). The introduction of "franchise" operations, in which universities in several countries are bringing their educational programs into new countries, pose questions for governments regarding stipulations and safeguards to protect students from low-quality providers.

As a further complication, many developing countries have found that outside agencies, including international bodies such as the World Bank or regional organizations such as the Asian Development Bank or the Inter-American Development Bank, are pressing them to develop mechanisms of quality assurance that may be more extensive or introduced more quickly than the country wants (Chapman, this volume; Inter-American Development Bank, 1997a). In contrast, countries with the most experience in quality assurance often took a slow pace with its development. In Western Europe, new initiatives emerged incrementally, at a different pace from one country to another, but from internally felt pressures and from indigenous efforts by universities and government agencies to address problems that were widely discussed (Association of European Universities, 1997; Westerheijden, Brennan, & Maassen, 1994).

Externally pressed or not, each country faces a similar task of policy formulation, whether with quality assurance or with other issues: the government must identify its primary objectives and what problem(s) most demand action. It must identify what actions or solutions offer an appropriate solution or way forward from current conditions. To accomplish this, most countries would benefit from developing a strategic planning process that defines their overall purposes and offers a strong basis for selecting both initial and long-term strategies for carrying out the plan.

This chapter discusses a range of policy objectives that might be used to respond to problems relevant to quality assurance in developing countries. What should be the focus of a quality assurance initiative? What problems are to be addressed? Is a comprehensive approach needed? Drawing on experience in many countries over the last few decades, this chapter offers framing questions designed to help narrow the choice of objectives. It also discusses how quality can be defined and identifies some components of quality that are applicable to higher education.

The discussion is meant to offer background, a resource that can contribute to the decision process for policy makers. It does not offer a single solution. Each country should make its own decisions about what components of an approach are most suitable to the country's circumstances. The chapter offers general points about policy objectives, rather than specific descriptions of current practice, out of concern that descriptions too quickly are taken to imply that current practices are optimal or are models. Although much can be learned from studying current practices, it should be recognized that they generally reflect a limited number of governmental objectives. Some are deeply flawed in concept, but exist because they are politically palatable. Even with those that are considered to be effective, it is difficult to sort out why they work or how they could be duplicated (Billing & Thomas, 2000). Context factors, often critically important, are usually not easily explained. Thus, the purpose in this chapter is to give perspective on individual country approaches by focusing on underlying purposes and the choices to be made with regard to policy objectives for quality assurance.

DEFINING OBJECTIVES

It is often difficult to understand the reasons why governments have chosen to foster quality assurance or why they have selected a specific approach. Such policy decisions are embedded in political negotiations, certainly, and it is likely that compromises were made from an earlier, logically constructed set of policy proposals (Kingdon, 1984). Often too, governments do not announce their policy rationales. The United Kingdom has been notorious in this respect, offering very little public rationale when it initiated its research and teaching assessments in the 1980s and 1990s (Kogan & Hanney, 1999). So too, the announced rationale may be only part of the story. In this age of "spin" by government agencies, the least objectionable reason may be stated while other reasons are not mentioned. There often are many overlapping, even inconsistent, objectives behind such policies.

Choosing a strategy is inherently difficult. The educational process beyond high school is complex, structured into degree programs differing in length and in the demands they make on students. While some study programs are general, most involve specialized professional training where restrictions are set by the profession or by licensing examinations. Although such professional programs may be subject to detailed external scrutiny, the general programs offered by the same university may receive much less scrutiny (El-Khawas, 1993).

Higher education in most countries is made up of institutions with diverse histories and constituencies, presenting varying issues with respect to quality. For some institutions, all of their students have been well prepared

Figure 10.2
Clarifying Overall Purposes

Broad questions about policy objectives

- Is the goal to monitor or to improve?
- Is the purpose to address an immediate need or to change institutional practice?
- Is the goal to improve all institutions or a few institutions, or certain types of institutions?
- What are the trade-offs: how do these goals conflict with or contribute to other goals? (Access and equity; research activity; regional development)

Choosing specific outcomes

- To monitor or control all institutions?
- To monitor or control specific study fields?
- To identify and curb inadequately performing institutions?
- To increase the number of "top" institutions?
- To reduce "weak" performance?
- To increase "average" quality?
- To spur innovation or adaptiveness?
- To increase responsiveness to national needs?

---

for university study; for others, most or all students have gaps in their preparation, which makes their progress at university more difficult. Still other institutions are in between, perhaps with students who range widely in their preparation. So what type of student population is to be targeted in an intervention effort?

Difficult decisions need to be made when quality assurance is being introduced at the same time that the country is introducing (or expanding) its provision of nonuniversity, vocational, or short-cycle higher education: should there be one quality assurance process, or several? Brazil and Portugal are among the countries that have had to confront this question (Amaral, 1995). A further dilemma arises in small countries or in countries with much land but small populations; in such settings, only one higher education institution, or one major institution, may exist, or the availability of study programs may be restricted to certain geographic locations (Chapman, this volume; Council of Europe, 1993).

Figure 10.2 offers a simplified outline of policy purposes related to quality assurance. This outline distinguishes among several possibilities. Thus quite different choices can be made at the first decision level, that of clarifying overall purposes. Once those purposes are sorted out, another level of choices must be made, forcing policy makers to be increasingly specific about the outcomes they seek and the necessary locus of any intervention they develop. Some comments on each of these levels may be helpful.

ADDRESSING BROAD QUESTIONS

First, some broad decisions need to be made: is quality assurance to be directed to an immediate need, a short-term problem that can be fixed in a short period? Instead, is there a long-term agenda, either to introduce monitoring that will become a regular part of institutional operations, or to change other aspects of institutional practice? Another broad question addresses the scope of needed effort: should all higher education institutions be affected? Instead, should there be some differentiation of effort in which certain institutions or certain types of institutions are targeted? If so, on what grounds? These questions are especially appropriate in countries such as Brazil where several, parallel systems of higher education—municipal, state, and federal—operate alongside a large and diverse private sector.

Other broad questions, more difficult to sort out, relate to trade-offs and side effects, that is, the prospect that activities in support of quality assurance may conflict with (or contribute to) other policy goals. Although it is very difficult to identify such conflicts, systematic planning efforts and questioning can help to identify possible repercussions. For higher education, a potential concern is for the impact of quality assurance on policy goals of achieving higher participation rates or greater access and opportunity for underserved populations. One can ask how various approaches to quality assurance restrict access, make degree completion more difficult, or narrow the availability of course offerings. Another question is how new policies could change the balance between the time instructors allocate to research, to teaching, and to other activities. Other consequences for the system of higher education might be considered: would certain institutions, or types of institutions, benefit by a policy? What other effects might a certain approach to quality assurance have, for example, on support for good instruction, on instructional time and resources, on institutional abilities to plan or to develop new programs?

Systematic questioning of a policy's likely effects on employers and on economic activity in an institution's surrounding community can also be addressed. Can an effect be anticipated in terms of increasing or decreasing the supply of trained workers? Does the policy facilitate or make it more difficult to foster regional development?

CHOOSING SPECIFIC OUTCOMES

Other questions relate to the specific objectives, or purposes for quality assurance. Quite generalized themes are typically stated as reasons for new initiatives related to quality assurance: improvement, enhancement, relevance, or excellence; raising standards or ensuring quality control; correcting deficiencies or avoiding unacceptable behavior. Such themes offer a vision or an aspiration but they are not specific enough to form the basis for a strategy.

In most policy debates on quality assurance, a dichotomy of purposes has become familiar: whether to improve or to monitor, whether to enhance or to hold accountable (cf. Brennan, de Vries, & Williams, 1997; Thune, 1996; Westerheijden, Brennan, & Maassen, 1994). Long and contentious debates, in diverse countries, have belabored this distinction. One faction argues that monitoring and compliance actions are cumbersome, too time consuming, mean-spirited, inappropriate for higher education, and counterproductive because they produce a compliance culture. Others, less vocal, point to the conservatism of universities and argue that, without external mandates, universities will continue with their traditional but inefficient methods, as well as their emphasis on research and institutional needs over student and employer concerns. In fact, however, the distinction between improvement and control is unsustainable in practice: both approaches may lead to improvements and, conversely, either approach may be unsuccessful in bringing about improvements. The debate is confusing means and ends. Any progress with improving education must somehow be monitored, or observed; any effective methods of monitoring would identify areas needing improvement. While a specific policy can emphasize one of these goals more than another, the full operation of a policy on quality assurance will necessarily include both improvement and monitoring purposes.

What the debates over improvement or monitoring can clarify, perhaps, is the fact that policies on quality assurance are inevitably based on some theory, however implicit, of how and why higher education institutions change. Planners should try to make these theories explicit: are they assuming that institutions change only when compelled to, or when deficiencies are exposed? Are they assuming, instead, that providing information to the public offers a sufficient basis for ensuring quality or that providing more resources to well-performing institutions will improve overall quality?

UNDERSTANDING DIFFERENCES IN QUALITY

Definitions of quality, or of quality assurance, are subject to various formulations, long essays, and debates over fine points (Harvey & Green, 1993; van Vught, 1997). As with the proverbial elephant described by nine blind men who each touch only one part of the animal, different policy makers may have quite different specific incidents or behaviors in mind as they, together, express the need for improved quality.

In most countries, the introduction of quality assurance has been accompanied by extended debates on definitions and underlying premises, aimed

Figure 10.3
Operating Definitions of Quality

- **Sufficient capacity (resources; effective planning and administrative procedures)**
- **Effectiveness (high achievement levels for graduates; achievements are relevant to society and to the economy)**
- **Efficiency (low unit costs; high completion rates; timely completion)**

both at clarifying what is intended and pointing out deficiencies of various approaches to quality assurance. In Scotland, as a result, officials have decided not to offer a general definition but to develop specific criteria for excellence that can be applied to each institution's own objectives.

For purposes here, quality is defined in terms of three characteristics: sufficient capacity, efficiency, and effectiveness (see Figure 10.3). The latter characteristic, which could also be described as quality of results, is an obvious choice; quality exists when results are excellent, when the institution is producing good results. The point here, however, is that, for an entire system to assure quality, the other two categories also matter. For an institution to sustain quality over time and in changing conditions, it must be self-aware and know what it is doing that produces good results; it must have adequate resources and must plan and administer those resources well. Each of these categories is discussed in the following paragraphs.

Sufficient Capacity

One aspect of quality is to have (and maintain) an infrastructure adequate to the accomplishment of objectives. This includes both physical and human resources. It includes the ability to operate with regularized administrative procedures, to conduct planning that allows the institution to monitor its operations and results, and to have the resources to improve those results based on what is learned. Effective planning and administration in higher education has two components: academic administration, so that courses, instructional staff, and support services fit into place in a coordinated way; and administrative practices, so that services and facilities are available as needed. For higher education, effective administrative procedures also address issues of whether curricula are up to date and whether textbooks or other support materials are right for the specific educational level and program for which they are being used.

In many countries, issues of capacity have been criticized as a potential focus for quality assurance policies. They have been described as narrow, only showing "inputs" that offer no insight on whether the inputs are well utilized and what results are achieved (Alstete, 1995).

After decades of disfavor, however, there is a new appreciation in several countries of the importance of "capacity" as one criterion of an institution's overall ability to offer academic programs of good quality. The accreditation community in the United States, for example, is giving renewed attention to capacity and inputs. The Western Association, in its recent restructuring of accrediting requirements for its member institutions, has organized its standards and review materials around two core issues: capacity and effectiveness (Council for Higher Education Accreditation, 1999; Petersen, 1999). Here, and in other settings, there is a new recognition that questions are properly raised about such matters as whether resources are sufficient for the intended program or whether instructors know their subject well.

Other countries, such as Scotland and New Zealand, include questions about inputs, processes, and environments in their quality probes and review the coherence and adequacy of an institution's strategic plans and objectives (Massy, 1997; Woodhouse, 1999). For many developing countries, these are pressing concerns. In the Czech Republic, for example, questions about the adequacy of resources and infrastructure, about the qualifications of teaching staff, and the appropriateness of curriculum content were explicitly addressed as planning got underway for accreditation and evaluation of universities (Council of Europe, 1995). Similarly, Argentina's improvement fund includes components designed to strengthen capacity, including the quality of libraries and the training of teachers; it also addresses objectives of effectiveness and efficiency in its support of program improvement and of efforts to reduce dropout rates (Ministry of Culture and Education, 1998).

Issues related to capacity and resources are especially pertinent in judging proposals for new institutions, whether they are public or private and whether they offer traditional classroom-based instruction or instruction by distance methods. Such questions about capacity are often raised about distance learning programs, but it is reasonable, too, to raise these issues with classroom-based instruction (Farnes, 1997). It is reasonable to verify whether they offer sufficient chance for students to discuss issues with instructors, for example. With new, private tertiary institutions, questions of sufficient capacity are also proper to raise: do the private owners show sufficient readiness to invest in good materials and in instructors likely to contribute to the long-term health of programs? Questions about capacity, and the ability to maintain capacity over an extended time, should also be raised about overseas franchises. Have they sufficiently adapted their program materials to the host country's needs and issues? Have they established a stable and efficient administrative structure? As should be obvious, these issues can be applied to traditional institutions as well.

A delicate question arises with respect to the capacity levels of publicly supported institutions: situations can and do occur in which underfunding of an institution, especially severe and chronic, precludes the possibility of performing well. Yet, the quality assurance process is typically sponsored by government. How can the quality assurance process come to an objective and honest position when capacity shortcomings are evident, and clearly due to underfunding? Although it may be politically unpopular to do so, quality assurance councils should ask questions about capacity and consider whether underfunding of publicly supported institutions have caused capacity to be compromised.

Effectiveness

Questions of effectiveness look to what the institution does with its resources, whether it has developed a good academic program, whether or not it is maintaining the right activities to accomplish its goals (Brennan, de Vries, & Williams, 1997; Dill et al., 1996). Such questions address fundamental issues of what institutions are doing and what they are accomplishing. Although some academics believe that these questions should be directed mainly to fledgling institutions, their general importance to higher education argues that they be directed to long-established institutions as well (Higher Education Quality Council, 1994).

Fundamentally, this requires a look at outcomes, what an institution accomplishes. It means questions about whether graduates are well-prepared, whether they have both the knowledge and skills that they—and society—expect as a result of their studies. To ask about outcomes inevitably raises related questions about the quality of the curriculum (understood as the sum total of planned studies and activities set out for each study field) and whether the quality of teaching is strong enough that students have attained high levels of knowledge in their subject. Thus, if gaps are found in what graduates have achieved, the institution should examine whether changes in its existing practices are needed to achieve a more satisfactory outcome (cf. El-Khawas, 1998; Harvey & Green, 1993).

Relevance can also be considered a separable issue that focuses on whether the information and skills that students have attained through their studies represent the right institutional choices (Salmi, this volume; Task Force on Higher Education and Society, 2000). Do graduates have the specializations and competencies needed for their career field? Do graduates, collectively, have the range of skills and information needed by employers to contribute to the nation's economic development, and for service to the larger public good? Are there, for example, sufficient graduates in fields critical to social welfare services, in fields that prepare them for the civil service, or for areas of science needed for further development?

A difficult aspect of quality oversight arises when problems are found in terms of educational effectiveness. That is, definitions and broad criteria generally fail to offer sufficient guidance about where to draw the line between what is adequate and what is not. Effectiveness is not unidimensional, but depends on the way that various resources work in combination. Many developing countries, among them Hungary, Argentina, Mexico, and Laos, suffer from the problem of low instructor salaries which cause instructors to take second jobs. Yet, in many such contexts, instructors still perform adequately. Funds for ancillary materials may be low, making it impossible to hold labs, class trips, tutoring support, and so forth, or even small classes. At what point do these shortages become inadequate to achieve effectiveness?

As difficult as these questions are, the quality assurance role is to hold institutions to their responsibility for meeting their core educational obligations. Budgets for equipment and facilities may be cut back, but they should not be allowed to compromise the institution's ability to offer effective teaching and learning.

Efficiency

Efficiency goals, which look to the provision of effective education at low unit cost, are sometimes considered an aspect of quality. Academics traditionally resist this view arguing that it has a narrow perspective on education. Yet in the same way that other public agencies have expectations for efficiency, higher education must accept responsibility for accomplishing its work in efficient ways. In fact, several measures of outcomes reflect both efficiency and effectiveness goals. High degree completion rates, for example, represent efficient use of resources but also reflect effective teaching and other academic practices. It is also true, however, that some government policies on quality assurance have given greater importance to the efficiency aspects of quality, perhaps because efficiency is the easier construct to measure and interpret. The key issue is that efficiency should not be the preeminent goal although it can be one among the several aspects of quality that are pursued (cf. Harvey & Green, 1993).

Several difficulties arise when efficiency goals are applied to higher education. The nature of the work involves sustained effort over the long term, dependent on the multiyear activities of many individuals, to conduct the degree programs that are the backbone of higher education. In such situations, efficiency can be achieved in many ways, not all of which involve good social or educational policy. Thus, if institutions of higher education are very restrictive, only admitting highly qualified students, or if large numbers of students drop out in their first term of study, the institutions could appear to be very efficient, i.e., keeping unit costs down. However, this may not serve societal goals of increasing the number of college-educated, professionally trained persons available to join the national workforce (Billing & Thomas, 2000). Other choices, for example, to depress instructor wages to such a level that staff turnover is disruptive of student progress, may also improve efficiency (that is, achieve low unit costs) but at the cost of effectiveness.

Indeed, in considering how efficiency relates to quality for higher education institutions, questions need to be raised about the interplay among the various aspects of quality. The relationship between capacity, efficiency, and effectiveness is not easily understood. Over the short term, capacity can be reduced, thereby increasing efficiency without doing harm to effectiveness. As already mentioned, resource cuts, over the short term, may not cause instructors to teach differently; in a longer perspective, however, low instructor salaries can dramatically affect recruitment of good instructors. To judge efficiency, then, it is critical to distinguish between short- and long-term situations, and to be able to ascertain whether apparent gains in efficiency are in fact only documenting declines in capacity.

PUTTING QUALITY INTO PERSPECTIVE

Apart from the issues in developing definitions of quality, a practical problem should be understood when thinking about quality for entire systems, such as with higher education. When problems with quality are being discussed, different and possibly contradictory assumptions are being made. For an entire system of higher education—multiple institutions, large numbers of students, many staff, programs of differing length—any overall evidence of quality is, in fact, showing an "average" that is explainable in quite different ways.

Most issues of quality for a large, complex entity such as higher education need to be examined in terms of how quality is distributed. Said differently, the problem can only be addressed if its components are considered. If it is believed that universities do not have high enough standards for their students, is this a problem of uniformly weak levels of achievement for all students or, instead, is the problem due to low levels of performance for only a certain segment of students? Are students in some fields, some institutions, or some programs not doing well?

Depending on the actual problem, quite different policy interventions are needed. Raising all institutions from "average" performance to higher performance may require quite different actions than needed to address the issues affecting a small number of low-performing institutions. So too, actions to raise the performance of low-achieving students (e.g., more drilling on fundamental skills) can be quite different from those that are needed to raise the performance of students of middling achievement (where, for example, successful strategies may call for more flexibility to accommodate student interests, not more drilling on what is already understood).

A realistic policy approach needs to identify how quality issues are "distributed" across a system. Once this is understood, policies can be fashioned that should address the actual underlying problems.

SUMMARY AND DISCUSSION

This analysis has reviewed the different objectives that are found in recent approaches to quality assurance for higher education. For countries wishing to develop, or change, their approach to quality assurance, several lessons follow from the perspective offered here. One implication is that, in view of the complexity of systems of higher education, it is unlikely that a single, comprehensive approach to quality assurance can be developed. Priorities must be set among the various objectives. If more attention is to be given to certain issues or objectives, less attention inevitably will be given to other aspects of what constitutes quality for higher education.

Another implication is that decisions need to be made in light of both short- and long-term goals. Staging may be inevitable in choosing among possible objectives. Some types of government action can be taken first but others can only be introduced later, as conditions allow. Such staging has benefits. By beginning with one important objective, institutions could be expected to give priority attention to that objective; once there is evidence of progress, attention can be turned to other objectives.

So too, different priorities will influence the choice of strategy. If concerns about employability of graduates are paramount, for example, a focus on specific academic programs, or faculties, is better than a focus on entire institutions. With a program focus, it is easier to gauge graduation rates and job-finding success, or to examine the effectiveness with which students are being prepared for specific careers. An institutional focus, in contrast, is best suited to an examination of management processes. Thus, if the major policy concern is with efficiency and good planning, an institutional focus is best able to address the effectiveness of a range of administrative operations and processes.

The choice of initial strategy may involve pragmatic considerations, such as the feasibility of one approach over another. Information reporting, for example, can be a very efficient method for gaining evidence on institutional operations, but such mechanisms work best in systems that have substantial experience with statistical information systems. To adopt such an approach too quickly, where the necessary infrastructure is not in place, just means that delays and incomplete reporting will be continuing problems.

Aside from focusing attention on certain objectives at different stages, a long-term perspective requires that planners also keep in mind that the larger purposes of quality assurance involve capacity-building. The long-term goal is to change core practices within higher education institutions, not only to ensure that sound procedures are followed but also to develop evaluative systems that allow the institutions to maintain strong programs and adapt them effectively to changing needs. For this long-term result to be achieved, various policy strategies will be needed, over an extended period, that will affect multiple levels of institutional operations.

In brief, strategies for quality assurance need to be seen as means, not ends. The larger goal is to have an effective system of higher education, one that allows students to have strong accomplishments that use their talents and that will help serve the nation's needs. As the recent World Bank/UNESCO report stated, "Higher education is focused on people—regulation needs to foster, not hamper, human potential" (Task Force on Higher Education and Society, 2000, p. 52).

REFERENCES

Alstete, Jeffrey W. (1995). *Benchmarking in higher education: Adapting best practices to improve quality* (ASHE-ERIC Higher Education Reports, No. 5). Washington, DC: George Washington University.

Amaral, A. (1995). The role of governments and institutions: The Portuguese and the Brazilian cases. *Quality in Higher Education, 1*(3), 249–256.

Association of European Universities. (1997). *Institutional evaluation as a tool for change*. Geneva: Committee of European Rectors.

Billing, D., & Thomas, H. (2000). The international transferability of quality assessment systems for higher education: The Turkish experience. *Quality in Higher Education, 6*(1), 31–40.

Brennan, J., de Vries, P., & Williams, R. (Eds.). (1997). *Standards and quality in higher education*. London: Jessica Kingsley Publishers.

Brennan, J., El-Khawas, E., & Shah, T. (1994). *Toward effective uses of peer review: A U.S.–European comparison*. London: Open University/Quality Support Centre.

Council for Higher Education Accreditation. (1999). *Quality review: CHEA almanac of external quality review*. Washington, DC: CHEA.

Council of Europe. (1993). *Accreditation and evaluation in higher education* (Report DECS-HE 93). Strasbourg: Council of Europe.

Council of Europe. (1995). *The organization of quality assurance* (Report DECS LRP 95/30). Strasbourg: Council of Europe.

de Wit, H., & Knight, J. (Eds.). (1999). *Quality and internationalisation in higher education*. Paris: OECD, Programme on Institutional Management in Higher Education.

Dill, D. D., Massy, W. F., Williams, P. R., & Cook, C. M. (1996). Accreditation and academic quality assurance: Can we get there from here? *Change Magazine, 28*(5), 16–24.

El-Khawas, E. (1993). External scrutiny, U.S. style: Multiple actors, overlapping roles. In T. Becher (Ed.), *Governments and professional education* (pp. 107–122). London: SRHE/Open University Press.

El-Khawas, E., with DePietro-Jurand, R., & Holm-Nielsen, L. (1998). *Quality assurance in higher education: Recent progress, challenges ahead*. Washington, DC: World Bank.

Farnes, N. (1997). New structures to reform higher education in Central and Eastern Europe: The role of distance education. *European Journal of Education, 32*(4), 379–396.

Gibbons, M., Limoges, C., Nowotny, H., Schwartzman, S., Scott, P., & Trow, M. (1994). *The new production of knowledge: The dynamics of science and research in contemporary societies.* London: Sage Publications.

Harvey, L., & Green, D. (1993). Defining quality. *Assessment and Evaluation in Higher Education, 18*(1), 9–34.

Higher Education Quality Council. (1994). *Learning from audit.* London: HEQC.

Inter-American Development Bank. (1997a). *Higher education in Latin America and the Caribbean.* Washington, DC: Inter-American Development Bank.

Inter-American Development Bank. (1997b). *Higher education in Latin America: Myths, realities, and how the IDB can help.* Washington, DC: Inter-American Development Bank.

Kingdon, J. (1984). *Agendas, alternatives, and public policies.* Boston: Little, Brown.

Kogan, M., & Hanney, S. (1999). *Reforming higher education.* London: Jessica Kingsley Publishers.

Massaro, V. (1997). Learning from audit? Preliminary impressions from a survey of OECD countries. In National Agency for Higher Education (Ed.), *Quality assurance as support for processes of innovation: The Swedish model in comparative perspective* (pp. 9–38). Stockholm: National Agency for Higher Education.

Massy, W. F. (1997). Teaching and learning quality-process review: The Hong Kong programme. *Quality in Higher Education, 3*(3), 249–262.

Ministry of Culture and Education (Argentina). (1998). *Fund for the enhancement of university educational quality.* Buenos Aires: Ministry of Culture and Education.

National Agency for Higher Education. (1997). *Quality assurance as support for processes of innovation: The Swedish model in comparative perspective.* Stockholm: NAHE.

Neave, G. (1998). The evaluative state reconsidered. *European Journal of Education, 33*, 265–285.

Neave, G., & van Vught, F. (1991). *Prometheus bound: The changing relationship between government and higher education in Western Europe.* Oxford: Pergamon.

Neave, G., & van Vught, F. (1994). *Government and higher education relationships across three continents: The winds of change.* Oxford: Pergamon.

Petersen, J. C. (1999). *Internationalizing quality assurance in higher education.* Washington, DC: Council for Higher Education Accreditation.

Schofield, A. (Ed.). (1998). *Benchmarking in higher education: An international review.* London: Commonwealth Higher Education Management Service.

Staropoli, A. (1987). The French National Evaluation Committee. *European Journal of Education, 22*, 123–132.

Stensaker, B. (1999, August). *Quality as discourse: An analysis of external audit reports in Sweden 1995–1998.* Paper presented at the annual meeting of the European Association for Institutional Forum, Lund, Sweden.

Swift, D., & Morejele, M. (1996). Quality in distance education. In A. H. Strydom, L.O.K. Kategan, A. Muller (Eds.), *Quality assurance in South African higher education: National and international perspectives* (pp. 116–130). Bloemfontein, South Africa: University of the Orange Free State.

Task Force on Higher Education and Society. (2000). *Higher education in developing countries: Peril and promise*. Washington, DC: The World Bank.

Thune, C. (1996). The alliance of accountability and improvement: The Danish experience. *Quality in Higher Education,* 2(1), 21–32.

UNESCO. (1998). *World declaration on higher education*. Paris: UNESCO.

van Vught, F. (1997). To innovate for quality. In National Agency for Higher Education (Ed.), *Quality assurance as support for processes of innovation: The Swedish model in comparative perspective* (pp. 80–102). Stockholm: National Agency for Higher Education.

Westerheijden, D. F., Brennan, J., & Maassen, P.A.M. (Eds.). (1994). *Changing contexts of quality assessment: Recent trends in West European higher education*. Utrecht: Lemma.

Woodhouse, D. (1999). Quality and Quality Assurance. In H. de Wit & J. Knight (Eds.), *Quality and internationalisation in higher education* (pp. 29–41). Paris: Organization for Economic Cooperation and Development.

World Bank. (1994). *Higher education: The lessons of experience*. Development in Practice Series. Washington, DC: The World Bank.

Part VI

Supporting Academic Staff in New Roles

Chapter 11

Context for Higher Education Reform in China: An Analysis of Faculty Issues

Yvonna S. Lincoln, Bryan R. Cole, Wang Xiaoping, and Yang "Sherry" Xiaobo

Framed in large measure by centuries of rich tradition and culture, Chinese higher education is being catapulted into a future of cataclysmic change that will raise many doubts, fears, and anxieties while it simultaneously offers great opportunities (Hawkins, 1992; Hu, 1993; Zuo, 1993). The forces driving and restraining these changes, as well as the implications for faculty and faculty worklife in higher education in China (Postiglione & Jiang, 1999), are the focus of this chapter. Specifically, the chapter discusses various higher education reforms that impact faculty worklife, faculty hiring and rewards systems, faculty roles in curricular change, and faculty workload.

The study contributing to this chapter was one of the outcomes from a two-year USIA funded exchange project between U.S. and Chinese higher education officials. The project was jointly administered by Texas A&M University and the National Center for Education Development Research (NCEDR) in the State Education Commission in China. The methodology for the research was qualitative in nature. Data were derived over a two-year period from in-depth interviews and discussions with Chinese higher education administrators and Chinese State Department of Education and provincial education officials, literature reviews, and institutional visits. On-site visits included Beijing University, Beijing University of Aeronautics and Astronautics, the National Academy of Educational Administration, Petroleum Industry University, Motorola China Ltd., Northwestern University in Xian, Guangdong Province Higher Education Bureau, Xijiang University (Guangdong Province), and the Shanghai Academy of Educational Sciences (which included the Shanghai Institute of Higher Education, Shanghai Institute of Educational Science, Shanghai Institute of Vocational and Technical Education, Shanghai Institute of Adult Education, and Shanghai Institute of Human Resource Development).

Documents, interviews, records, and notes from policy briefings and discussions were subjected to content analysis procedures and organized into categories and themes. As themes were compared and political, social, cultural, and economic tensions, contradictions, and stresses identified, competing forces affecting faculty were arrayed into dichotomous force-fields (Lewin, 1951).

CONTEXT, CHALLENGES, AND TENSIONS

Higher education in China consists of three types of institutions: specialized undergraduate programs lasting two to three years; undergraduate programs lasting four years; and postgraduate programs including two-year, nondegree graduate studies, master's programs that take two to three years, and Ph.D. programs that require three to four years. In addition to regular colleges and universities, China has developed a very good system for adult higher education (continuing professional development), commonly called "the big five" schools. These include universities for workers and staff, radio and television universities (including distance learning), correspondence universities and colleges, evening universities, and a higher education examination system for people studying on their own, commonly called self-study. In the higher education examination program, students may pass examinations course by course, and when all required courses are passed, university diplomas are awarded.

Reform of higher education is underway in China. Guiding principles to direct reform were enunciated in the Central Committee of the Communist Party of China and State Council's *Outline for Reform and Educational Development*, adopted on February 13, 1993. The overarching goal of the Chinese government for higher education was to prepare graduates "to meet the needs of economic, scientific, technological, and social development." Additionally, the report urged:

> Major efforts must be made to run certain important colleges and universities well and teach certain major disciplines well. Experts should mainly be trained in China. The quality of instruction, the level of science and technology and educational efficiency should be noticeably improved. (Central Committee of the Communist Party of China and State Council, 1993, p. 2)

The fact that great segments of the Chinese society never participated in the industrial and postindustrial revolutions creates monumental infrastructure and education challenges for the decades ahead. So far, reform in higher education has had three major emphases. The first, a financial revolution, devolved some of the responsibility for financing onto provinces, local control, and institutions themselves. The second revolution was in the way institutions had been traditionally administered. The new cadre of administrators and mid-level managers is now far more autonomous but also enjoys a much higher level of responsibility for funding their own institutions. The third revolution is currently underway and includes curricular reform and the reform of faculty worklife, hiring and promotion policies, workload assignments, and retirement arrangements. Following a discussion of the expansion of higher education in China, these three aspects of reform are considered.

Expansion of Higher Education

Since UNESCO's (1998) World Conference of Higher Education, China has moved proactively toward mass higher education for various social, economic, and political reasons. The annual growth rate of enrollment, originally projected at 5 to 6 percent in the 1990s, actually rose much faster than either planned or projected (Essential Statistics of Education in China, 1995) in the second half of the decade to 20 percent and beyond. The result was a total enrollment in the year 2000 more than three times that of 1980. In recent years, higher education institutions have been recruiting annually an average of about 600,000 regular college students for undergraduate programs and about 40,000 candidates for master's and doctor's degrees (Huang & Mao, 1991). In 2000, regular (traditional) colleges and universities admitted a total of 1.6 million first-year students. Enrollments for 2000–2001 in some form of postsecondary or higher education were expected to stabilize at 15 to 21 percent.

This staggering growth can be attributed to pressures from socioeconomic development, young people's aspirations for higher education, international competition in higher education, and political pressures to expand higher education at a much faster growth rate (Hao, 1995). The country is moving to provide mass higher education primarily through three means: institutional mergers, new facilities (e.g., the new campus of Shanghai University located 40 km outside the city because the older campus has no room for expansion), and increasing the student-faculty ratio. The decision to pursue mass higher education seems likely to remain unchanged for the foreseeable future, although the central planning committee of the Politboro could decide otherwise if conditions change.

Financial Reforms

Beginning in 1985, financial reforms in education shifted financial responsibility to lower levels of government, diversified the funding of education to more government agencies, and created new sources of funding in the nongovernment sector (Hartnett, 1993). The burden of financial responsibility continues to shift, although from 1998 to the present, the central government has increased its expenditures for higher education, primarily to improve research facilities and productivity.

Another element in financial reform has been the creation of a tuition-based system for postsecondary education and a concomitant growth in the number of fee-paying students who find higher education a worthwhile investment. In a national conference on higher education in November 1992, Zhu Kaixuan, the deputy chairman of the State Education Commission, set forth the ultimate aim of government policy regarding higher education:

> The whole society's concept of higher education should be changed. It should be made clear that higher education does not fall into the category of compulsory education and, in principle, all university students should pay their way. (Qiping & White, 1994, p. 221)

Administrative, Governance, and Structural Reforms

The second "Decision on the Reform of the Educational System," in May 1985, asserted that successful higher education reform would involve

> transform[ing] the management system of excessive government control over the institutions of higher education, expand[ing] the autonomy of institutions under the guidance of the state's unified educational policies and plans, strengthen[ing] the links between institutions of higher education and production organizations, scientific research organizations, and other social sectors, and enabl[ing] the institutions of higher education to take initiatives to meet the needs of economic and social development. (Qu, 1991, p. 806)

Despite a trend toward reducing "excessive government control," the political will at the central level still plays a key role, especially as China is still moving from a centrally planned economy to a market economy. Even though far less than before, many directions and policies are still dependent on administrative measures rather than on market drive. For example, as noted earlier, last year China's higher learning institutions enrolled the unprecedented number of 1.6 million freshmen, due to a decision made by the Politboro, rather than because of planning or a decision made by the Ministry of Education.

Another structural and management issue that constitutes an important force affecting higher education is the ongoing consolidation and merger of higher education institutions. This is part of an effort to strengthen the universities to become "comprehensive universities," a reversal from the previous Soviet specialized higher learning model, which China copied in the 1950s. It is also a part of the China 211 Project, focused on building about 100 top-level universities or higher learning institutions in the twenty-first century. Some of these universities should reach world-class level. As a result, some Chinese universities are now superlarge: Sichuan University (the result of a merger of the former Sichuan University and Chengdu University of Science and Technology), Zhejiang University (a merger of the former Zhejiang University, Hangzhou University, and Zhejiang Teachers University), and Jilin University (created by the merger of five universities). The mergers seem to be the outcome of political decision rather than natural academic choice. The effects of such mergers are not yet clear.

These structural reforms, especially with respect to financing institutions of higher education and decentralizing administrative structures, are creating new forms of diversification in institutional structure, faculty governance, administrative decision making, and curriculum and pedagogy. In addition, these reforms are, to an extent, remaking the face of higher education (Hu, 1993). While new institutions are being created every year to handle demand and to situate institutions where major population growth is occurring (e.g., Fudan University on the China–Hong Kong border), it is also the case that institutions formerly under ministry control have now merged and operate under state (provincial) or local control (e.g., Yangzhou University, Shuzhou University, or the merger of Beijing Medical University into Beijing University). Even when universities have not merged, economies of scale have been created through mergers of extremely small departments with other small departments (for example, history and philosophy have now merged at Beijing University). Administrative costs are saved and faculties have gained strength as they have acquired more human resources for meeting student needs. As a consequence, many institutions in China now look more like U.S. comprehensive universities. Faculty roles have necessarily grown more complex as a result, with increased responsibilities for curriculum planning and for extended governance mechanisms.

An area where reform is not evident is in capital plant development and capital investment accounting. Capital plant and capital investment accounting are extremely important concepts, but money has been in such short supply that facilities have eroded seriously. Some facilities probably cannot be upgraded and will need to be replaced. Two important considerations are missing in this thinking: forward-looking investment, including human and physical plant capital investment, and improvement in utilization of available resources. In other words, little attention has been paid, in the immediate past, to both the external and internal efficiency of the higher education system (World Bank, 1994).

Curriculum Reform

Current higher education reform policies revolve primarily around issues of finance (Jiang, 1994) and employment (Cao, 1991). The reform policies were not intended to relax state control in other realms of higher education, particularly in areas which are seen as sensitive to ideological debates (such as history and philosophy). Nevertheless, curriculum polices are changing, and departments of liberal arts, history, philosophy, and literature are currently growing. Reforms in such areas have come to be understood as essential to the long-term development of the nation (*Higher Education in China*, 1994). The revitalization of the liberal arts is a strong positive sign, a signal that China values its long tradition of culture and philosophy, and its rich tapestry of history, as elements worthy of research, serious scholarly study, and transmission through higher education (Hayhoe, 1995; Hayhoe & Pan, 1996).

Nevertheless, higher education policies are still somewhat conceived within the boundaries of manpower supply (King, 1995). Goals such as the exploration of new thought are not at the forefront of the reform agenda. The formal curricula in the social sciences maintain a Marxist outlook and the research agenda remains fairly political. The involvement of students in voluntary organizations is still seen as unwanted by the government (Cheng, 1995).

Each of the issues and tensions discussed profoundly affects faculty members and their worklife. The rest of this chapter examines specific issues and challenges confronting faculty members due to the changes in society and higher education in China.

FORCES IMPACTING CHANGE IN FACULTY WORKLIFE

From 1966 to 1976, China's education system was the target of the most radically reactionary programs in any nation. Today, almost no one in China has anything good to say about that period. Most, in fact, say it was the most destructive decade faced by the Chinese people since the founding of the People's Republic in 1949 and blame it for destroying almost a whole generation of promising young and midrange scholars. In fact, China has few midrange faculty in institutions of higher education, relatively speaking. As a result of the disappearance of thousands of faculty from institutions of higher education during the Cultural Revolution, many faculties are not "diversified" in terms of including young, midrange, and senior faculty members. The current balance among faculty is approximately 70 percent senior faculty and 30 percent junior faculty members. It will be a generation before China's faculty members are once again diversified in terms of rank and age.

Current reforms are, in part, directed toward creating a cadre of new, young faculty members that does more than merely replace retiring faculty (Cao, 1991). The new professional cadre is intended to be both broad (covering all the disciplines well) and deep (including sufficient diversity to extend capacity across the next several decades). "Human capital" accounting (which, in the case of faculty, would argue for extensive faculty development opportunities) is still considered too "Western"—and far too expensive—to make many inroads into planning for higher education.

To date, many of the younger faculty members in the universities have been trained abroad, in Western Europe, the United States, Canada, and Australia, principally (World Bank, 1994, 1996). They bring with them Western ideas of how to teach and what constitutes appropriate curricular scope and sequence, as well as intricate knowledge of state-of-the-art laboratory equipment, and new models for faculty-student interactions and relationships. Their experiences will subtly shape how curricula—whether in the hard sciences (Jiang, Mao, & Zhang, 1993), the social sciences, the humanities, or education (Shen, 1994; Yang, 1990)—are revised, expanded, or remodeled to accommodate a shifting focus on the global economy.

The assumption underlying curricular reform and modernization is that faculty members, rather than the ministry or the central planning committee, will be their primary architects, importers, and shapers. The central planning bureau's proposal reflects a belief that newly minted doctorates will be those chiefly responsible for curricular reform. Thus, as the number of early career faculty members increases, Western forms of curricular reform will likely be integrated into the curriculum. Further, faculty exchanges are proposed to facilitate curricular updating and upgrading. Thus, new young faculty must both carve out their own research and teaching careers and also assume responsibility for overhauling, modernizing, and restructuring their departmental curricula. At the same time, many of these faculty members, though they studied as undergraduates in a system with faculty-to-student ratios of approximately 1:5–6, will face ratios of nearly triple the number of students, about 1:15–16.

Against this contextual backdrop, the implementation of higher education reforms in China presents significant challenges for Chinese policy makers and educators. In order to better understand these issues and forces, the following subsections focus on specific challenges that competing demands, forces, and counterforces place upon faculty.

Faculty Manpower Needs

Before 2005, 80 percent of the full professors nationwide in China will be eligible for retirement. As the number of retirements increase, it is possible that fewer dollars will be available to address other ongoing programmatic and faculty needs, since each institution has traditionally been responsible for the retirement (including housing and retirement stipend) for all faculty members. Faculty are likely to see a shift in the way their retirements are funded, and over time, faculty housing for retirees is likely to be phased out, especially in more urban universities. The major implications for faculty members are that they will have to relocate and pay for their own housing (as newer faculty are currently doing), they will need to save for and fund a portion of their own retirements, and systems will be created for establishing retirement funds (to operate, presumably, as Chinese versions of the TIAA-CREF pensions and annuities in the United States). Clearly, this is not only a fundamental systemic change for institutions of higher education and their faculties, it is a quality-of-life issue for those who will look toward retirement in the future. This decision will impact and interact with other issues confronting both institutions and the central government. Whole organizational structures will need to be created to administer a pension plan similar to those in the West.

The positive outcome of this "generation gap" in the professoriate has been the opportunity for new, young scholars to move into vacant positions and rise swiftly through the ranks. This "new blood" will bring new ideas and new methods for teaching into the curriculum (Postiglione & Jiang, 1999). China has been sending a record number of graduates overseas for advanced graduate and postgraduate work in order to augment rapidly the number of individuals prepared for faculty careers. In Beijing University, for example, more than 30 percent (300+ out of 1,000) of the faculty members have been trained abroad. The situation is similar at Qinghua University. In addition to gaining linguistic and idiomatic fluency in another language, those individuals who study abroad return with decidedly Western ideas regarding the possibilities of a capitalist economy and its contribution to individual wealth.

Individuals who have studied abroad are highly sought after for multinational corporation positions. Global multinational corporations can and do pay far larger salaries, and frequently offer more perquisites, than institutions of higher education can currently offer. Thus, the market economy in the business and industry sector competes with institutions of higher education to siphon off the best and the brightest of returning graduates with offers of higher salaries than they might earn as faculty members and with more attractive retirement packages. Higher education will have to move flexibly and rapidly to keep faculty positions attractive to those with advanced graduate degrees and the training and skills to be able teachers and research faculty.

Manpower needs, and the competition for manpower between business and industry and higher education institutions, is likely to continue for the foreseeable future. This competition will—and should—shape the programs that are developed to fund and manage faculty retirements. For China's older faculty, the systems with which they matured are likely to remain in place; for China's new, young faculty, new systems must be developed in order to cope with the high costs of retirement. In the meantime, those costs will continue to rise, resulting in a persistent shortage of funds for new and emergent programmatic and faculty hiring needs.

Faculty Roles in Teaching, Research, and Governance

China has managed to absorb the rapidly expanding demand for higher education throughout the last two decades principally by increasing faculty teaching and advising loads (Seebert, 1993). In the early 1990s, faculty teaching loads were still roughly 1:7–8 for undergraduate education, and, at some institutions, 1:5 for graduate education. Both central provincial planning authorities and the new cadre of institutional administrators were planning, and have moved, to somewhat higher faculty teaching ratios. In some places, they have risen to roughly U.S. and British ratios (1:15 for undergraduate education and 1:7–8 for graduate and advanced education) over the past decade. Within the next two decades in China, they are expected to rise to these levels throughout virtually the entire system of higher education.

As well as assuming teaching roles with larger student-to-faculty ratios, faculty will face two other sets of rising expectations. First, a larger number of faculty members, in a larger set of universities, will be expected to create and pursue research agendas. If fulfilled, such expectations should make China highly competitive in the knowledge and information economies globally. This set of rising expectations will likely, however, give rise to an interesting contradiction or tension: how can scholars pursue new knowledge with creativity and freedom and at the same time *not* have a profound effect on China's culture and political structure? The very changes needed in the structure, direction, and pace of faculty worklife necessarily imply a certain lack of central control and inherent disorder. High creativity and research initiative are almost never amenable to routinized processes.

A second impact of rapid modernization and the relaxation of central (Politburo) control will be the necessity for faculty members to take an increasingly active role in governance structures: promotion and tenure systems, selection and hiring committees, policy development structures, admissions decisions, financial decisions, and corporate partnerships. Such unprecedented responsibility carries with it a strong sense of autonomy. The sense of autonomy will no doubt create concomitant stresses and anxieties as institutions of higher education, faculty members, and the central government move together in creating new forms of work and new work relationships.

Faculty Roles in Curriculum Development

Faculty and curricula interact in ways that can be understood pedagogically, but also intuitively. Many of the older faculty now in institutions survived the Cultural Revolution with a clear understanding of what would be taught, and how. Course content, and indeed the entire knowledge structure, needs updating in many institutions of higher education. While the curriculum in the liberal arts, particularly history, philosophy, and literature did not expand for many years, and while graduates of those programs and departments were kept to a small number because of their perceived lack of contribution to a planned economy, those departments now are undergoing a slow broadening and expansion. The ability of an information and industrial economy to absorb liberal arts graduates is uncertain, but it would appear that in addition to professors trained in the hard sciences and business, institutions of higher education are now looking toward their languishing liberal arts programs to expand. Even in the hard sciences, however, curricular content, structure, and methods need steady updating and upgrading.

The implications for overseas universities—which are now doing a large portion of the advanced graduate and postdoctoral training of future Chinese faculty—are significant. U.S. universities, which are now thinking much more seriously about the pedagogical training future Ph.D.'s receive prior to taking faculty positions, should also be thinking seriously about their international students and the needs of China and other rapidly developing nations with strong demands for faculty manpower. Adjustments in doctoral program curricula in American universities may be needed to provide adequate preparation for future faculty from developing countries as well as for Americans aspiring to the professoriate.

Faculty Needs for Laboratories and Equipment

One of the most pressing needs in China's universities today (particularly the so-called "Top 100," or largest research universities) is for updated, upgraded laboratories and equipment and additional space to ensure capacity growth in scientific facilities (Chenru & Zhang, 1996; Jiang, Mao, & Zhang, 1993) over the coming decades. As well as constructing more buildings, or creating entirely new campuses, simply to cope with increasing capacity, the major research universities will confront demands by new faculty for more modern and updated facilities and equipment, both for teaching their students and for conducting their own research. Some collaborative arrangements exist in Beijing and Shanghai (and perhaps in other cities) where modern equipment, particularly in engineering, computing, and communications fields, has been lent or given by global corporations that hire the graduates of the programs. Not only students, but also research-oriented faculty, have profited by such arrangements. Nevertheless, major infrastructure needs exist in virtually all research-oriented universities in China (and in non-research-oriented, teacher training, or liberal arts institutions as well). The lack of uniformly modern research facilities sometimes slows or limits the more ambitious research programs of faculty. Rapidly modernizing facilities and equipment will create a geometric expansion in Chinese higher education's research capabilities and production. Chinese researchers are as anxious and eager as the Central Planning Committee to have their departments be recognized as world-class.

SUMMARY AND CONCLUSIONS

A clear understanding of the competing forces and tensions affecting higher education institutions is fundamental to China's ability to address effectively the critical issues and challenges involved in the proposed higher education reforms. This chapter has focused particularly on the impact of competing forces and tensions, as well as reform efforts, on the work and worklife of faculty members. Faculty members are critically important to the quality of higher education institutions and the impact of these institutions on the societies of which they are a part. Policy makers and institutional leaders cannot afford to overlook the roles, challenges, and issues pertaining to their academic staff.

Analysis of the forces affecting higher education in China and the reform efforts in that country point to several specific issues and challenges for faculty members. In a larger sense, all reform efforts must take place within a context of competing, "push-pull" forces. It is clear that higher education reform efforts are tightly coupled to economic reforms, most directly the effort to become a global economic power. This almost certainly means moving China toward a less planned, and more open, market-oriented, capitalist economy. With a market-oriented economy, however, comes an openness which undermines central control. *Newsweek* magazine (Clemetson, 2001), reporting on the detention of Western scholars by China, observes that

> Many China watchers say [China's] arrest of the scholars has little to do with Washington. Next year the Communist Party will choose new leaders, and Chinese President Jiang Zemin and others are embroiled in an internal power struggle. By detaining freethinking Western scholars, party leaders are sending a warning to reform-minded activists that democratic insurgence comes with a price. (p. 40)

While Western China watchers may occasionally put a spin on interpretation which favors democracy at the expense of deep understanding of internal politics, nevertheless, it is instructive to observe what moves toward democratic activities prompt on the part of the central government. Competing in a global marketplace, expanding capitalist ventures in China, and their relationship to democracy is unclear; however, the camel of democracy has its nose in the tent of capitalism, and the tensions are bound to be reflected in higher education reform in China.

Second, there is an inherent tension between China's traditional policies of elitist higher education, and the clear need to begin to offer "mass" higher education. High technology workforce needs demand a broad base of highly skilled manpower. By the same token, a highly skilled manpower pool creates and drives its own needs for expression—economic, democratic, political. The demands for expression and increasing participation by an educated citizenry will undoubtedly spawn its own tensions. Some of these tensions are already reflected in the central committee's disturbance at student activity organizing, even for social organizations, within higher education. What further contradictions will be created as a result of an ever-larger pool of college graduates is, both in theory and in practice, unpredictable. But the tensions will clearly be felt in higher education arenas first.

Third, instructional methods, course content, and course structure, as well as the structure of knowledge in institutions of higher education, need updating. There is a disconnect between what is taught and what is actually happening in the social and work life of the Chinese. There will be some interaction between higher education course content and a broadening of the media access to and within China. As faculty and students have wider access to international media and the Internet, the flow of information—long controlled by the central government—will grow increasingly unimpeded. How the Chinese professoriate deals with current globalized and international events will prove a litmus test for reform efforts; whether information and news grows more restricted, or less impeded, will determine China's ability to move freely into the trade of goods, services, and markets. Whatever decisions are made by the central planning committee, higher education (and its reform efforts) is likely to be a barometer for all reforms, since college students are those most likely to be in the forefront of challenges to restrictive policies.

Fourth, China must protect the new, young Ph.D.'s being educated now for membership on faculties. Specifically, institutions must find ways to attract highly qualified faculty members who are willing to invest energy and creativity into reform efforts, even though other sectors in society may offer more attractive benefits. Faculty members need to be supported and must have opportunities to expand their skills if they are to engage in new kinds of teaching, revise curricula, and expand their research contributions. In contrast to the past, when administrators and faculty members responded reactively to state government plans, higher education leaders and faculty members now must take a proactive role in designing new educational systems. Of note also, even as faculty members must learn new roles, higher education institutions themselves also must adjust to alternative visions for academic work and institutional priorities and practices that new faculty, especially those who have studied abroad, introduce into their universities.

These issues and challenges pertaining to faculty members in China are similar to the issues that arise in other countries as higher education institutions seek to respond to societal needs. Some challenges which confront Chinese higher education may be more similar to those faced by other socialist economies (e.g., Russia, the Newly Independent States), but some of the challenges are strikingly parallel to those in even nonsocialist economies. Included in the latter would be alterations in administrative structures, alterations in pay scales (for instance, in various South American countries, where faculty must frequently hold down several posts in order to support their families financially), and in the kinds of roles which faculty can and should assume. Effective reform in higher education cannot occur without careful attention to the roles and responsibilities of faculty members, and the ways in which academic staff are supported as they learn about and assume those new responsibilities.

REFERENCES

Cao, X. (1991). Policy making in the improvement of university personnel in China under the national reform movement. *Studies in Higher Education, 16*(2), 103–115.

Central Committee of the Communist Party of China and State Council. (1993, February 13). *Outline for reform and educational development.* Beijing, China: Central Committee of the Communist Party of China and State Council.

Chen, G. (1994). *Education restructure and institutional innovations: Latest developments of Chinese education reform in the 1990s.* Shanghai: Shanghai Institute of Human Resources Development.

Cheng, K. (1995). A Chinese model of higher education? Lesson from reality. In L. Buchert & K. King (Eds.), *Learning from experience: Policy and practice in aid to higher education* (pp. 197–210) (CSEO paperback number 24). The Hague, Netherlands: Centre for the Study of Education in Developing Countries.

Chenru, S., & Zhang, S. (1996). Impact of opening up and reform on university science and technology education in China. *Impact of Science on Society, 41*(4), 367–376.

Clemetson, L. (2001, July 2). The crayon that roared. *Newsweek, 88*(1), p. 40.

Essential statistics of education in China for 1994. (1995). Beijing, China: State Education Commission Department of Planning and Construction.

Hao, K. (1995). *Issues in China's higher education development towards the 21st century.* Beijing: National Center for Education Development Research.

Hartnett, R. (1993). Higher education funding in open-door China. In P. Altbach & D. Johnstone (Eds.), *The funding of higher education in international perspectives* (pp. 127–150). New York: Garland Publishing.

Hawkins, J. (1992). China. In P. Cookson, A. Sadovnik, & S. Semel (Eds.), *International handbook of educational reform* (pp. 97–114). Westport, CT: Greenwood Press.

Hayhoe, R. (Ed.). (1995). *Knowledge across cultures: Universities East and West.* Changsha: Hubei Education Press and Toronto: Ontario Institute for Studies in Education Press.

Hayhoe, R., & Pan, J. (Eds.). (1996). *East-West dialogue in knowledge and higher education*. London: M.E. Sharpe.

Higher education in China: Current status and demands and prospects. (1994). Shanghai: Shanghai Institute of Human Resource Development.

Hu, R. (1993, June). *Chinese education: Development and perspectives*. Paper presented at the International Conference on Education and Development in the Asian/Pacific Rim, Hong Kong.

Huang, Z., & Mao, Y. (1991). People's Republic of China. In W. Wickremasinghe (Ed.), *Handbook of world education: A comparative guide to higher education and educational systems of the world* (pp. 167–171). Houston, TX: American Collegiate Service.

Jiang, M. (1994). *China: Education financial system reform under economy*. Paper presented to the International Conference on Economy and Education Reform, Beijing, China.

Jiang, M., Mao, H., & Zhang, C. (1993). Science research: Capacity, production, and effects. *Human Resource Development, 22*, 312–323.

King, K. (1995). World Bank traditions of support to higher education and capacity building: Reflections on higher education: The lessons of experience. In L. Buchert & K. King (Eds.), *Learning from experience: Policy and practice in aid to higher education* (pp. 19–40) (CESO paperback number 24). The Hague, Netherlands: Centre for the Study of Education in Developing Countries.

Lewin, K. (1951). *Field theory in social science*. New York: Harper and Brothers, Publishers.

Postiglione, G., & Jiang, M. (1999). Academic culture in Shanghai's universities. *International Higher Education, 17*, 223–237.

Qiping, Y., & White, G. (1994). The "marketisation" of Chinese higher education: A critical assessment. *Comparative Education, 30*(3), 213–237.

Qu, B. (1991). *Selected documents on Chinese educational reform*. Beijing: People's Education Press.

Seebert, V. (1993). Access to higher education: Targeted recruitment under economic development plans in the People's Republic of China. *Education, 25*(3), 169–188.

Shen, A. (1994). Teacher education and national development in China. *Journal of Education, 176*(2), 57–71.

World Bank. (1994). *Higher education: The lessons of experience*. Washington, DC: The World Bank.

World Bank. (1996). *China higher education reform*. Washington, DC: The World Bank.

Yang, D. (1990). China's crisis in education: Inadequate investment, low returns and slow reform. *Chinese Education: A Journal of Translations, 23*(2), 15–17.

Zuo, X. (1993). Reform in Chinese higher education in 1992. *International Journal of Educational Reform, 2*(4), 370–376.

Chapter 12

Academic Staff in Times of Transformation: Roles, Challenges, and Professional Development Needs

Ann E. Austin

Faculty members, or academic staff, as they are called in many countries, constitute a critical ingredient influencing the quality and effectiveness of higher education institutions. Universities in the developing world cannot respond to external changes and pressures without the involvement of capable, committed, and knowledgeable faculty members. The challenge for many faculty members, however, is that they are being asked to fulfill tasks and assume roles for which they may not be adequately prepared. Furthermore, policies in some countries and institutions actually may undermine the commitment of faculty members to their institutions and constrain the time that they can allocate to institutional matters. This chapter takes up the issue of institutional response to changing contexts from the perspective that faculty members are a critical resource who must be supported. The central argument is that, while faculty development may, in times past, have been viewed as an institutional and individual luxury, it is now essential for organizational effectiveness, creativity, and successful transformation.

The chapter begins with a discussion of the forces at work affecting higher education institutions in many developing countries that converge to make attention to faculty development an institutional imperative. It then illustrates the argument with an analysis of higher education in South Africa, focusing on important contextual factors at national and institutional levels that affect the work of academic staff, and thus, their professional development needs. As higher education institutions in South Africa in the postapartheid period strive to transform themselves into democratic, accessible institutions that address the social and economic needs of a rapidly changing country, faculty members need support for the many responsibilities they are expected to fulfill. Third, the chapter describes a range of effective professional development strategies that can help faculty members handle challenging demands. With adaptations to fit specific situations, these strategies have potential to be useful in higher education institutions in many countries.

DEMANDS ON FACULTY MEMBERS

Across countries, the pressures confronting higher education institutions, discussed in previous chapters, are creating new demands and difficult challenges for faculty members. Five trends, in particular, affect faculty members and create the need for faculty development strategies. First, the move to a market-based economy in many countries requires university instruction to become more relevant and better linked to the job market. Improving the relevance of course work usually requires curriculum revision or development, often with tight timelines. Additionally, the trend in higher education in many countries to develop United States–type course credit systems to facilitate student transfer across institutions requires course and program design adjustments. Most faculty members, however, in both the developing and developed world, have not had any specific preparation in how to systematically develop course and program curricula.

Second, as access to higher education is extended in a number of countries, faculty members face a broader range of students with diverse educational preparation and qualifications. In some countries, such as South Africa, young people in some population groups received far better educational preparation at the primary and secondary levels than did students in other population groups. The broadening of access also means that, in some countries, student bodies include people from a range of cultural backgrounds. Faculty members may need opportunities to learn more about teaching strategies that are effective with diverse learners.

Third, the move toward privatization of higher education institutions in some countries creates competition for students among universities. One way to attract students in an increasingly privatized environment is to emphasize the quality of instruction that an institution provides. Faculty development programs that help academic staff to enhance instructional quality and effectiveness can be part of an institution's strategy to assure market attractiveness.

Fourth, the trend toward greater institutional autonomy in a number of countries places new demands on academic staff for involvement and leadership. While strong government control and firmly embedded hierarchical structures within universities were the dominant features of organizational life in previous eras, faculty members in many countries are now asked to serve on committees, take leadership roles, and participate in new ways in institutional decision making. When faculty members assume such new roles, they can benefit from opportunities to develop relevant leadership and organizational skills.

Fifth, in some countries, higher education institutions are seeking ways to recapture faculty time and attention in the face of the attractiveness of supplemental income-producing activities. In Chapter 5, David W. Chapman has explained how policies to encourage faculty members to supplement their modest institutional incomes with entrepreneurial teaching endeavors can undermine faculty members' attention to internal institutional responsibilities. In some institutions, faculty development opportunities may serve as a strategy to strengthen the commitment and involvement of faculty members in institutional priorities and activities.

The following section focuses on higher education in South Africa to illustrate how external factors affecting faculty members result in the need for faculty development. Institutions of higher education in South Africa are striving to transform themselves by broadening access to students, restructuring to provide more democratic governance and organizational structures, and, in some cases, reconceptualizing the curriculum. The contributions and efforts of faculty members, as they carry out the day-to-day work of the academy, are essential if the transformation process is to succeed. In fact, efforts to truly transform South African universities and technikons into democratic institutions responding to the needs of the full population will require new ways of thinking and working on the part of faculty members.

The examples discussed in this chapter are based on experience and knowledge gained by the author during a year spent working in higher education in South Africa. Interviews, observations, and institutional visits contributed to the analysis and conclusions.

CHANGES IN HIGHER EDUCATION IN SOUTH AFRICA

Prior to the first democratic elections in South Africa in 1994, the higher education system reflected the beliefs of the apartheid government that individuals of different races should be separated. Thus, the higher education system today must deal with a legacy of inequitable resource allocation, fragmentation, and redundancy. That is, under apartheid, institutions were identified as serving a particular race group. Several institutions might be in close proximity in a particular area, each serving a different group of people. Historically White institutions were funded far more generously than African, Coloured, or Indian institutions. Following the end of apartheid and the change of government, the new national government under President Nelson Mandela appointed a National Commission on Higher Education to analyze and prepare recommendations concerning the system of higher education which should be created in South Africa (Department of Education, 1996, 1997). The work of the commission ultimately resulted in the 1997 Higher Education Act, which laid out the goals, structures, and values to guide higher education in South Africa. Key values articulated in the Act include equity, democracy, development, effectiveness and efficiency, and quality.

For the past several years, higher education institutions throughout South Africa have been engaged in significant institutional transformation to respond to the values and specific recommendations presented in the Higher Education Act. Most institutions are working to ensure that access is available to all members of the community, to democratize their governance and decision-making structures, to develop new curricula, and to develop new, more mutually beneficial relationships with the immediate communities in which they are located.

Certainly contextual factors affecting universities are filtered through particular institutional contexts and histories. For example, in the historically disadvantaged institutions, academic staff typically must grapple with grave needs for physical resources, such as adequate laboratories and libraries and appropriate educational technologies. In the past few years, the enrollments in a number of historically Black institutions have fallen significantly as students who could not access the historically White institutions under the apartheid system are now moving into the more advantaged universities and technikons. For example, Fort Hare University, renowned as the institution where many Black leaders, most notably Nelson Mandela, were educated during the apartheid period, has fallen in enrollment from approximately 5,000 students a few years ago to about 2,500 in 1999. Charges of mismanagement and corruption also have been levied against some of the historically Black institutions in the past two years.

The crises specifically experienced by the historically disadvantaged institutions create an environment where the challenges confronting academic staff are especially acute. The environment is different in historically White institutions, which have enjoyed considerably better resources for many years. A particular challenge in these institutions is that Black faculty members often report that organizational cultures still must change in significant ways if they are to be hospitable and welcoming for all members of the staff and student body. Nevertheless, while acknowledging the important differences associated with institutional type and specific circumstances, it also is possible to identify various issues and trends important throughout the higher education sector and influencing faculty work at a number of institutions.

This section discusses these key contextual factors affecting higher education institutions and their abilities to transform in ways that enable them to more fully serve the needs of the society. The analysis then turns to the specific implications of these factors for faculty members and their work.

The Roles of the University in Society

As in other countries, higher education institutions in South Africa are critically important to the future of the country. Given recognition that universities play a significant role in recreating the country, a key issue has become what it means to be "an African university" and a "South African university." National policy is emphasizing the responsibility of tertiary institutions to address community and labor market needs. In a country where unemployment figures typically are cited around 40 percent, this expectation facing the higher education system is not surprising. Historically disadvantaged institutions face particular challenges in responding to this national imperative since under apartheid they were required to focus degree offerings primarily in the humanities and social sciences (especially education and theology) rather than in the sciences and technical areas. However, while historically advantaged institutions have more developed science and technical departments, they also now must face the expectation to be directly responsive to the huge national need to strengthen the economy.

A second issue for higher education institutions is how to balance the participation of universities and their academic staff in global intellectual and international disciplinary conversations with expectations that universities and their faculty members will address significant local concerns. What should be the responsibilities of universities and technikons to South Africa and the African continent? What should be the roles of higher education institutions to their immediate communities? A number of higher education institutions are engaged in important exploration of how to interact with local communities in mutually beneficial ways (rather than relationships characterized by inequities in benefits and power). Discussions of what roles universities should play (workplace preparation, disciplinary advancement, and community involvement, for example) lead to questions about "what knowledge" and "whose knowledge" the institution should advance. Each position concerning the contributions tertiary institutions should make to society holds crucial questions and implications for the roles, responsibilities, and work of academic staff.

Tight Fiscal Conditions

A second contextual factor affecting the work environment for South African academic staff work is the tight fiscal environment. In a country with many demands to which public monies can be directed, allocations to higher education are far smaller than needs require and have decreased in real terms over the last decade (Vergnani, 1999). In the historically Black institutions, drastically dropping enrollments in 1999 have added to severe fiscal shortfalls—and the historically disadvantaged institutions are in the least advantageous position to deal with such problems given the lack of resources they received under the apartheid system. Many universities and technikons, grappling with unmet budget needs, have been faced with student unrest as they require students to pay their fees rather than continue enrollment with unpaid bills. In addition to student pressures for increased financial assistance, higher education institutions are coping with growing competition from private providers of educational opportunities, many of which offer distance education options and some of which have their bases in other countries. All told, all higher education institutions must find ways to meet the needs of their students, relate to their communities in effective, mutually beneficial ways, make progress toward significant curriculum reform, and enhance their quality—all in the context of tight budgets. These funding issues affect the professional development opportunities offered to faculty members, and the salary levels available to attract highly qualified individuals to faculty positions in the academy.

Movement toward Democratizing Organizational Structures and Processes

Encouraged by commitment to democracy throughout the country and expectations from the Department of Education, many South African universities and technikons are striving to transform their organizational structures and their policy-making strategies. Specifically, many are making efforts to move from hierarchical and authoritarian leadership and decision-making modes toward more participatory and open processes. National education policy calls for the establishment of Broad Transformation Forums, which are democratic governance structures with representatives from a wide array of stakeholders both within and external to the institution. At many institutions, restructuring toward greater democracy has taken place at the levels of institutional council, senate, and executive management.

Prior to the new era in South Africa, academic staff were accustomed to defer to the senior leaders of the university. In the old regime, institutional Councils had typically been very authoritarian and closed to all but a small group of members. Now faculty members are being asked to offer their views, participate as full stakeholders in institutional decisions, and bear responsibility for the direction and transformation of the institution. The movement toward more participation and democracy in both formal governance and informal decision making requires academic staff to develop and use new skills in decision making, teamwork, and institutional planning. The process of transformation toward greater democracy also invites faculty members to think in new ways about their relationships to the institution and their roles and responsibilities.

Broadening of Access

Particularly in the historically advantaged institutions, the end of the apartheid period has led to widening access and more diverse student bodies. Some historically White institutions now have student populations where Black students are the majority. The composition of the student body at the University of Port Elizabeth, for example, shifted from about 3 percent Black students in the early 1990s to between 55 and 60 percent Black students currently. Opening of access is an important symbol in post-apartheid South Africa and has been a cornerstone of the transformation process in most of the historically advantaged institutions. Diversifying the racial/ethnic mix, however, is only part of the process of institutional transformation. As discussed further below, institutional cultures must change and become welcoming, supportive places for all students, faculty, and staff. For academic staff, more diverse student bodies, especially in the historically White institutions, mean the responsibility and challenge to cultivate teaching and learning environments that provide for the needs of all students and serve as models of mutually respectful communities.

At the historically Black institutions a related but different problem is emerging. As large numbers of Black students shift from the historically disadvantaged institutions to the historically advantaged institutions, there is concern that the disadvantaged institutions will find themselves left with an imbalanced proportion of the most disadvantaged students who need substantial academic support. In this scenario, those institutions with the least resources, due to apartheid period inequities, are facing some of the greatest challenges in terms of student academic need. Clearly, this situation represents a serious challenge for academic staff in these institutions.

Extensive Curricular Change

When South African higher education leaders discuss institutional transformation, they often are referring to more diverse student bodies, flatter organizational structures, and curriculum change. Several factors are at work in fostering attention to curriculum development. First, the Report of the Commission on Higher Education (Department of Education, 1996, 1997) and the 1997 Higher Education Act encourage the development of programs that link academic study directly with labor market needs and career opportunities. Qualifications and programs of study must be registered with the National Qualifications Framework, and guidelines for program development call for learner-centered approaches, flexible entrance and exit points, opportunities for credit for life and prior experiences, more flexible delivery structures, emphasis on preparing students for knowledge application, and possibilities for greater articulation between programs.

Second, on a number of campuses, serious discussions are underway about curricular approaches and content specifically appropriate for South Africa, and furthermore, curricula that relate directly to community needs. Such discussions often revolve around the issues of the meaning of "Africanizing the curriculum" and the question of what being a university on the African continent might mean. These issues relate to the challenge of how institutions should balance global involvement and competitiveness with local commitments.

Third, the increased use of distance technology options at many institutions, especially through linkages with private providers, raises curriculum design issues. Distance learning has a long tradition in South Africa. The University of South Africa (UNISA) has provided its degrees for many years through correspondence, and many of the formerly imprisoned antiapartheid leaders, now elected leaders, took their degrees through UNISA. However, with many more departments and colleges (faculties) at some higher education institutions entering into distance learning and technologically assisted modules, this aspect of curriculum change represents serious challenges for faculty members who must learn how to teach in new ways.

Fourth, the national policy emphasis on outcomes-based education is opening the conversation at some institutions about ways to shift from teacher-centered to more learner-centered approaches. Such a shift involves immense challenges to academic staff, particularly since many students have come from primary and secondary educational experiences based on highly teacher-centered models where students take fairly passive roles. Faculty find they must think of learning in new ways, envision new roles for themselves, and develop expanded repertoires of professional strategies that include more interactive teaching. Simultaneously, they realize that students must also learn new ways of thinking and acting.

These issues are not playing out in exactly the same way at all higher education institutions. For example, institutions are responding in different ways to the national emphasis on outcomes-based learning, with some faculties taking on major curriculum revision and restructuring and others responding at a minimal level to the implications of the government's National Qualifications Framework guidelines. Similarly, interest in exploring new, more interactive ways to work with students is not shared across all campuses. Yet, these are themes that challenge academic staff across a number of institutions.

Quality

Commitment to ensuring excellence and quality is another factor that permeates the rhetoric of the Higher Education Act and informs policy guidelines from the Department of Education. Appointed in early 1999, the new Minister of Education, Kader Asmal, has publicly stated his commitment to raising standards, increasing efficiency, and increasing professionalism. Program evaluation plans are to be included in curriculum design and reported to the national department. A number of universities have appointed quality officers, who seek models and approaches for institution and program-level assessment, quality assurance, and evaluation strategies. The expectation that major transformation will at its heart mean enhanced quality puts heavy pressure on the academic staff, the ones whose work will determine the level of quality. Furthermore, increasing quality and monitoring progress become even more challenging amidst fiscal constraint, which is especially keen at the historically disadvantaged institutions.

Challenges of Creating New Institutional Cultures

While transformation often is interpreted to mean restructuring and expanding access, deeper level transformation is requiring cultural change that challenges how people live and work each day. The question is how to create institutional cultures that are truly welcoming and respectful of all people. A critical issue in the creation of new institutional cultures at historically White institutions is the very small number of Black faculty. Debate is strong about the reasons that historically White institutions do not yet have diverse faculties. Some argue that there is an insufficient number of Black individuals qualified for academic posts and that those qualified are often attracted to more lucrative positions in the new postapartheid government or in entrepreneurial organizations. Others assert that uninviting or unsupportive environments are the key reason that more Blacks are not taking university posts in historically White institutions. While elements of each argument are undoubtedly part of the problem, continued cultural change to create inclusive institutional environments is necessary if goals of democracy, equity, and redress are truly to be achieved.

Highlighting another kind of change that must occur, one dean interviewed called for efforts to shift from a "culture of conflict" to a "culture of post-adversary encounters." In contrast to the imbalanced power relationships and high conflict that characterized the apartheid period, faculty, administrators, staff, and students now must find new ways to interact that recognize often significantly different points of view and experience but that seek points of common commitment and interest. Efforts to create dramatically new kinds of institutional environments carry many challenges for academic staff.

Leaders across institutional types also emphasize the need to cultivate "cultures of research." Currently many faculty members hold only a bachelor's or a master's degree. In order to expand the qualifications of academic staff and to strengthen the capacity for quality teaching, many faculty members need opportunities to study for and complete advanced degrees. In sum, for deep level transformation to occur, extensive cultural change will be required that goes beyond creating new organizational structures and increasing the numbers of students from previously underrepresented groups, as important as those changes are.

SPECIFIC PROFESSIONAL DEVELOPMENT NEEDS OF FACULTY MEMBERS

Each of the issues, factors, and trends affecting higher education institutions in South Africa holds particular implications and challenges for academic staff. As institutions deal with important aspects of transformation at the level of structural change and broader access, the stresses and concerns of academic staff are sometimes overlooked. Some faculty members undoubtedly are resisting transformational change; others may hope new expectations and environmental features may ultimately fade away. Yet, many are striving to meet changing circumstances and new expectations in creative, quality-oriented ways. Often, however, they have uncertainties and questions about how to enact new roles and responsibilities. The discussion at the start of the chapter presented contextual characteristics and developments that are affecting higher education institutions in South Africa and the faculty members within them. The following discussion considers more specifically the implications, challenges, and resulting professional development needs that these contextual factors hold for academic staff.

Working with Diverse Students

As access is broadened and as institutions become more diverse (which is particularly occurring in the historically advantaged institutions), academic staff find that they need to learn about students different from themselves and the students they have taught previously. Understanding students' cultural traditions, expectations, and concerns is part of the learning required. Knowing more about the diverse ways in which students learn (a range which crosses cultural, racial, and ethnic lines) is a second area for professional growth. A third challenge and area for professional development concerns how to manage cultural diversity within a classroom. That is, students need to be supported as they learn to work in collegial, respectful ways with individuals different from themselves. Faculty members working with classes of diverse students must help students learn these new ways to relate to each other.

Moving from Teacher-Centered to Student-Centered Paradigms

As national policy encourages more learner-centered approaches to teaching and learning, faculty members at some institutions report the need to learn new strategies to encourage active learning, especially in large classes. Faculty members must not only increase their own repertoire of skills, but also find ways to develop new learning skills in students, many of whom have had primary and secondary education experiences based on rote learning and expectations that students should be quiet and passive. Academic staff at some institutions report that they want to learn more about teaching large classes in ways responsive to individual learners' needs and to use small groups effectively as alternative approaches to teaching and learning. Furthermore, disciplinary differences need to be considered as academic staff explore and seek to implement new approaches to teaching.

Engaging in Curriculum Design

As academic staff find themselves involved in developing new programs, some report a need to learn how best to approach curriculum design, especially for outcomes-based modules, courses, and programs. Understanding more about the implications of "contextualizing the curriculum" for the South African context is an interest among some. Since curriculum design often requires collective work, some faculty members report an interest in learning more about negotiation, conflict resolution, and team management skills.

Using Technologies to Support Learning

With more institutions adopting technologically mediated distance education options, academic staff must learn about computer technologies, resource-based learning, and other strategies to support learners at a distance. The particular challenges associated with distance teaching and learning vary by discipline. While this challenge does not pertain to all higher education institutions and to all academic staff members, it is likely to become more of an issue as technological resources are more widely available.

Addressing Quality Issues

Accompanying the creation of new programs is growing concern about and commitment to ensuring quality. In fact, when programs are registered with the Department of Education's National Qualifications Framework, plans for providing "integrated assessment of student learning" are expected. The challenge facing faculty members is to learn various strategies for providing integrated assessment, including on-going formative feedback during course work. Furthermore, the provision of multiple entrance and exit points in the educational system, which is a theme in national education policy, requires faculty members to provide evaluation of prior learning (life experiences) for those learners who make such a request. Also, as institutions develop quality assurance plans, faculty members require training in self-assessment and colleague assessment, as well as effective and trustworthy ways to collect and interpret students' evaluations.

Ensuring One's Disciplinary Expertise

Faculty members teaching with only a bachelor's or master's degree want to expand their disciplinary expertise and credibility by gaining an advanced degree. Those pursuing a doctoral degree find themselves very stretched as study time must be squeezed around institutional responsibilities. Other faculty members, especially those who already hold doctorates, express concern about how to stay current with and maintain the quality of their disciplinary knowledge and expertise. Some worry that the time required to learn new skills and assume new roles and responsibilities diminishes the time available to do discipline-based scholarship. Scientists in historically advantaged institutions seem more likely than other faculty to express this view. Some White faculty also worry about participating in disciplinary meetings outside South Africa. They had not felt welcome at such meetings during the apartheid period of isolation and now fear that they are very out-of-date.

Another issue at some institutions is the development of outreach and community-based learning experiences that link disciplinary work with opportunities for application of knowledge in real societal contexts. Those faculty members striving to link teaching, research, and community service need support as they engage in their disciplinary work in new ways.

Living and Working in a Changing Environment

Given the rapidly changing contexts in tertiary institutions in South Africa, the great challenge for many faculty members is simply getting everything done. In universities and technikons engaged in significant transformation, teaching, institutional governance, curriculum design, and meetings with students often require more time than usual. Just grappling with the extent of reform efforts requires considerable coping skills. There is great need for academic staff development that helps faculty members to cope with major change and to manage their time well in the face of excessive demands.

Since Black faculty members in historically advantaged institutions are still few in number, they face daily challenges about being accepted, respected, and welcomed. One faculty member, an African man who joined the faculty at a historically White institution as a senior professor, explained that during his first year, he was often mistaken for a member of the cleaning staff. While most historically advantaged institutions now have large proportions of Black students, the proportion of Black faculty has not increased in parallel ways. As discussed, various reasons are at play, including the lure of high salaries in government posts for the relatively small proportion of Black people with advanced degrees. However, the comments of Black faculty who work in historically White institutions make clear that the environments, though changing in many institutions, still often include subtle, if not explicit, unwelcoming or hostile messages. All faculty members must learn new behaviors and ways of interacting in the new South African environment.

APPROACHES TO FACULTY DEVELOPMENT IN TIMES OF CHANGE

Higher education institutions in many countries, both developed and developing, are grappling with changing environments, new societal expectations, new institutional roles and responsibilities, and changing student bodies. Some of the major questions for all universities right now are how to conceptualize the role of the university in society, how to create institutional environments that support learners and staff from diverse cultural backgrounds, how to better link the discovery, dissemination, and application of knowledge, and how to respond to and balance pressing immediate national needs and priorities with long-term disciplinary traditions and commitments within the academy. For many institutions in a number of countries, these issues must be handled in situations of considerable fiscal constraint.

Higher education institutions cannot transform internally or respond effectively to external pressures without the involvement and commitment of their faculty members. The energy, commitment, and talents of faculty members are needed as higher education institutions grapple with new societal expectations, new institutional roles and responsibilities, and changing student bodies. Faculty members are the central players as universities strive to create institutional environments that support learners and staff from diverse cultural and educational backgrounds and to balance disciplinary traditions, institutional capabilities, and national economic and workplace needs. Yet, as this chapter has explained by using South Africa as an example, the changing contexts for higher education institutions in developing countries create new and complex challenges for academic staff for which they are not always adequately prepared. Efforts to help faculty members make adjustments, develop new skills, and function effectively in new environments are strategically wise choices for institutional leaders and agencies supporting higher education innovation in developing countries (Moyo, Donn, & Hounsell, 1997).

Academic staff development can take a variety of forms. Some professional needs, such as earning advanced degrees, may require faculty members to travel elsewhere or make significant adjustments in their lives to accommodate formal study. Other professional needs, however, can be addressed quite effectively, in modest ways, within an institution. This section begins by describing modest "in-house" strategies that are having some impact at some South African universities and technikons. The second part of the section describes a set of strategies that South African institutional leaders and academics have suggested would be helpful in situations where international partnerships around academic staff development are possible. The strategies offered here, while based on South African examples, are relevant and adaptable in other national contexts. Modest yet strategic plans that meet real needs, draw on the interests, experiences, and ideas of the academic staff themselves, and build both capacity and colleagueship are likely to be most effective in meeting significant professional development needs.

In-House Institutional Strategies

"In-house" staff development strategies are most likely to contribute to real capacity building if they meet several criteria. First, they must be perceived by academic staff as truly addressing significant challenges and worthy of the investment of time and energy. In order to achieve this criterion, they must provide ideas and tools that can be used in the near future to address clearly identified issues, problems, concerns, and goals. Second, staff development should provide opportunities for reflective practice within which ideas for improvement can be nurtured. Third, staff development plans should be designed to draw out the talents and experiences that reside within the staff themselves. In this way, faculty members come to see themselves as empowered to support and assist each other, rather than dependent on one or two professional staff members whose job it is to design professional development opportunities. This approach also creates a professional development program that faculty members feel they "own." Fourth, at virtually all higher education institutions, cost is an important factor to consider, so modest strategies that build on the skills and talents of those within the institution are very appropriate.

At the University of Port Elizabeth in South Africa, the use of "collegial conversation" as a metaphor for faculty development has led to an array of fruitful strategies. Faculty development based on collegial interaction provides opportunities for academic staff to exchange ideas, work together to explore new possibilities, and nurture accountability and cooperation with each other. Collegial conversation involves inquiry (asking questions and reflecting on aspects of academic work), dialogue (opportunities for faculty to exchange ideas and explore questions within and across departments), and connection (an environment for faculty to develop relationships with new colleagues or deepen ties with others). Four kinds of collegial conversations have worked well.

Topical Lunches

During once-a-month topical lunch seminars, interested academic staff gather to discuss specific, previously agreed upon topics such as issues around student learning, changing roles and responsibilities for academic staff, and new societal expectations of higher education.

Peer Partnerships

Peer partnerships, originally established with considerable success in the United States, involve pairing two colleagues to explore, discuss, and improve their teaching. Pairs visit each other's classes, interview each other's students, meet for regular discussions about their teaching experiences, and occasionally meet with other peer partner groups.

Career Stage Groups

A third form of faculty development, career stage groups, involves colleagues at similar career stages (early career, midcareer, and senior stage) who gather for monthly meetings to discuss shared concerns and to offer each other support, ideas, and colleagueship.

Action Research

Action research involves a cycle of issue identification, question formulation, data gathering and interpretation, and use of data to guide new approaches to practice, followed by another similar cycle (Zuber-Skerritt, 1992a, 1992b). At the University of Port Elizabeth, several groups of academic staff have worked in action research teams to explore important issues of teaching and learning. The emerging findings and subsequent adjustments to their practice, coupled with the collegiality and exchange of ideas as teams met to discuss their projects, was very stimulating for all involved and led to changes in practice.

Building Partnerships to Foster Faculty Development

In addition to in-house strategies, higher education institutions in developing countries can benefit from entering institutional partnerships designed to foster faculty development. Across countries, many of the issues, questions, and problems confronting faculty are similar. They are concerned with how students learn most effectively, how to work with classes of diverse students, what it means to contextualize the curriculum, and why, how, and for what purposes assessment is done. Academic staff also must grapple with internationalizing the curriculum, the roles and responsibilities of the university in society, and the implications of these issues for academic work. Certainly, national histories and contexts are unique in significant and highly important ways. In South Africa, the depth of disadvantage experienced by many students, two decades of severe disruption of the school systems and the consequent undermining of a "culture of learning," and the cultural gaps between historically disadvantaged and historically advantaged universities are highly important particularities of the higher education context. Yet, since the underlying, critical questions for higher education are quite similar across countries, the potential benefits from institutional partnerships organized around faculty development bear consideration.

Institutional partnerships for academic staff development may be most beneficial when they are organized explicitly around questions of mutual interest, rather than simply around skill development. Using questions of mutual interest to frame partnerships for faculty development enables all participants to acknowledge that they are grappling with vexing issues and looking toward their partners for new insights that may emerge from efforts to address a question from a context different from one's own. When partners are working together to explore and address common concerns, power and responsibility are equally shared, an important characteristic of successful partnerships.

Around what questions or problems might partnerships for staff development usefully be organized? The issues presented in this chapter are possibilities: (1) working with classes composed of diverse students with an array of needs, (2) developing curricula responsive to societal needs, (3) moving from teacher-centered to learner-centered teaching and learning paradigms, (4) effectively handling distance learning, resource-based learning, and new technologies, and (5) ensuring quality in all institutional endeavors. Department chairpersons often serve both as academic staff and as key institutional mid-level leaders who must link institutional priorities and the interests, priorities, and concerns of their unit colleagues. They face specific challenges around which partnerships for professional development might be formed. These concerns include (1) organizing and engaging a department as a working team, (2) leading curriculum and program development, planning, and change, and (3) taking on new responsibilities for budgeting and evaluation.

Partnership approaches may be of particular interest to foundation and institutional leaders working to conceptualize and develop activities to support academic staff development in developing countries. These ideas would be rather difficult to implement in higher education institutions in developing countries without financial support from external agencies.

Teaching Fellows Partnerships

While faculty members often participate in research-oriented exchanges to work with colleagues at other universities, exchanges focused specifically on teaching could be effective as well. In such a program, a group of academics would be appointed as fellows for a semester or year and would teach at a participating partner university. Additionally, each fellow would participate in departmental meetings at the host institution, assist as much as possible with advising, and, through daily involvement, learn about how teaching and learning, as well as other responsibilities, are handled in the partner institution. A faculty host for each fellow would ensure that the visit was as productive as possible.

Partnerships for Degree-Awarding Programs

Many faculty members and administrative leaders in developing countries want opportunities to pursue graduate degrees focused on their areas of specialty or on management and leadership issues. Some South African universities are selecting promising Black undergraduates to send at institutional expense to pursue graduate work at selected institutions in other countries. The hope is that these individuals will return to the South African university to share their expertise and to contribute to the diversification of the faculty.

This "grow your own faculty" strategy is a slow process but has been fairly successful. Institutional leaders at the University of Port Elizabeth in South Africa have found it especially helpful to focus strategically on cultivating specific American institutions to which they send promising young scholars. The young scholars can expect to be welcomed and supported in more personal ways than if they were to attend universities without particular links with their home institution. Since the costs of sending scholars to other countries to study is daunting, South African university leaders are interested in developing partnerships with universities in other countries willing to explore innovative graduate study. Presumably such arrangements would be attractive to faculty members in other developing countries also. For example, some universities might offer opportunities for faculty members from other countries to engage in periods of intensive coursework punctuated by periods of time back on their home campuses where they can continue their study through special projects even as they handle their professional responsibilities.

Exchanges and Team Visits

When colleagues travel together to spend time at other institutions, they learn not only from their hosts at the institution being visited but also from each other as they discuss and debrief about what they are observing and the implications or possible ways to adapt ideas to their own institutions. Trips by teams to visit other institutions internal or external to the country offer another way for colleagues to connect across institutions for possible long-term collaborations. Back at their home campuses, team colleagues are a source of support as individuals engage in change related to ideas developed through the visit.

SUPPORTING ACADEMIC STAFF AS PART OF A SYSTEMS APPROACH

A systems approach to understanding organizational change emphasizes that all organizational players, not only senior leaders, have an essential role. Faculty members are key institutional players whose concerns and needs must be addressed in order to ensure institutional quality. The changes in higher education in South Africa illustrate how contextual factors affecting higher education institutions have specific implications for academic staff. Faculty members need opportunities to develop new skills and abilities if they are to assume new roles. This chapter has offered a set of faculty development strategies aimed to meet specific faculty professional needs.

In sum, the thesis of this chapter is two-fold: (1) across countries dealing with changing external contexts, similar challenges are likely to confront faculty members; (2) when specific institutional strategies are implemented to support academic staff development, the institution as a whole, not only individual faculty members, benefits. The development of strategies to address the needs of academic staff should be on the agenda of policy makers concerned with supporting transformation in higher education, institutional leaders who recognize academic staff as a key resource in the face of demanding external contexts, and faculty members themselves seeking to understand their individual experiences in a wider context.

REFERENCES

Department of Education. (1996). *Transformation: The report of the National Commission on Higher Education.* Pretoria: Government Printer.

Department of Education. (1997). *White paper on higher education.* Pretoria: Government Printer.

Moyo, C., Donn, G., & Hounsell, D. (1997). *Academic development and strategic change in higher education.* A final report of a South African Association for Academic Development Project funded by the Kellogg Foundation with the support of the British Council and the University of Edinburgh. Battle Creek, MI: W. K. Kellogg Foundation.

Vergnani, L. (1999, March 12). South Africa's Black universities struggle to survive in a new era. *Chronicle of Higher Education.*

Zuber-Skerritt, D. (1992a). *Action research in higher education: Examples and reflections.* London: Kogan Page.

Zuber-Skerritt, D. (1992b). *Professional development in higher education: A theoretical framework for action research.* London: Kogan Page.

Part VII

Conclusion, Lessons, and Directions

Chapter 13

Balancing Pressures, Forming Partnerships

Ann E. Austin and David W. Chapman

The sharply increasing demand for higher education across the developing world has occurred, not because of actions taken by colleges and universities, but largely as a result of demographic, political, and economic changes at the national level. These changes have triggered a complex set of interconnected pressures on government and higher education leaders to accommodate larger enrollments while encouraging more diversity in student populations, raising the quality of instruction, and either doing these things at a lower unit cost, generating new sources of funding, or both. Even as enrollments are growing, the pressures introduced by globalization, the rapid creation and dissemination of knowledge, and the information and communication revolution are leading to intense demands on higher education institutions to develop new structures and modes of operation. These changes are occurring in national contexts in which governments are less able and less willing to continue funding higher education at former levels and are seeking ways of devolving more financial and administrative responsibility to the institutions themselves.

The underlying thesis of this book is that a systems approach is necessary for understanding how these pressures are reshaping higher education in the developing world. Universities are complex organizations, composed of multiple subsystems and serving multiple constituencies. At the same time these institutions operate within broader social, economic, and political systems that pose an array of often conflicting demands, expectations, and pressures. Any effort to understand how higher education institutions respond to their changing environments must recognize the complex interplay of these broader pressures. Government and educational leaders must consider the context within which institutional efforts at reform and innovation occur.

To be successful, efforts to reform higher education require leaders who have both the technical knowledge and skills associated with institutional and system management and a sound understanding of the societal dynamics within which these reforms are occurring. The history of educational development is littered with good ideas that failed, not because they lacked merit, but because their implementation overlooked important cultural and contextual factors that limited their success. In debates about the most effective strategies for development, there is often a tension between the policy mechanics who look for technical fixes to the problems of development and the social constructivists who seek to understand local meaning and symbolism of actions (Fuller & Clark, 1994). While the policy mechanics search for generalizable solutions that apply across contexts and countries, the social constructivists try to understand the unique factors that shape a particular institution. In reality, both perspectives are important inputs to the planning process, but the balance between them is sometimes illusive. The systems approach advocated in this book requires drawing from both perspectives to analyze the dynamics of higher education reform.

The preceding chapters support five observations about fostering innovation in higher education across the developing world.

1. *Many of the most pressing issues facing higher education institutions in the developing world are not directly educational issues.*

Issues are not always what they appear to be. Several of the preceding chapters have documented the noneducational derivation of many of the seemingly "education issues" now facing higher education systems. In Chapter 2, Jamil Salmi argued that three powerful forces—economic globalization, the importance of knowledge production, and the wide-spread use of high-speed information and communication systems—are creating a major turning point for higher education institutions. While these forces are far more than "education issues," they certainly have huge implications for higher education institutions and systems.

Moreover, the reform of higher education is often not the primary goal that governments or international assistance agencies really seek. Rather, governments and external agencies often urge changes in higher education as a means of strengthening the work force, supporting economic development, improving the national budget, or appeasing politically powerful constituencies. One consequence of these goals is that demonstrably ineffective educational policies are sometimes supported by governments and other organizations because those policies are well-aligned with larger national initiatives that those groups support.

To be effective in this political milieu, education leaders must understand the embedded nature of the issues with which their institutions must contend. More importantly, they need to be adept at formulating institutional strategies that address the real issues of concern to national policy makers while, at the same time, serve to strengthen their institutions. They need to be astute analysts of economic, social, and political issues and how those may interact in ways that affect their institutions. They must be alert to realize that institutional initiatives to respond to one set of pressures may create other difficulties.

2. *Successful reform processes require more than the formulation of clear goals. Pursuing one set of goals may mean neglecting or undermining others. Specific institutional goals that seem noble and necessary may interact with each other in ways that produce undesirable outcomes.*

Not all goals can be achieved simultaneously. A major challenge confronting institutional leaders is to decide which goals to address and to correctly anticipate how those goals may interact with each other. For example, one might expect that lowering tuition and encouraging privatization of education might contribute to national goals of increasing access. As Darrell R. Lewis and Halil Dundar (Chapter 9) showed, however, this strategy actually may undermine opportunities for access among low-income students. Similarly, using the national language in university level instruction seems reasonable as a way to enhance national pride within a country. Unfortunately, as David W. Chapman's analysis of the Lao situation explained (Chapter 5), this decision diminished the ability of scholars and students to participate fully in the international community of scholars, an equally important goal. Efforts to achieve one goal may actually negate another.

As another example, D. Bruce Johnstone and Olga Bain (Chapter 3) explained that trends toward privatization, decentralization, and institutional autonomy in Russian universities may lead to more responsive, more accessible, and better managed higher education institutions. These same trends, however, may be accompanied by diminished government support and increased fiscal constraint, which undermine institutional quality. Goals that seem attractive may have unintended effects.

3. *Autonomy breeds new tensions when key constituencies lack consensus about institutional goals and priorities. To build the needed consensus, institutional leaders must forge new alliances and build support from key groups, both inside and outside the institution.*

A recurring theme across many of the preceding chapters was that, in many countries, fiscal and managerial responsibility are being shifted away from central governments and vested at the institutional level. As a result, colleges and universities are under intense pressure to forge new partnership arrangements with government, other civil society institutions, and with each other. Their financial survival frequently depends on it. Yet as Jairam Reddy explained in Chapter 6 in his analysis of the shifts in government-university relationships in Africa, and as John C. Weidman and Regsurengiin Bat-Erdine discussed in Chapter 7 in regard to Mongolia, forging new and satisfactory external relationships is extremely difficult for higher education leaders. In Mongolia, for example, the government's decision to cap tuition levels led to other institutional income-making ventures which were met by government claims to the new funds. These developments do not describe a relationship without tension. In Africa the story varies by country, but in many the struggle for an appropriate balance between government control and institutional autonomy is very difficult and continues.

As fiscal and managerial responsibilities devolve to the institutional level, education leaders also must create alliances and build support among key groups inside the university. For some education leaders and for faculty members asked to assume new institutional leadership and decision-making roles, thinking in this way is new ground. Particularly for institutions emerging from heavy central government control, where effective procedures and traditions around faculty decision making are not yet well developed, the challenge of building consensus among constituencies is enormous.

The main challenge for institutional leaders is that some policies that they must support often contradict the interests of the very constituencies from whom support is essential. For example, several chapters discussed the shift of the cost burden for higher education toward students and their families. This move, while important to institutional survival and widely accepted as an appropriate action, does not contribute to smooth relationships between institutional leaders and student groups. In South Africa, for example, much of the student unrest that has occurred is a direct result of institutional decisions to require student payments. Another example concerns faculty work. When faculty members are urged to increase their workload within the institution and expand into entrepreneurial work on behalf of the university, even as salaries remain low, they do not view institutional leaders as supportive partners.

Greater institutional autonomy would seem to be a desirable goal for most institutional leaders. In some countries, such as Brazil, the shift toward institutional autonomy undermines long-standing arrangements that particular constituencies have found beneficial. In that situation, as analyzed in Chapter 4 by David N. Plank and Robert E. Verhine, reform will require the various constituent groups to see the value of relinquishing individual advantages for the greater good of the institution, the higher education system, and the nation. In that country as in others, the shift toward more institutional autonomy and responsibility challenges institutional leaders and faculty members to assume new roles, new perspectives, and new alliances.

4. *While raising the quality of higher education is one of the most widely acclaimed items for the agenda of the next decade, it is one of the most difficult to achieve.*

Virtually all colleges and universities identify higher instructional quality as a central goal of higher education reform—but this has been true for many years. Given the persistent and near universal value placed on higher quality, why do universities have so much trouble achieving it?

Three reasons help explain the resistance to quality improvement efforts. First, quality is a particularly tricky issue because the desire for high quality is, in practice, "capped" by an intense interest in efficiency (Chapman & Adams, 1998). Governments and universities both claim they want high quality but always mean they want as much as they can get for the amount of money they want to spend. The search for quality is constrained by the willingness to pay the price. As funding for higher education becomes more problematic in many countries, the emphasis on improving quality is sometimes deferred. Second, high quality is an elusive target. Seeking higher quality is always a popular cause, but it is a safe political goal in that it is never satisfied—it continues to be an effective rallying cry.

Finally, raising quality has its enemies: Few argue against higher quality. However, raising quality involves tradeoffs (Chapman & Adams, 1998). Quality interventions usually require additional resources; those who lose in the transaction may see quality improvement as secondary to what they value. For example, there is generally a tension between expanding access to higher education and increasing quality. Absorbing more students requires resources that might otherwise be spent on quality. Moreover, increased access results in a wider range of student abilities and prior preparation. Increased enrollments tend to include more academically average students so that teachers are confronted with more heterogeneous classes. Consequently, during times of rapid enrollment expansion, quality indicators tend to decline.

Improving quality, then, is as much a political issue as a technical one. Universities already know a great deal about what factors increase student learning. Implementing them is another matter. Moreover, emphasizing access and offering greater inclusiveness are more politically acceptable. Spending money on improving quality is viewed by some as exclusive and elitist. Yet, as Elaine El-Khawas argued in Chapter 10, both national governments and higher education institutions have a responsibility to ensure minimum standards—and there are various strategies from which to choose to fulfill this obligation.

5. *In the midst of changing national agendas for higher education, it is still the day-to-day effort of the faculty that gets the work done. Thus, institutional priorities should include attention to recruiting, training, and supporting faculty members.*

Countries cannot achieve their goal of strengthening higher education without the time and commitment of their academic staff. Many of the most widely advocated reforms to higher education can be seen to have a potentially negative impact on—or at least to create significant challenge for—faculty members' worklives. That is, faculty members face pressure to teach differently, engage in curriculum reform, work longer, and diversify their entrepreneurial efforts on behalf of the university. This book has provided several analyses of the implications of institutional change and reform for faculty members. Both Gerard A. Postiglione (Chapter 8) and Yvonna S. Lincoln and her coauthors (Chapter 11) explored the forces affecting faculty members in China, and Ann E. Austin (Chapter 12) analyzed how postapartheid transformation in higher education in South Africa requires academic staff to assume new roles. In many cases, faculty members have had little training or experience to undertake new teaching, research, curriculum, entrepreneurial, or institutional leadership roles.

The need for professional development and training is not the only concern regarding faculty members. In some countries, if higher education reform is to be effective, institutions must recapture the time and attention of academic staff and focus it in institutionally productive ways. For example, in Laos and China, many academic staff have operated outside of institutional priorities in an effort to offset low salaries. Encouraging faculty members to turn their attention back to institutional roles is a formidable challenge.

A third issue is attracting and recruiting faculty members, as Lincoln and her colleagues (Chapter 11) noted. Each of these issues—new roles, recapturing faculty time, and attracting new faculty members—can be addressed, at least partially, through strategic faculty development plans, as Austin argued in Chapter 12.

How can education leaders in the industrialized world and international agencies usefully support the reform efforts now underway in the developing world?

The responsibility for the growth and strength of higher education in the developing world falls largely on the government and education leaders of the countries themselves. Nonetheless, external support continues to be an important input. While countries must chart and negotiate their own solutions, international expertise can make a useful contribution.

In the past, the development of higher education institutions has been left largely to government. The involvement of universities in the more industrialized world in the affairs of higher education institutions in the developing world has generally taken three forms: student and faculty exchange programs, participant training, and participation in bilateral or multilateral technical assistance contracts (Chapman & Claffey, 1998). However, the faculty and student exchanges and the participant training programs have tended to be rather narrowly focused on academic goals, and the contract work has often been viewed by institutions from the sponsoring countries as entrepreneurial ventures.

Another common form of cross-national participation has been in leadership training. For the most part, this has concentrated on training aimed at improving internal institutional management. While this is important, it is not enough. The need now is for leadership in forward-looking strategic planning and in establishing effective working partnerships with business, industry, and government.

Training is necessary, but only up to a point. It is a solution only to the extent that lack of training was the underlying problem. Leaders of many higher education institutions across the developing world are already well trained and have a sophisticated understanding of political dynamics, both at the campus and the country levels. What they often need now is international collaboration in actually implementing some of the development strategies, particularly in building their working relationships with the larger civil society in which they operate and in responding to the forces of the market economy in which many now participate.

Another useful form of participation by the international community would be with networks of higher education, government, and private sector groups in developing countries to conduct interdisciplinary applied research in areas of high public concern (e.g., health, energy, education). These networks should focus on the cross-disciplinary, integrated research needed to address the complex issues that countries face. For example, while environment is a key concern in many countries, the research needs go well beyond pollution, to include the identification of impacts associated with proposed solutions, the economic consequences of alternative courses of action, and the social marketing of environment-friendly practices (Chapman and Claffey, 1998). Higher education institutions in the developing world can contribute much to their countries by addressing such important research questions. The international community can provide opportunities and support for scholars in the developing world to conduct the necessary research.

An additional focus for collaboration builds on the experience of many institutions in the industrialized world in accessing and communicating scientific and technical information, particularly in the areas of electronic data storage and retrieval, professional conferencing, and electronic networking. While universities in the developing world are being radically reshaped by information technologies, these institutions will need international support and assistance to become leaders in this new field in their own geographical spheres.

Over the next decade, it is likely that more of the important country-to-country sharing will be across institutions within the developing world. The sharing of expertise between universities in the developing world and in more industrialized institutions is likely to be formulated as more equal partnerships, as Austin recommended.

CONCLUDING COMMENTS

The thesis of this book is that higher education institutions throughout the world are facing changing external environments and that a systems approach provides a useful perspective for understanding these changes and formulating appropriate responses. Institutional leaders need to analyze how these forces interrelate and, in turn, how institutional responses can yield implications that flow beyond the specific issues being addressed.

A growing pressure on higher education systems worldwide is that they contribute to national development. For their part, higher education institutions in developing countries may harbor a healthy skepticism about becoming closely involved in the applied aspects of national development. Institutions get politicized, governments change, and punishments are exacted. But the risks are changing. The growing danger now is that universities will be judged irrelevant by their own national governments and will have increasing difficulty competing for public funds. In too many cases, graduates' skills have been poorly matched with labor force needs, faculty have disdained involvement in community outreach activities, and institutional status has been viewed as more important than program relevance (Chapman & Claffey, 1998).

Increased university involvement in national development initiatives can provide multiple benefits to the colleges and universities involved. Long-term institutional strength requires financial self-sufficiency that, in turn, depends on a strong national economy. Helping foster a strong economy is a way of creating a necessary condition for long-term institutional revitalization. In addition, the involvement of educators in key development issues increases the relevance of both the research faculty engage in and the instruction they provide. This contributes to further benefits. Attention to development priorities builds political support as the public and private sectors come to value higher education as a first-line resource in solving complex national issues. The result may be the political support institutions need in the competition for public and private funding.

Higher education institutions in developing countries face critical issues: finding a workable balance in government-institution relationships, managing new levels of autonomy, meeting the needs of an increasingly diverse range of students, ensuring quality in teaching and research while holding down costs, and supporting faculty members who must assume new roles. Expecting simple solutions to these complex issues is unrealistic. Each higher education institution is a complex organization situated in a unique national system. These institutions and their leaders deserve the support of colleagues around the world. At the same time, the strategies they employ—both successful and not—offer useful lessons and examples for other institutions in developing and developed countries, since all are confronted with the task of interacting with a rapidly changing external environment.

REFERENCES

Chapman, D. W., & Adams, D. (1998). The quality of education in Asia: The perennial priority. *International Journal of Educational Research, 29*(7), 643–665.

Chapman, D. W., & Claffey, J. (1998, September 25). Higher education and international development: some new opportunities worth taking. Point of View commentary. *Chronicle of Higher Education*, p. B6.

Fuller, B., & Clark, P. (1994). Raising school effects while ignoring culture? Local conditions and the influence of classroom tools, rules, and pedagogy. *Review of Educational Research*, *64*(1), 119–157.

Index

About the Contributors

ANN E. AUSTIN is Associate Professor of Higher, Adult, and Lifelong Education at Michigan State University, where she is also a member of the core faculty of the African Studies Center. Her research and teaching concern higher education, with emphasis on organizational change, academic cultures, faculty professional development, and teaching and learning issues. In 1998, she was named as one of the 40 Young Leaders of the Academy by *Change: The Magazine of Higher Education*. During 1998 she held a Fulbright fellowship in South Africa, where she worked at the University of Port Elizabeth on issues of institutional transformation, curriculum development, faculty development, and innovations in teaching and learning. She also spent time working with academic staff and institutional leaders and conducting research at twelve other South African higher education institutions. She has authored or edited eight books and monographs and numerous journal articles and book chapters.

OLGA BAIN, who received her Ph.D. in comparative and higher education at the University at Buffalo, State University of New York, was formerly a lecturer and an Associate Dean at Kemerovo State University. She holds a degree of Candidate of Sciences from St. Petersburg State University. Dr. Bain has served as consultant to the Council of Europe on issues of local governance, especially as they relate to the support of education. Her research interests include the sociology of educational change and comparative policies of higher education finance and governance, with a focus on postcommunist nations.

REGSURENGIIN BAT-ERDENE is the former State Secretary of the Ministry of Science, Technology, Education and Culture of Mongolia. He has written extensively on higher education reform in Mongolia and has been involved in both the 1993 and 1999 education sector studies funded by the Asian Development Bank. He holds a master's degree in higher education from the University of Pittsburgh and is currently a doctoral student there.

DAVID W. CHAPMAN is Professor of Education in the Department of Educational Policy and Administration at the University of Minnesota. His specialization is international development assistance. In that role, he has worked in over 30 countries for the World Bank, the U.S. Agency for International Development, UNICEF, the Asian Development Bank, the InterAmerican Development Bank, UNESCO, and similar organizations. He has authored or edited six books and over 100 journal articles, many of them on issues related to the development of education systems in international settings. He served as the guest co-editor for the December 1998 issue of the *International Journal of Educational Research.*

BRYAN R. COLE is Professor and Head of the Department of Educational Administration and Human Resource Development at Texas A&M University. Dr. Cole also served as Associate Dean of Undergraduate Studies in the College of Education for ten years and Assistant Dean for five years. He served as the director of the Summer Seminar on Academic Administration for 25 years. Dr. Cole's professional interests include continuous quality improvement in educational systems, educational law, and higher education administration. He is a frequent speaker and consultant on the implementation of continuous quality improvement in educational systems.

HALIL DUNDAR, who is currently a program manager and education economist at the World Bank, holds a Ph.D. in higher education from the University of Minnesota. Previously he was an Assistant Professor at the Middle East Technical University in Ankara, Turkey, and Research Associate at the University of Minnesota. He has published extensively in international journals on the related issues of cost, equity, and productivity in higher education in the United States, Turkey, and other developing countries.

ELAINE EL-KHAWAS is Professor of Educational Policy at George Washington University. Her research and publications address issues of higher education policy and organizational change, with special attention to policies for quality assurance and the ways that universities respond to pressures for accountability and educational effectiveness. Dr. El-Khawas has lectured widely, has authored more than 60 publications, including book chapters, monographs, and articles, and was principal author of a 1998 World Bank report on quality assurance. She serves on the editorial boards of three international journals in higher education and has served as a consultant to many U.S. universities and national associations, as well as the World Bank, OECD, and UNESCO. She is a Vice President of the Society for Research in Higher Education (U.K.), a member of the Scientific Research Committee of the Association of African Universities (Ghana), and a member of the governing board of the Consortium of Higher Education Researchers (Europe). A sociologist with master's and doctoral degrees from the University of Chicago, she also has served as Vice President for Policy Analysis and Research at the American Council on Education, and as Professor of Higher Education at the University of California, Los Angeles.

D. BRUCE JOHNSTONE is University Professor of Higher and Comparative Education at the State University of New York at Buffalo. His teaching and research interests combine economics, finance, and governance of colleges and universities in both domestic and international contexts. He is Director of the Learning Productivity Network, which studies productivity from the perspective of enhancing higher education's outputs and is currently studying college-level learning in high school. He has studied and written about student finance, particularly tuition policy and student loans, and has been tracking the shift of the higher education cost burden from governments and taxpayers to students and families in other countries. Dr. Johnstone has served as President of the State University College at Buffalo and Chancellor of the SUNY system. He received his B.A and M.A.T. degrees from Harvard University and his Ph.D. from the University of Minnesota.

DARRELL R. LEWIS, who holds a Ph.D. in economics, is Professor of Educational Policy and Administration at the University of Minnesota. Professor Lewis has over 30 years of experience in the employment of economic analysis to examine evaluation and policy questions in the fields of education and disability. He currently teaches courses in the economics of education, economic evaluation, and higher education. His current research interests include the economics of higher education with special attention to developing countries. He has authored or coauthored more than 150 books, monographs, journal articles, and book chapters, including publications in nearly 20 different scholarly journals, such as the *American Economic Review*, *Economics of Education Review*, *Journal of Higher Education*, *Higher Education Policy*, *Educational Evaluation and Policy Analysis*, and *Journal of Disability Policy Studies*. He also has served on the board of editors for three journals and as a reviewer for 14 journals. He has been a frequent consultant on matters of policy, research, and evaluation to international, national, state, and local agencies, including eight foreign universities or ministries in developing countries over the past five years on issues relating to the economics of higher education.

YVONNA S. LINCOLN is Professor of Higher Education and Program Director, Higher Education Program Area, Department of Educational Administration and Human Resource Development at Texas A&M University. She has done pioneering work in alternative-paradigm methodology and philosophy, and currently co-edits *Qualitative Inquiry*, a journal directed toward exploring and expanding the range of qualitative methods for the human and social sciences. She is the coeditor of the first and second editions of the *Handbook of Qualitative Research* and the coauthor or editor of six other books. Her current research includes exploring student, parent, and alumni perceptions of higher education, tracing whether unfavorable media representations of higher education are shared by those who are the major consumers of its services, and exploring perceptions of quality service in libraries which serve Research I institutions (funded by a grant from the Fund for the Improvement of Postsecondary Education). She has recently completed editing a four-volume set of both classic, unheard, and fugitive voices in qualitative research.

DAVID N. PLANK is Professor in the College of Education at Michigan State University. He earned his Ph.D. at the University of Chicago. He specializes in the areas of educational policy and educational finance and has conducted research and served as a consultant in these areas in numerous countries in Africa and Latin America. His most recent book is *The Means of Our Salvation: Public Education in Brazil, 1930–1995.*

GERARD A. POSTIGLIONE is Associate Professor in the Department of Education of the University of Hong Kong. In the field of higher education, he has written for the American Council on Education, the Carnegie Foundation for the Advancement of Teaching, *Comparative Education Review, Higher Education Management*, and the *Chronicle of Higher Education.* He also edited *Asian Higher Education.* He has produced nine books and numerous articles on education and society in Hong Kong, China, and East Asia. He was General Editor of *Hong Kong Becoming China: The Transition to 1997*, and is now editing a new series entitled *Hong Kong Culture and Society.* He is Associate Editor of the journal *Chinese Education and Society* and Editor of *China's National Minority Education: Culture, Schooling, and Development.* He has been a consultant to the United Nations Development Programme and the Asian Development Bank on education projects in mainland China, and in Hong Kong for the Carnegie Foundation for the Advancement of Teaching. He also serves as Associate Director of the Centre of Research on Education in China and Director of Advanced Studies in Education and National Development of the University of Hong Kong.

JAIRAM REDDY is a researcher and consultant in higher education and has recently completed six months as a Fulbright Fellow at Michigan State

University. He holds a bachelor's degree from the University of Birmingham, England, a Master of Science from the University of Manitoba, Canada, and a Ph.D. from the University of the Western Cape, South Africa. From 1990 to 1994, he was the Vice Chancellor of the University of Durban–Westville, and previously he held academic posts at the University of London, Temple University, the University of Washington, and, in South Africa, the University of the Western Cape. In January 1995, he was appointed to chair the National Commission on Higher Education of South Africa, whose report formed the basis of the White Paper on Higher Education and the Higher Education Act, which framed the higher education system in postapartheid South Africa. He also has served on the boards of the African Center for the Constructive Resolution of Disputes, the Health Systems Trust for Planning and Development, and the Center for the Advancement of Science and Mathematics. Dr. Reddy has lectured widely, presented more than 50 papers in various congresses, and authored numerous refereed articles published in local and international journals.

JAMIL SALMI, a Moroccan education economist, is presently the Education Sector Manager for the Latin American and Caribbean region at the World Bank. He is also the coordinator of the World Bank's network of higher education professionals and was the World Bank's official representative at the UNESCO World Conference on Higher Education in Paris in 1998. In the past few years, Mr. Salmi has provided technical advice on higher education development and reform in Brazil, Colombia, the Dominican Republic, Uruguay, Venezuela, Nicaragua, Peru, China, Vietnam, Thailand, Poland, South Africa, Kenya, and Senegal. Before moving to the World Bank's Latin America and Caribbean vice-presidency in October 1993, Mr. Salmi worked for four years in the Education and Social Policy Department of the World Bank doing policy research in the field of higher education. Mr. Salmi was responsible for the preparation of the World Bank's Policy Paper on Higher Education, published in July 1994 under the title "Higher Education: Lessons of Experience." Prior to joining the World Bank in December 1986, Mr. Salmi was a Professor of Education Economics at the National Institute of Education Planning in Rabat, Morocco. He also worked as a consultant to various ministries, national professional associations, and international organizations. Mr. Salmi holds a master's degree in Public and International Affairs from the University of Pittsburgh and a Ph. D. in Development Studies from the University of Sussex. He is the author of five books and numerous articles on education and development issues. Over the past five years, he has written extensively on higher education reform issues.

ROBERT E. VERHINE holds a Ph.D. in Comparative Education from the University of Hamburg and has worked in Brazil since 1977 as a Professor of Education at the Universidada Federal da Bahia. He is currently the director of a university research institute that focuses on public sector governance and is President of the Brazilian Comparative Education Society. His research and writing addresses the organization, structure, and financing of public education in Brazil at all levels. He has published in a variety of international journals and has consulted for such organizations as the World Bank, UNICEF, the U.S. Agency for International Development, and the Brazilian Ministry of Education.

JOHN C. WEIDMAN is Professor of Higher Education and of Sociology at the University of Pittsburgh. He specializes in issues of comparative education management and policy analysis. In addition to graduate teaching and research in these areas, he has consulted for the Asian Development Bank on projects in Mongolia and Laos, the Academy for Educational Development, and the German Academic Exchange Service (DAAD). His visiting professorships include the UNESCO Chair of Higher Education Research at Maseno University College in Kenya and Fulbright Visiting Professor of the Sociology of Education at Augsburg University in Germany. He has published numerous articles on comparative higher education reform and recently coedited a book on higher education in Korea.

YANG "SHERRY" XIAOBO is a researcher and lecturer at the National Academy of Educational Administration in Beijing, China. She is currently on leave, working on her doctoral degree in higher education administration at Texas A&M University. She received a bachelor's degree in history from Peking University and a master's degree from the Institute of Higher Education Research in Beijing. She has authored a book and six research papers on issues related to comparative and higher education.

WANG XIAOPING is currently employed by the Nike Corporation in Beijing, China. Dr. Wang earned his doctorate at Teachers' College, Columbia University, and upon returning to China, worked as a senior researcher and policy analyst with the National Center for Education Development and Research (NCEDR), a bureau of the State Education Commission of China.